27/6

£32

CENTRAL BANKING
IN THE
EMERGING COUNTRIES

By the same Author:

1. *Industrial Finance in India* (Fourth Edition),
   Calcutta University, 1961.

2. *A Survey of Contemporary Banking Trends* (Third Edition),
   The Book Exchange, Calcutta, 1965.

3. *The Managing Agency System*,
   World Press Private Ltd., Calcutta, 1958.

4. *Theory and Practice of Development Banking*,
   Asia Publishing House, Bombay, 1965.

CENTRAL BANKING IN THE EMERGING COUNTRIES

A STUDY OF AFRICAN EXPERIMENTS

by

S. K. BASU, M.A., PH.D.

Research Director, Indian Institute of Social Welfare and Business Management, Calcutta
Formerly Professor of Banking and Industrial Finance, Department of Economics, Calcutta University

ASIA PUBLISHING HOUSE

LONDON

PRINTED IN INDIA

BY S. N. GUHA RAY AT SREE SARASWATY PRESS LTD., 32, ACHARYA PRAFULLA CHANDRA ROAD, CALCUTTA-9 AND PUBLISHED BY P. S. JAYASINGHE, ASIA PUBLISHING HOUSE. 447 STRAND, LONDON, W.C. 2

To My Grandchild

RAJA

Life of my Life

As a token of my Love

Preface

THE PRESENT study is concerned with a review of the experiments in central banking that have been made in the newly independent African colonies and dependencies during the decade 1955-1965. The object is to analyse the structure, policies and problems of a sample of Eight Central Banks, in the context of the 'new' concept of central banking that has evolved during the past 20 or 25 years, and against the background of the so-called 'central banking in underdeveloped countries', as developed earlier in the Latin American and some Asian countries. The Eight Banks under discussion here have not been selected haphazardly, but have been deliberately chosen as a representative series by virtue of their geographical location, socio-political heritage, mode of gestation, membership of particular currency areas and the developing nature of the export-oriented dependent economies in which they operate. As for the material upon which the work is based, major reliance has been placed upon authoritative sources, such as the Banks' Charters, Annual Reports and Statements of Accounts, Economic and Financial Bulletins and Reviews, Statistical and other publications. The Annual Reports of the Currency Boards where these were the precursors of the central banks have also been drawn upon. In some cases unpublished mimeographed notes on various aspects of the respective countries' money and capital markets, indigenous banking systems and development finance institutions, which have been generously provided by the authorities of the Banks concerned, have been important source material. Use has also been made of the Statutes and Articles of Association of various Development Banks operating in some of these African countries, their annual reports and explanatory memoranda etc. Letters from the management of some of these central and development banks in reply to my queries have, in addition, been very helpful material. Thanks are particularly due to the authorities of the Central Banks of Nigeria, Ghana, Rhodesia and Nyasaland, Southern Rhodesia, Tunisia, Morocco, Libya and the Sudan and those of the Industrial Bank of Sudan, the National Investment Bank of Ghana, the Industrial Development Bank of Nigeria, *Societe Tunisienne De Banque* of

Tunisia and *Banque Nationale pour le Developpment Economique* of Morocco for the kind co-operation they have extended to the research project. To Dr. S. Dhar, a former pupil of mine, at present Chief Advisor of Libya's Ministry of Planning and Development, I am indebted for all the material relating to the Libyan I.D.O. and I.R.E.B. Apart from the text, there is an Appendix which contains a sample of Central Bank charters processed and analysed with respect to certain distinguishing features. It would serve as a kind of reference material supplementing the textual analysis. The entire material relating to the Bank of Morocco and the Central Bank of Tunisia and the Tunisian STB and the Moroccan BNDE, however, was available only in French. I am deeply indebted to Mr. R. Dutta, my former pupil and colleague in the Department of Economics, Calcutta University for translating the contents thereof into English for my benefit. I have also to acknowledge with thanks the statistical assistance received from Mr. H. N. Sinha who has prepared all the graphs presented here.

As regards published literature which is admittedly meagre on the subject of our study, I must acknowledge my great indebtedness to the well-known work of Dr. Erin Jucker Fleetwood on "Money and Finance in Africa".

The work has grown out of a paper presented to the Seminar on Monetary-Fiscal Policy held in January 1966 under the auspices of the University Grants Commission of India and the Department of Economics, Calcutta University. I had to secure the necessary material from the different African countries which inevitably took a long time. That explains the delay in publishing the work in the present form.

Finally, I must express my gratitude to the University Grants Commission for granting me a financial award and to the authorities of the Indian Institute of Social Welfare and Business Management, Calcutta for providing me with the necessary facilities to do my work.

23 January, 1967 S. K. Basu

Contents

Chapter One

Rise of Central Banks in the Newly Independent African Countries

The traditional concept of central banking as embodied in the structures and practices of the old established central banks has passed through several stages of evolution, and during the last twenty-five or thirty years has radically changed. In its place a new concept of central banking has come to hold the field. The concept is found to be embodied in the relations of the central banks with the government, the public and the financial and banking communities, in the new role assigned to monetary reserves, in the changed pattern of monetary control and last but not least in the banks' attitude towards economic development.[1] The details of this modern conception have indeed varied from one country to another according to its historical, political and financial set-up and in the context of its stage in economic development. But it is clear that this new philosophy has not only dominated the laws and practices of the younger central banks in underdeveloped economies and newly independent territories but has even permeated the older banks in the mature and advanced countries.[2] This new concept found an expression, for the first time, in the pattern of central banking which evolved in the underdeveloped countries of Central and South America. The drafters of the charters of these Banks made no attempt to transplant the classical model on their own soil by a slavish imitation of the rules and practices developed in the hands of the Bank of England. They were fully aware of the peculiar economic and financial structures of the countries where the new central banks would have to operate. They were clear in their minds as to the aims and objectives of the institutions they were promoting and the responsibilities that would be entrusted to them. They also profited from the experience of the earlier central banks establishd after the First World War following the advice of the Brussels Conference of 1920. These banks, it may be recalled, were set up as part of a *scheme of currency stabilisation and*

[1] Lord Cobbold, *Some Thoughts on Central Banking*, Stamp Memorial Lecture 1962.

[2] *A Survey of Contemporary Banking Trends*, (Third Ed). Ch. 1 by the present writer.

prevention of inflation.[1] But in most cases they were not adjusted to the money and capital market conditions of the respective countries. The founders of the central banks in the underdeveloped countries of Latin America appreciated that their banks would function in mono-culture export-oriented economies, characterised by imperfectly developed banking systems and non-existent or rudimentary money and capital markets. These institutions could not be modelled on the lines of their "elder brothers" in mature industrially advanced countries with diversified economic structures and sophisticated money and capital markets. The banks had to be adapted to meet the concrete needs of their own economy.[2]

The general concept of "central banking in underdeveloped countries" has been hitherto applied by and large to the form of central banking as evolved in the Latin American countries in the years after the great depression through the end of the Second World War. The same model was built up under foreign advice in some Asian countries. But in the mid-1950's a new phase in the evolution of central banking patterns could be witnessed in the emerging countries of Africa and South East Asia. With the crumbling of the old colonial system to pieces and the achievement of political independence by the dependencies and protectorates, a battery of new central banks came to be established in almost all these newly independent territories.[3] These were underdeveloped countries but in some important respects the basic economic situation and the socio-cultural heritage of these territories were different from those in Latin American countries. As is well known, underdeveloped countries may have the same basic characteristics but coming to details various categories of such countries may be distinguished. Each category may have special problems of its own. Central banking policies will have to be formulated in such a manner as to cope with the special problems of each country. So we may have a type of central banking in the underdeveloped countries of Africa which may not conform to the standard Latin American pattern. A detailed

[1] C. H. Kisch and W. A. Elkin, *Central Banks*, 1932, p. 2.

[2] Robert Triffin, *Monetary and Banking Reform in Paraguay*, pp. 72-73.

[3] To mention only a few of them—Ghana, Guinea, Malaya, Nigeria, Rhodesia and Nyasaland, Southern Rhodesia, Zambia, Malawi, Morocco, Tunisia, Sudan, Sierra Leone, Somalia, Libya, Jamaica, Mali, Algeria, Cyprus, States of West Africa, States of Equatorial Africa and the Cameroon, Lebanon, Rwanda, Burundi and the Kongo, all during 1956-1964.

examination of the structure, objectives, functions and policies of these new central banks as well as the problems that are facing them in the perspective of the classical as well as the Latin American model—would be a fruitful line of research. But the scope of the present work and the time and space at our disposal will not permit a detailed study of all the new Afro-Asian institutions in their various aspects. It is proposed, therefore, to confine our study to the African scene, selecting only seven from the long list of newly established central banks—three operating in the South of the Sahara, in Nigeria, Ghana, and Rhodesia, two in the North of the Sahara, in Morocco and Tunisia, and two in the East of the Sahara, in the Sudan and Libya. These seven banks selected for our study have not been chosen haphazardly. They do present a representative series and exemplify the new concept of central banking. Although the central banks in these newly independent countries conform to a broad underlying pattern, they differ in detail with regard to their organisational set-up, problems, policies and practices. The differences arise from their political and social heritage, their membership of particular currency areas, their precursors and mode of gestation, stages of their economic growth and last but not least the manner in which their senior and technical staff were recruited. The institutions chosen for our analysis are representative in that they exhibit one or more of these distinctive characteristics. All these factors have served to develop individual traditions and shape individual practices. Their influence is clearly reflected in the respective statutes in respect of their structure and organisation, relations to the respective governments and the commercial banks, and machinery of monetary-credit control. Thus Nigeria, Ghana, Rhodesia and the Sudan may be said to be of British heritage and Morocco and Tunisia of French heritage. The first four were dependencies of Britain while the last two were protectorates under France. Nigeria, Ghana and Rhodesia belonged to the sterling area and Sudan is said to have been an honorary member of the sterling area. Morocco and Tunisia, on the other hand, were members of the French franc area. While the precursors of the central banks in Nigeria, Ghana and Rhodesia were currency boards, the Western African Currency Board in the case of the first two and the Central African Currency Board for the third, Sudan especially created such a board for the transition period to facilitate the succession of its future central bank. The Libyan central bank also had for its predecessor a Currency Commission, more or less on the lines of the British Currency Boards, which was set up under the advice of experts from the IMF by the passage of a Currency Law in October 1951. The precursor of the Bank of Morocco was the Banque d'Etat du Maroc (State Bank of Morocco), a private international institution formed by the Treaty of Alegeciras in 1906. It had been functioning both as a note issuing and a commercial bank with a long established tradition. When the agreement on independence was signed in Morocco in 1956, the Bank of Morocco became its successor and received a new charter in 1959. While the central bank of Morocco was the successor of the State Bank of Morocco, the Central Bank of Tunisia was established as a new bank in 1958, as a result of negotiation with the Banque d'Algerie et de Tunisie which had previously managed the monetary system of Tunisia. Prior to the establishment of the Bank of Sudan, some of the traditional functions of central banking were exercised between themselves by the Ministry of Finance and Economics, the Sudan Currency Board and the National Bank of Egypt, while others were either not performed at all or only inadequately performed. The Currency Board was entrusted with the management of the currency; by its very nature it was precluded from performing other central banking functions. It held only that part of the country's foreign exchange reserves which served as currency cover. The rest of the official reserves was mostly held and administered by the Ministry of Finance and Economics. The National Bank of Egypt acted as banker to Government and as lender of last resort to the commercial banks. The National Bank was not in a position to act as adviser to the Government on matters of monetary and financial policy, nor as supervisor of the commercial banks. Its Sudanese offices were merely branches of the headquarters at Cairo and as such they were not equipped for either of these tasks. Some measure of control over the borrowings of the ordinary banks from the National Bank was exercised by the Ministry of Finance which also operated certain qualitative controls over the banks' credit policies. All these functions came to be centralised in the hands of the Bank of Sudan on its establishment.[1]

[1] *Bank of Sudan*, Report for the year ending 31 December, 1960, pp 1-2

Ghana was one of the four territories which were members of the West African Currency Board before the establishment of a central bank in the country. The Bank of Ghana was established under an ordinance of March 1, 1957 which was subsequently replaced by a consolidating law, viz. the Bank of Ghana Act May 14, 1963. The influence of socio-political heritage is reflected in its original organisational set-up in that the Ghanaian Bank was split up on the lines of the Bank of England into two departments, the Issue and the Banking Departments.[1] The Banking Department commenced its operations on August 1, 1957, but a great deal of preparation was necessary before the Issue Department could function. This department had to undertake the responsibility of replacing the West African Currency Board notes and coins by a new national currency for which a considerable amount of planning had to be made. Notes and coins issued by the West African Currency Board were to remain legal tender in Ghana until such day, as the Bank giving three months' notice appointed.[2] This could be done, obviously, after the major portion of the estimated circulation of the Board's notes and coins in Ghana had been withdrawn, and arrangements for the delivery, distribution and storage of the new currency could be made. Thus the Issue Department could commence its operations eleven months afterwards on July 14, 1958. The West African Currency Board had only four effective centres in Ghana—Accra, Kumasi, Tamale and Sekondi where issues and redemptions of currency were undertaken. The commercial banks had to move large amounts of cash between their various branches at their own expense and also to hold unduly large cash balances involving them in loss of interest and the public as a consequence in high internal exchange rates. With the gradual introduction of a national network of currency agencies, maintained and replenished at the expense of the central bank, the commercial banks, it was expected, would be able to reduce their rates.

The Bank of Southern Rhodesia presents a unique case as one of the three "successor" Territorial Central Banks born out of the dissolution of the Bank of Rhodesia and Nyasaland when the Federation came to an end on December 31, 1963. The various functions of the Federal Government reverted to the territories

[1] The Bank of Ghana Ordinance, 1957, Sec. 6.
[2] *Ibid.*, Sec. 49.

of Malawi, Rhodesia and Zambia each of which decided to issue its own currency and establish its own central bank.[1] The new Bank of Rhodesia was established only in 1964 and has just commenced its operations. It is not known now how it will formulate its monetary policies and what further contribution it will make to the economic growth of its territory. The original Bank of the Federation of Rhodesia and Nyasaland which was established by an Act of March 13, 1956 had commenced its operations towards the end of the same year. As such, it is older than any of the banks studied here and has evolved its own tools of monetary policy and contributed significantly to the development of the money and capital markets in the three territories comprising the Federation. Appropriately a review of the activities of this Institution should be our main concern. But in discussing the legal framework reference will be made from time to time to the charter of the new Bank of Southern Rhodesia which is closely patterned after the lines of the parent bank.

[1] *Bank of Rhodesia and Nyasaland, Annual Report for the year* 1964, pp. 1-2.

Chapter Two

Economic and Financial Structure of the Countries

The territories in which the central banks under review operate possess relatively the most developed institutional, social and legal framework among all emerging countries in Africa. Admittedly there are important differences in size, wealth, stage of economic development reached and potentialities for further development but they bear by and large common economic and financial characteristics. The case of Libya is somewhat different and is being studied separately. Their political structure also varies from country to country. Some of the countries are monarchies while others are republics. Some of them again which were originally monarchies have transformed themselves into republics; others again have passed through political upheavals and military coups. They have low levels of *per capita* income, are industrially backward and have a large proportion of their population engaged in subsistence agriculture and their economies are dependent for their prosperity on a few articles of export subject to wide fluctuations of a cyclical or accidental character. Their chief exports are primary products, such as, cocoa, groundnuts, palm kernels and palm oil as in Nigeria; cotton (ginned), gum arabic and groundnuts as in Sudan; tobacco, white maize and copper as in Rhodesia; olive oil, phosphates and wines as in Tunisia; phosphates, grain, wine, vegetables and fish as in Morocco; and cocoa as in Ghana.

GHANA

The State of Ghana was born on March 6, 1957, when the former colony of the Gold Coast and the Trusteeship Territory of Togoland attained Dominion Status. On July 1, 1960 the country was declared a republic within the Commonwealth. The Constitution provided for a Parliament, consisting of the President of the Republic and the National Assembly. In January 1964, President Nkrumah introduced the one party state in which only his Convention Peoples' Party was allowed to function. The state has an area of 287,480 sq. Km. and a population of 6,726,000 according to the 1960 census. In January 1963 the population was estimated at 7.1 million. As the result of a military coup the National Liberation Council took over the reigns of government in Ghana on 24th February, 1966 under the chairmanship of Lt. General Joe Ankrah. The National Liberation Council has since published a decree on the suspended constitution of the country, providing for Ghana's continuance as a sovereign unitary republic, until a new constitution was promulgated by the people of Ghana. It was announced on August 23, 1966 by Dr. K. A. Busia, Vice Chairman of the political committee of the National Liberation Council, that Ghana would have a democratic constitution and might return to civilian rule in a year or two's time.

As observed in the Trevor report, the Gold Coast (present-day Ghana) was a producer of primary commodities for export. By far the most important of these exports was cocoa which in 1950 constituted about 70 per cent of the value of the total. Other products in order of their importance were gold (11.6 per cent), manganese (6.7 per cent), timber (5.2 per cent), diamonds (2.4 per cent) and bauxite (0.3 per cent)[1]. In the 1960's as in the fifties, cocoa beans still comprised by far the bulk of the exports amounting by value to 61.1 per cent in 1961, 60.0 per cent in 1962 and 63.7 per cent in 1963. The percentage distribution of the exports is given in Table No. 1.

TABLE[2] No. 1

GHANA

Percentage Distribution of Exports of Domestic Produce

	1961	1962	1963
Cocoa beans ..	61.1	60.0	63.7
Cocoa paste	0.9	0.8	0.2
Cocoa butter	0.4	2.5	3.2
Timber	13.5	11.0	12.1
Bauxite	0.4	0.6	0.5
Manganese	5.4	4.9	3.7
Diamond	6.3	6.7	2.1
Gold	9.5	10.1	10.7
Kolanuts	0.9	1.3	0.8
Others	1.6	2.1	2.0
	100.0	100.0	100.0

[1] Report by Sir Cecil Trevor on "Banking Conditions in the Gold Coast and on the Question of Setting up a National Bank," 1951, Para 32.

[2] SOURCE: *Bank of Ghana,* Report of the Board of Directors for the financial year June 1964, Table X, p. 17.

The weakness of the economic structure of these dependent economies exporting primary products is revealed in the recent sharp drop in Ghana's export earnings by 2.5 per cent at current prices and 5.5 per cent in real terms as a result of the decline in the volume of exports. The higher prices obtained for some of the exports such as cocoa were inadequate to offset the decrease in the value of the country's other exports. The world price index for both primary agricultural commodities and minerals having fallen between 1951-61 from 119 to 91 and from 104 to 100 respectively, the deteriorating trend in the terms of trade of these dependent economies is closely associated with the structure of their exports. It is diversification of the countries' economy which can reduce the dependence of the countries' exchange earnings on the value of one or two articles of export. The percentage distributions of the exports in Nigeria, Sudan, Morocco and Tunisia as given in the following four tables bring out clearly the same pattern of an export-oriented economic structure with a few articles of export dominating the foreign trade of these countries and thereby rendering their economies inevitably vulnerable.

NIGERIA

On October 1, 1960 the Federation of Nigeria became sovereign and an independent member of the Commonwealth. Three years later it became a republic. It is comprised of three regions, Northern, Eastern and Western Nigeria and the Federal Territory of Lagos. A fourth region called the Mid-West was created in July 1963. Before the army coup in 1966 each region of the Federation was self-governing and had its own constitution. The Federal Parliament consisted of a Senate and a House of Representatives which functioned on the pattern of the British House of Commons. The executive was a Council of Ministers under the Prime Minister of the Federation. The Federal Republic had its own President. The area of the country is approximately 923,773 sq. kilometres. According to the census the population was 55,653,821 in November 1963.

Nigeria witnessed several army revolts since January 15, 1966. Following the last revolt Col. Yakubu Gowon, Head of the National Military Government, announced that an Advisory

Council would soon be established to deal with the main issues of national interest. The vacuum created by a total ban on all political organisations could be partially filled that way. He further declared that the National Military Government under his leadership would be a continuing effort and would continue the policy laid down in the statement made by the former Supreme Commander. A three stage plan to return to civil government ensuring a rapid restoration of the former Federal Structure of Government was also envisaged. On August 31, 1966 the Head of the National Government issued a decree in Lagos that Nigeria would revert to a federal form of government. By the same decree the federal system was restored throughout the country.[1]

It will be interesting to note that neither in Ghana nor in Nigeria the political upheavals have disturbed the existing monetary-banking systems as is evidenced by the uninterrupted flow of the publications of the central and development banks to the writer from the respective countries. In the case of Ghana it is reported that the country is being kept, under the present regime, strictly to the path laid down by the International Monetary Fund. By the middle of 1968 it is officially hoped that the economy will begin to take off again with a projected growth rate of 3 per cent. There is evidence also of renewed co-operation with the Sterling Commonwealth Countries in West Africa—Nigeria, Gambia and Sierra Leone.[2]

SUDAN

The Sudan was proclaimed a sovereign independent republic on January 1, 1956. The government was however taken over by the Army on November 17, 1958. The Council of State and Cabinet were dismissed, Parliament and all political parties were dissolved and the constitution was suspended. The Supreme Constitutional Authority was vested in the Supreme Council of the Armed Forces. A civilian cabinet was appointed by General Ibrahim Abour, on October 30, 1964 with Ser al-Khatm Khalifa as Prime Minister. The area of the republic comprises 2.5 million

[1] *Africa Research Bulletin*, August 1-31, 1966, p. 590.

[2] Art. by R. W. Howe entitled "Ghana Sheds no Tears for the God that Failed", in *The Statesman*, December 3, 1966.

sq. kilometres. The population according to the 1955-56 census was 10,262,674. It was estimated at 13 million on January 1, 1964.

MOROCCO

From 1912 to 1956 Morocco was divided into a French protectorate, a Spanish protectorate and the International Zone of Tangier.

The treaty of Fez, which had established the French Protectorate, was terminated on March 2, 1956. On April 7, 1956 Spain relinquished her protectorate and on October 20, 1956 the international status of the Tangier Zone was abolished.

Hassan II succeeded on March 3, 1961 his Father Mohammed V with the title of His Majesty the King.

The Kingdom of Morocco is a constitutional Monarchy with a legislature of two Houses. The King as sovereign Head of State appoints the Prime Minister and other Ministers. The House of Representatives is elected directly by the people; and the House of Counsellers elected by members of local authorities, trade unions, chambers of commerce, etc.

Its area is 443,680 sq. km. and population according to the census June, 1961 was 11,598,070. It was estimated on July 1, 1965 at 13.32 million.

TUNISIA

Tunisia is a sovereign independent Republic. The monarchy was abolished by the Constituent Assembly on July 25, 1957. The National Assembly was elected on November 8, 1959 when all the 90 seats were won by the National Front. The constitution of the Republic was promulgated on June 1, 1959, The President and National Assembly are elected simultaneously by direct universal suffrage for 5 years.

The country is bounded on the South by the Sahara and Libya; on the North and East by the Mediterranean; on the West by the Algerian Province of Constantine. Its area is 164,150 sq. km. Its population according to the Census of 1956 was 3,783,169. It was estimated on January 1, 1965 at 4.63 million.

TABLE[1] No. 2

NIGERIA

Value in £ thousand and Percentage Distribution of Exports of Major Commodities

Period	*Cocoa*	*Ground-nuts*	*Ground-nut oil*	*Palm Kernels*	*Petroleum*	*Natural Rubber*	*Raw Cotton*	*Palm Oil*	*Tin Metal*	*Timber*
1960										
Value	34916	21906	5295	25024	4408	14378	5909	13189	6025	..
Percent	20.57	12.91	3.12	14.74	2.6	8.47	3.48	7.77	3.55	..
1961										
Value	33744	32233	4992	19889	11545	11021	11120	13226	6643	..
Percent	19.45	18.58	2.88	11.47	6.66	6.35	6.41	7.62	3.83	..
1962										
Value	33358	32349	6177	16886	17210	11359	5852	8843	6609	..
Percent	19.96	19.36	3.7	10.11	10.3	6.8	3.49	5.29	3.96	..
1963										
Value	32359	36646	6528	20818	20177	11794	9500	9564	8104	..
Percent	17.09	19.36	3.45	10.99	10.66	6.23	5.02	4.95	4.28	3.5
1964										
Value	40100	34056	8102	20963	32056	11986	6104	10755	12498	..
Percent	18.74	16.0	3.8	9.8	15.0	5.6	2.9	5.02	5.83	4.0
1965 Percentage Jan-June	14.2	17.4	4.7	8.4	22.5	5.0	1.6	4.4	5.7	3.2

[1] Report for the financial years, 1964 and 1965 p. 54. Also Economic & Financial Review, Central Bank of Nigeria Vol. 4. N. 1, 1966. Table 4, P. 10.

TABLE[1] No. 3

SUDAN

Selected Exports: (Percentage Distribution of the Total Exports)

Items	1960	1961	1962 (*Jan-Nov*)	1963	1964
Cotton ginned sakel	50.68	46.48	52.84	54.35	45.12
Gum Arabic	10.99	9.88	5.97	7.23	9.90
Groundnuts	6.93	8.64	8.62	8.14	13.35
Sesame	7.24	6.72	7.15	6.11	9.45
Cottonseed	4.39	5.85	7.14	4.83	1.74

TABLE[2] No. 4

MOROCCO

Percentage Distribution of Exports

	1962	1963	1964
1. Food, beverages and tobacco	46.37	48.54	49.13
2. Mineral products	36.21	34.33	36.83
3. Gross animal & vegetable products	7.55	9.26	6.63
4. Power and oil	0.79	0.77	0.73
5. Intermediates	5.28	3.96	3.29
6. Finished products (consumption)	3.18	2.68	2.73
7. Finished products (industry)	.62	.46	.46

TABLE[3] No. 5

TUNISIA

Value in Dinars and Percentage Distribution of Total Exports

Export Items	1962		1963		1964	
	Value in thousand	*% of the Total*	*Value in thousand*	*% of the Total*	*Value in thousand*	*% of the Total*
Olive oil	1,072	26·42	827	18.75	1,407	27.96
Cereals (wheat, oats)	110	2.93	326	7.39	19	0.38
Wines	638	15.73	853	19.34	281	5.58
Agrumes	152	3.75	151	3.42	278	5.52
Phosphates	573	14.12	635	14.4	929	18.46
Superphosphates	196	4.83	255	5.78	266	5.29
Iron	198	4.88	200	4.54	101	2.01

[1] *Annual Reports of the Bank of Sudan* 1960-1964.

[2] Calculated from the data given in the *Report of the Bank of Morocco* 1963, p. 61 and 1964, p. 71.

[3] *Bulletin Banque Centrale de Tunisie,* January 1964, p. 21 and March 1965, p. 22.

In Nigeria cocoa, palm kernels and groundnuts between them comprised 48.22 per cent of domestic exports in 1960 rising to 49.43 per cent in 1962. Thereafter there was a steady decline to 44.41 per cent in 1964 and 42.6 per cent in 1965 (six-month period). In Tunisia olive oil, mines and phosphates between them made up 56.27 per cent, 42.49 per cent and 52.00 per cent of exports of domestic commodities in 1962, 1963 and 1964 respectively. The dependence on these few articles for their export earnings is quite clear.

FEDERATION OF RHODESIA AND NYASALAND

The Federation of Southern Rhodesia, Northern Rhodesia and Nyasaland was brought into existence on August 1, 1953 when the Queen signed the order in Council proclaiming the Federal statute. The Federation was dissolved with effect from 31 December, 1963, but the Federal monetary area was to continue under the administration of the Bank of Rhodesia and Nyasaland till the establishment of the new central banks. With break up of the Federation, all Federal functions returned to their respective territories, with the exception of the following which would be kept under common administration: Central African Airways, Rhodesian Railways, Federal Power Board and African Research Council. On the South the Federation is bordered by the Republic of South Africa; on the West by the Bechuanaland Protectorate and Portuguese West Africa; on the North-West and North by the Congo; on the North by Tanganyika and on the East by Port East Africa. The area and population of the territory are given below:

At December **1962**	*Sq. Miles*	*Sq. Kilometres*	*Population*
S.R.	150,333	389,300	3,930,000
N.R.	290,323	751,900	2,580,000
Nya	46,066	127,400	2,980,000
Federation	486,722	1,267,800	9,490,000

Thus the total population of the Federation on December 31, 1962 was 9,490,000 and the area 1,267,800 sq. kilometres. Nyasaland became the sovereign independent state of Malawi in July 1964 and Northern Rhodesia became Zambia in October

1964. Southern Rhodesia changed its name to Rhodesia and has since declared independence unilaterally, posing an intricate political problem.

In the Federation of Rhodesia and Nyasaland upto November 1961 primary products made up 89.1 per cent of exports other than gold. Of the primary products minerals constituted 61.3 per cent (copper 53.9 per cent) and agricultural produce, 27.8 per cent (tobacco 21.5 per cent).[1] The Federation was a heavy importer of agricultural products, mainly food stuffs. In 1961 such imports were 10 per cent of its total imports. The authorities of the central bank realised the imperative need to diversify agricultural production, agriculture being unduly dependent on one crop.[2]

Following dissolution of the Federation and the consequent conversion of the two northern territories of Malawi and Zambia into external markets, an even greater proportion of Rhodesia's productive effort became oriented towards exports with increased dependence on external demand.

Tobacco, beef and sugar (upto October 1964) amounted to 30 per cent of total exports; mineral products accounted for 24 per cent; manufacturing industry, which had been growing along with traditional sectors, made an important contribution accounting for 25 per cent. With the separation of the territories Rhodesia is now largely dependent on the export market. The United Kingdom was the most important single market taking up 28 per cent, Zambia, the second most important single market with 25 per cent and S. Africa, 7 per cent. Imports of producer goods such as plant and machinery accounted for 70 per cent of the total and consumer goods, for 25 per cent (durables 8 per cent, nondurables 17 per cent). Protective tariff policy accounted for the relatively small proportion of consumer goods imports.[3]

The Federation, within a few years of its formation, had been able to achieve a high rate of economic growth, indeed the highest attained by any other country in the world during the early stages of its development. Another remarkable achievement of the Federation was a unified monetary area with an integrated financial system.

[1] *Annual Report of the Bank of Rhodesia and Nyasaland*, 1961, p. 14.
[2] *Annual Report of the Bank of Rhodesia and Nyasaland*, 1962, p. 12.
[3] *Annual Report of the Bank of Rhodesia and Nyasaland*, 1964.

Rapid diversification of economy is taking place in most of these newly independent countries. In Rhodesia new agricultural commodities like sugar have been figuring in the recent exports and developments have also been taking place in mining and industry. The emergence of crude petroleum as an important article of export in some countries like Nigeria and more particularly Libya has been on such an increasing scale that the traditional economic characteristics of these countries may be said to be undergoing a remarkable change. Thus crude petroleum which accounted for 10.5 per cent of Nigeria's exports in 1962 shot up to 22.5 per cent in 1964 and 27.56 per cent in 1966. While much of the export trade improvement can be attributed to the growth of crude petroleum exports, decline in some traditional lines of exports, such as rubber and raw cotton in Nigeria, is to be explained by a rapid growth of local industrial consumption and expansion of the indigenous cotton textile industry. Ghana also has been making efforts to diversify its economy so as to reduce its dependence on cocoa as a principal foreign exchange earner.

The main items of import in these countries had hitherto comprised cars and textiles. Recent trend in many countries is for growth of raw material and capital goods imports and decline of imports of consumer and nondurable goods (food stuff, beverages, tobacco and cement). In all these countries national money income depends on the level of export earnings. Their economy is basically dualistic, a large static tradition-oriented "folk-like society" with a small but important modern sector, the former using barter or money substitutes and the latter money and credit. Some commentators would prefer to speak in terms of a "trialistic" economy with an intermediary transitional sector in between the two major sectors comprising a small group of indigenous entrepreneurs who have their roots in the traditional sector but who have re-acted somewhat to the call of incentives from the modern sector.[1] But this feature is not peculiar to the developing countries of Africa alone. The existence of such "layers" is to be witnessed in every underdeveloped country with the cultural and behavioural gaps between the layers shading into each other. Thus in between the sophisticated westernised industrial or commercial urban elite and the village-like urba-

[1] E. E. Jucker Fleetwood, *Money and Finance in Africa*, p. 46.

nites there is an intermediary group composed of a hard core of professional people and intellectuals who serve to narrow down the gaps between the two extremes.[1]

A brief review of the banking infrastructure in the countries under discussion is worthwhile at this stage. It consists mostly of expatriate banks which are in effect branches of large overseas banks with head offices in the important international financial centres. Most of these foreign banks in the former British colonies are "supra-territorial" banks in the sense that they operate in a number of political areas and hold funds in London. The colonial banking system has thus inevitably been based on the London money market.[2] There are indigenous banks in some cases but their share of the total banking business of the respective countries is small. Since independence central banks and national governments have been making attempts to establish new indigenous commercial banks or to bring them under indigenous ownership and control. A brief review of the banking structure in the different countries at this stage will be not only of interest but also useful in understanding the relationship of the central banks to the money and capital markets there.

THE BANKING SYSTEM OF SUDAN

In Sudan, the first commercial bank under Sudanese control and financed almost wholly from indigenous sources was established in 1960. The paid up capital of the bank at that stage amounted to LS 547000, being 50 per cent of the capital subscribed. The division of the capital into LS 1 shares facilitated widespread subscription from all over the country. Six foreign banks were then operating in the country. There were altogether 36 banking offices concentrated in the large towns and cities. The total number of the banks' branches and agencies increased to fifty-one during 1964. There was no change in the number of branches, and agencies in 1965.[3] A copy of the consolidated balance sheet of the banks is given below for the years ending 31 December, 1964 and 1965.

[1] See Bert Hoselitz, *Sociological Aspects of Economic Growth*. Chs. 7 and 8.
[2] *Banking in the British Commonwealth* (Ed. R. S. Sayers), pp. 436-40.
[3] *Bank of Sudan*, Annual Reports for the years 1960, pp. 22-23 and 1964, p. 35. Also Economic and Financial Bulletin, Bank of Sudan, January-March 1966 Vol. VII. No. 1, p. 24.

TABLE[1] No. 6

(*LS. 000's*)

Liabilities 31.12.64		31.12.65	*Assets* 31.12.64		31.12.65
	Deposits				
1,074	Government	1,137	1,334	Cash	1,277
35	Boards	16		Balances with Banks	
1,577	Local government	1,063	1,509	Bank of Sudan	6,405
28,175	Private	32,667	37	Other Banks	20
	Bankers				
11,946	Bank of Sudan	4,398		Foreign Correspondents:	
67	Other Banks	63	237	Scheduled Territories	218
			7	Egypt	7
			116	Others	178
	Foreign Correspondents				
2,306	Scheduled territories	855			
5,163	Egypt	3,269			
856	Others	946			
3,776	Capital	5,984	55,355	Advances, etc. to Private Borrowers	45,748
6,896	Other Accounts	7,477	3,276	Other Accounts	4,022
61,871		57,875	61,871		57,875

It is observed from a sectorwise analysis of Sudanese bank advances that in the earlier stages of the development of the economy bank advances in Sudan to industrial enterprises constituted a very small percentage of the total of such advances, being LS 1,171,000 only out of LS 26,549,000 or 4.4 per cent of the total. These advances included working capital requirements and finance for imports of equipments. Advances to the primary sector, agriculture, (chiefly cotton cultivation) and the tertiary sector, commerce (chiefly cotton exports) at LS 3,768,000 and LS 8,416,000 accounted for the greater portion of their advances and constituted 14.2 per cent and 31.7 per cent respectively of the total. As the economy tended to grow, advances to the industry no doubt increased in absolute terms to LS 7,575,000 in

[1] *Bank of Sudan*, Annual Report for the year ending 31 December 1965, p. 36.

December 1965 but relatively speaking they constituted still a very small portion of the total of LS 45,748,000 viz. 16.5 per cent. Advances for cotton cultivation have significantly declined and amounted to LS 806,000 only at the end of 1965 or 1.8 per cent of the total.

An interesting feature of the Sudanese banks' loan portfolio to be observed is the item, medium and long term advances which accounted for LS 5,401,000 out of a total of LS 26,549,000 in December 1958 or 20.3 per cent and LS 6,756,000 out of a total of LS 45,748,000 in December 1965 or 14.8 per cent.[1]

THE BANKING SYSTEM OF NIGERIA

Seventeen commercial banks were operating in Nigeria in 1964. They fell into three distinct groups.[2] First, the indigenous group comprising six banks of which two were co-operatives under the management of two regional governments. Although the history of indigenous banking in Nigeria can be traced to the year 1914, most of the banks had either failed or never commenced business. Thus of the 18 banks started during 1952-1961, only three have survived. They owed their survival to the patronage of the regional governments and confined their operations to the regions of their origin. Thus the African Continental Bank operates in Eastern Nigeria and the National Bank of Nigeria in Western Nigeria.

The patronage extended by the Nigerian Regional Governments to indigenous banks was motivated by the belief that the expatriate banks operating in the country deliberately discriminated against Nigerian business men, however credit-worthy they might be. Further, there was an undercurrent of feeling that these bankers tried to create a monopoly in banking business by ruthless competition with the indigenous banks. In the course of a study of the policy of encouragement of indigenous banking adopted by one of the Regional Governments, the Western Nigerian Government, a recent commentator has shown how the government attempted to foster the growth of national banking by providing financial assistance to individual commercial

[1] See Table Appendix 12. Report of the Bank of Sudan (6) for the year ending 31 December, 1965, pp. 80-81.

[2] *The Bankers' Magazine*, January, 1965. Art. entitled "Commercial Banking in Nigeria" by O. Olakanpo", pp. 17-19.

banking institutions. Government assistance generally took the form of deposits and their subsequent conversion into shares. This was well illustrated in the case of the Agbonmagbe Bank and the Merchants Bank which received deposits from such public corporations, as the Marketing Board, Production Development Board, Nigerian Ports Authority, Western Region Finance Corporation and Federal Loans Board. In the case of the former bank, which was a private company incorporated in 1945 and owned wholly by an African Chief, a deposit of £200,000 was made by the Marketing Board in pursuance of this policy of encouragement of indigenous banking in October 1959. A year later £80,000 of this deposit was converted into shares. The second bank received its first official deposit of £10,000 in 1955. In its zeal, however, to encourage indigenous banking the government evidently did not make any careful investigation into the affairs of the banks, for the banks fell into serious difficulties immediately afterwards as a result of their inefficient management and illegal practices, reflected in poor liquidity ratios and extraordinarily high advance-deposits ratios. Mr. Brown has argued that the banks had been rendered 'worse off' by the government policy of giving aid; and indeed they would have been 'better' off if they were not recipients of government aid.[1]

But it has been claimed by the Nigerians that the banks made some positive contribution to the development of the economy. The IBRD Mission has also supported the nationalistic aspirations to build up an indigenous banking system in the context of the growing economy of the country.[2] The responsibility of providing credit to African business had to be undertaken by the African banks themselves. As the IBRD Mission observed, the expatriate banks could not be expected to contribute much to meeting the increased demand for credit facilities from the developing economy. The national banks could not only provide the credit facilities but could also offer financial advice to their customers which no expatriate banks would have done. In the circumstances the policy of state encouragement pursued by the Regional Governments could not be open to any objection. But they should have taken a little more care in making an appraisal

[1] C.V. Brown, *Government and Banking in Western Nigeria*, O.U.P. 1964, pp. 34-42.

[2] IBRD Mission, *The Economic Development of Nigeria*, p. 96.

of the financial position and credit policies of the banks to be assisted before any such assistance was given.

Second, the expatriate group, consisted of seven banks of which two were British, two American, one Indian, one Arab and one French. Of the two British institutions, the Bank of West Africa was established as early as 1894 and the Barclays Bank D.C.O. in 1912, both of them in Lagos. The other five banks were new entrants and were established during 1960-1965. In the third group four banks are to be witnessed which are all registered in Nigeria and have their head offices there. This group may indeed be divided into two sub-groups. One of the sub-groups comprises two banks whose capital is entirely foreign-owned—viz. the United Bank for Africa Ltd., and the Barini Bank Ltd. The former, started in 1961, is Nigeria's largest international bank. The other sub-group also comprising two—the Bank of the North Ltd., and the Bank of Lagos Ltd.,—have a mixed ownership. Their capital is held by both foreigners and nationals. The Government of Northern Nigeria holds the controlling share in the Bank of the North Ltd.

Of the seventeen banks functioning in Nigeria in 1964 the Big Five comprising three expatriate and two national banks controlled nearly 80% of the total banking business and owned between them 192 out of a total of 218 branches. Of these five, again, the two long-established expatriate banks controlled between them nearly 50% of the country's banking business and operated 125 branches. Acceptance houses, building societies and hire purchase finance companies also operate in Nigeria. Net hire purchase credit increased from £42,79,000 in January 1963 to £60,37,000 in May 1965.

The banking system of Nigeria witnessed certain interesting developments in 1965. The number of commercial bank branches increased by 14 in the year to 240 as compared with 160 in 1959. The B.A.O. (Banque de L' Afrique Occidentale) was reorganised as Banque Internationale Pour L' Afrique Occidentale with a subscription to its capital from the First National City Bank of New York. The continuing movement towards bank mergers in the U.K. and the U.S.A. had its impact. The Nigeria branch of the Chase Manhathan Bank merged with the Bank of West Africa Ltd. which itself had amalgamated with the Standard Bank of London earlier in the year. The Bank of Lagos surrendered its licence and from September 17, commenced operations as the Finance Company of Lagos Ltd. With these developments the number of commercial banks operating in Nigeria was reduced from seventeen to fifteen at the end of 1965.

Judging by the volume of business and expansion of physical facilities the banking industry in Nigeria has been growing fairly rapidly in the past few years. [Speech of the Governor of the Central Bank of Nigeria at the First Annual General Meeting of the Institute of Bankers 25 Feb. 1966.]

The growth of capital accounts, loans and advances and total deposits of the Nigerian banks over the period 1960-65 is given in Table No. 7.

TABLE[1] No. 7

(£'s thousand) s

At the End of	*Capital Accounts*	*Loans and Advances*	*Total Deposits*	*Investments*
1960	2,966	57,000	68,512	2855 (1847)*
1961	10,209	59,990	76,914	4329 (2971)
1962	13,060	77,036	86,940	5001 (3370)
1963	12,757	89,468	96,908	2342 (1190)
1964	15,111	1,22,406	1,15,045	6989 (5363)
1965 (April)	15,178	1,15,956	1,20,766	9418 (7858)

The above figures indicate the same trend towards increase of loans and advances on the one hand and the growth of deposits on the other as are to be witnessed in the other emerging countries. The bulk of the investments similarly is held in treasury bills. An analysis of the Nigerian Commercial Banks' advances to the various sectors is given in Table No. 8, p. 23.

[1] Economic and Financial Review, Bank of Nigeria July 1965, pp. 28-29 and December, 1965, pp. 28-31.

* The figures within brackets in the last column relate to Treasury Bill holdings.

TABLE[1] No. 8

(In per cent)

Class of Borrower	1958 Dec.	1959 Dec.	1960 Dec.	1961 Dec.	1962 Dec.	1963 Dec.	1964 Dec.	1965 June
Government	.43	.75	1.86	1.42	.96	.78	.76	.76
Public Utilities	.39	×	.92	.17	.23	1.09	.64	.29
Credits & Financial Institutions ..	4.32	8.31	5.14	4.05	1.13	1.48	2.98	1.69
Agriculture	30.73	22.94	19.79	21.03	23.42	21.99	24.69	17.02
Mining	.85	1.00	.95	.79	.68	.64	.47	.34
Manufacture	4.79	4.04	4.26	5.49	7.60	9.98	10.73	13.72
Construction	6.45	7.51	6.31	9.24	6.73	7.20	4.71	6.39
Gen. Commerce	34.98	33.20	36.87	32.40	36.00	34.31	27.33	28.88
Bills Discounted	×	1.48	2.23	1.86	4.02	8.32	12.30	11.49
Misc.	17.06	20.77	21.67	23.55	19.23	14.21	15.39	19.42
Total	100.00	100.00	100.00	100.00	100.00	100.00	100.00	100.00

[1] *Economic and Financial Review, Bank of Nigeria, July,* 1965, p. 45.

THE BANKING STRUCTURE OF MOROCCO

The banking structure of Morocco is well diversified. Twenty commercial banks originally affiliated to the expatriate banks (banques étrangères) have now been established under Moroccan Law and have associated nationals in their financial control and administration work. Between them they collect 90% of the deposits of the banking system. There are six banques d'affaires which also act as deposit banks. The distinction between the two types is not rigid. The Moroccan Bank of External Commerce (BNEC) was deliberately created by the government in September, 1959 to promote possible foreign markets for national output and to facilitate the programme of imports of capital goods into Morocco. As a specialist institution for medium-term credit it has access to central bank credit. The bank also engages in short-term credit operations like ordinary commercial banks. Besides commercial banks there is a variety of financial intermediaries under indigenous control operating in Morocco of which the following may be particularly mentioned:

1. Le Credit Populaire (one central and nine regional banks), reorganised in February 1961 with a view to remove some lacunae of the old structure, to endow them with important technical means and to enlarge their activities. They provide credit to small and medium-sized enterprises, co-operatives, artisans and associations of trade and industry.
2. National Bank of Agricultural Credit formed as a part of the agricultural reform of 1961 out of three previous institutions has eight regional banks with a central office.
3. The National Bank for Economic Development (BNDE) organised in 1959 specially for stimulating capital formation and accelerating economic progress.
4. Bank of Markets (Acceptance Houses)—created in 1950 as an affiliate of the National Bank of Markets of the State, passed into Moroccan control in 1961. Their business is to put their signatures, make endorsements and accept bills of exchange.
5. Mortgage Bank of Morocco (CPIM), originally created in 1920, was rehabilitated in 1962 to discount and hold medium term bills of exchange relating to credits granted by other credit institutions, to enlarge its activities generally and

liberalise its interest rates. Although it is authorised to take part in all branches of economic activity it has allowed the BNCE (the Bank of External Commerce) and the BNDE (Development Bank) to participate in the mobilisation of credit for export trade and industry.[1]

THE BANKING SYSTEM OF TUNISIA

At the end of December 1964, 9 banks were found to be working under Tunisian Law with the Central Bank of Tunisia (BCT) at the top. The banks may be classified under the semi-public and private sectors. The banks in the semi-public sector comprise three organisations, the STB (La Societe Tunisienne de Banque), the BNA (La Banque Nationale Agricole), and the SNI (La Societe Nationale d' Investissement. The Caisse Mutelle de Credit Agricole en Tunisie (Mutual Bank for Agricultural Credit in Tunisia) which belonged to this sector has gone into liquidation.[2]

1. The STB was established in 1957 originally with a registered capital of 400,000 dinars. Under Resolutions of the Extraordinary General Assembly its capital was raised from time to time until it reached 2,000,000 dinars on June 28, 1964. This registered capital of 2 million dinars is composed of 400,000 shares of 5 dinars each as follows:—2,000 registered shares representing the initial capital; 78,000 registered shares representing the increase in capital on October 9, 1957—120,000 shares representing the increase in capital on June 26, 1960—and 200,000 shares representing the increase in capital by incorporation of Special Reserves on June 28, 1964.[3] The creation of the Bank has been an interesting social experiment. It ranks to-day as the foremost financial institution in Tunisia. It may be characterised as a development-cum-commercial bank for it combines in itself the two functions of a promotional institution as well as those of an ordinary bank. But there is clear segregation of the two functions which are not at all mixed up. Generally speaking, fixed capital is provided by the development wing and working capital in the form of a short-term credit line is arranged by the commercial section.

[1] A Note on the Structure and Distribution of Credit in Morocco. (A mimeographed copy kindly provided by the Bank of Morocco) (In French).

[2] *Annual Reports of the Bank of Tunisia 1958-59 and 1964. Also Statistical Bulletins* published by the Bank No. 17 April, 1963, pp. 5-11.

[3] *Status.* Titre II Art. 6 STB 1957-1964.

This short-term credit may be renewed from time to time so that it is really of the nature of term finance. The provision of short-term working capital by a development bank may be necessitated by the very fact that the fixed capital provided would certainly enlarge the operations of the loanee company. As we have argued elsewhere, a co-ordination between development and commercial banks in the matter of industrial financing may be useful in various ways.[1] As a commercial bank its main business consists of acceptance of demand and time deposits and all other banking operations including the granting of short and medium credit and rediscounting of all types of papers. The short-term credit provided by it is limited to a maximum period of nine months. Its medium term credit should bear a strict proportion to its medium and long-term funds made up of deposits, loans, special funds etc. As a development bank it participates in industrial, commercial and financial enterprises, which serve some public interest, with the prior approval of the Secretary of State for Planning and for Finance in proportion to its own resources. A more detailed review of the STB will be attempted in a subsequent chapter.

2. Banque Nationale Agricole (BNA) or the National Agricultural Bank established in April 1959 with a capital of 400 million dinars of which 50% was contributed by the State, commenced operations on June 2, 1959. It has two principal objectives, first that of encouraging the development of agriculture to which it has a special duty and secondly, that of pursuing all banking operations. It will be observed that its statutes do not limit its operations to the agricultural sector nor debar it from performing all other banking operations. As a matter of fact the industrial and commercial sectors have not been neglected by the institution.

3. Societe Nationale d' Investissement (SNI) was established by an Act of February 28, 1959 with a capital originally of 400 million dinars which was increased to 2,000 million dinars in 1960-61. Its objective is to study and create industrial enterprises. In this connection it can participate in their equity capital and can also grant long-term loans. Since the beginning of the 3 year plan, the Society has been entrusted with the responsibility of

[1] See *Industrial Finance in India* by the present writer (4th Ed. 1961, p. 445, p. 473).

screening of the rediscounting of medium term credit. To enable the society to obtain stable resources so necessary for the fulfilment of this role, it has been permitted to float loans in international markets and to generate long-term resources connected with the foreign aid received by the country.

As regards banks in the private sector they comprise among others the following:

1. Banque Franco Tunisienne (Franco-Tunisian Bank) established in 1879 with a capital of 30 million dinars.
2. Banque de Tunisie (Bank of Tunisia) established in 1884 with a capital of 300 million dinars.
3. Union Bancaire pour le Commerce et l'Industrie (Banking Union for Commerce and Industry) established with a capital of 250 million dinars. (1961)
4. Banque d'Escompte et de Credit a l'Industrie en Tunisie (Discount and Credit Bank for Tunisian Industry) with a capital of 350 million dinars.

Of five Banks of French origin two had been nationalised viz. Credit Lyonnaise (established 1912) and Societe Generale (established 1912). The other three are Compagnie Algerienne de Credit et de Banque, Societe Marseillaise (1919) and Credit Foncier d'Algerie et de Tunisie (1907). The other foreign banks are the British Bank of the Middle East (1957) and the Arab Bank (1960).

With the exception of the first one (BFT) all the banks in the private sector are strictly deposit banks. Medium term credit provided by these banks constitutes less than 5 per cent of their total accommodation (Portfolio and Advances). BFT is a specialist Institution since two-thirds of its operations relate to loans on mortgages.

As regards the solvency of the banking system, the co-efficient of solvency which is defined as the ratio of the banks' own funds to their liabilities was 6 per cent in 1964, there being no change from the 1963 position. The co-efficient of liquidity is the ratio of the assets currently realisable and disposable to current (short-term) liabilities. This ratio which had stood at 69 per cent at the end of 1963 declined to 63 per cent in 1963.

The table No. 9 on p. 28, brings out the number of banks of different origins in different sectors together with their capital and reserves:

TABLE[1] No. 9

	Number			(In millions of dinars) Capital			Reserves		
	1962	1963	1964	1962	1963	1964	1962	1963	1964
Tunisian Banks	8	8	9	2053	2562	5305	3217	4085	5181
French Banks	7	4	3	1227	998	778	323	262	123
Other foreign Banks	2	2	2	344	344	344	133	74	30
Banks in the Private Sector	14	11	10	2182	2453	2976	1181	1253	1074
Banks in the Semi-Public Sector	3	3	4	1442	1451	3451	2492	3168	4260

THE BANKING STRUCTURE OF RHODESIA AND NYASALAND

The Federation of Rhodesia and Nyasaland was fortunate in possessing a wide range of financial intermediaries, including a central bank, commercial banks, merchant banks, discount houses, hire purchase companies, building societies, development corporations and land banks. The emergent economy could derive a great advantage from the variety of the financial services offered by them. Before the establishment of the Bank of Rhodesia and Nyasaland in 1956, the note issue of the Federation which comprised the three territories of Southern Rhodesia, Northern Rhodesia and Nyasaland was managed by the Central Africa Currency Board, formerly known as the Southern Rhodesia Currency Board. The Standard Bank Ltd., was the oldest commercial bank to be established in the Federation and had opened an office in Salisbury in 1892. The Barclays Bank D.C.O. began operations in 1925 after taking over the National Bank of South Africa, formerly the Bank of Africa. Until the end of World War II these were the only two banks which operated in all the territories of the Federation through a wide network of branches. The last few years have witnessed the establishment of three smaller commercial banks, the Netherlands Bank of South Africa, the Ottoman Bank and the National and Grindlays Bank. Two merchant banks resembling their British counterparts were established in Salisbury (Southern Rhodesia) in the same year as the Central Bank of the Federation. They are the Merchant

[1] SOURCE: *Rapport Annuel, Banque Central de Tunisie* for 1964, p. 86.

Bank of Central Africa Ltd., and Rhodesian Acceptance Ltd., which accept deposits at call and for longer terms and provide acceptance credit facilities for commerce and industry. They also issue letters of credit and sometimes function as issue houses and underwriters. In more recent years building societies and hire purchase companies have also been formed, both of which accept deposits from the public. It was not till 1957 when the central bank, as the agent of the government, began to issue treasury bills on a regular weekly tender basis that there could be an outlet for the large liquid resources accumulated by the banks and other credit institutions. Thus the nucleus of a money market came to be built up in 1959. The establishment of two Discount Houses, the Discount Company of Rhodesia and the British and Rhodesian Discount House Ltd., in the same year strengthened the foundations of the market.[1] Although the market cannot be said to have reached such a stage of maturity that it could function as a sensitive instrument for central bank operations, there is no doubt that Rhodesia possesses a more sophisticated money and capital market and a more diversified economic structure than any other African territory discussed here.

An analysis of the loans and advances of commercial banks in the Federation sector-wise is given in Table No. 10:

TABLE[2] No. 10

RHODESIA AND NYASALAND

Analysis of Loans and Advances of Commercial Banks by Different Sectors

(In per cent)

	1961	*1962*	*1963*	*1964*
Agriculture	15.8	20.0	18.1	20.7
Mining	1.8	2.0	3.7	4.0
Manufacturing	25.6	25.0	23.9	21.1
Distribution	19.4	18.4	18.4	20.5
Construction	3.0	2.6	2.1	2.2
Financial	14.5	13.5	12.2	10.8
Private accounts ..	11.9	11.3	11.7	10.7
Services	4.6	4.6	4.9	6.7
Others	3.4	2.6	5.0	3.7
Total	100.0	100.0	100.0	100.0

[1] *The Bankers' Magazine* December 1962, pp. 401-402. Art. by V. P. Romilly entitled "The Money Market of Rhodesia & Nyasaland".

[2] SOURCE: *Annual Reports, Bank of Rhodesia and Nyasaland* for *the years 1961, 1962 and 1964.*

The above table highlights the relatively large proportion of bank advances to the primary and secondary sectors as against the tertiary sector in sharp contrast with most other underdeveloped countries under discussion. This feature reflects comparatively more advanced nature of the country's economy. In spite of the rapidly developing economy of the country, however, the expansion of the deposits of the commercial banks has been rather slow. During 1962-1964 when gross national product increased by 64% and advances by 79%, total deposits grew by only 11%.[1] The chief explanation for this disparity is to be found in the rapid growth of various categories of non-banking financial institutions like post office savings banks, merchant banks, hire-purchase companies and building societies. All these institutions were accepting deposits from the public and by offering higher rates of interest were able to divert a good deal of savings and liquid resources away from the banking system to themselves. There has in fact been a remarkable expansion of total liquid resources. This rise of a large number and variety of non-banking financial institutions again reflects the growing maturity of the economy.

THE BANKING SYSTEM OF GHANA

At the time of the Trevor Report in 1951 the banking system of Ghana comprised besides the Post Office Savings Bank and the Gold Cost Co-operative Bank, two expatriate commercial banks, Bank of British West Africa Ltd., and Barclays Bank D.C.O. which maintained a limited branch network in the principal towns only. These banks conducted all normal commercial banking business. It is interesting to notice the existence of an Industrial Development Corporation and an Agricultural Development Corporation to facilitate, promote and assist in the financing of industrial and agricultural undertakings. The former had at the time eleven branches and the latter seven.[2] Since the publication of the Report three National Financial Institutions with specifically defined functions have been established in addition to the above-mentioned banks. They are the

[1] Art. by R. I. Grant Suttie in the *Commonwealth Banking Systems* Ed. W. F. Crick, p. 144.

[2] See *Report by Sir Cecil Trevor op. cit.* Ch. V.

Ghana Commercial Bank (1952), the National Investment Bank (1963) for the provision of long-term finance for approved development projects in the country and the Agricultural Credit and Co-operative Bank (1965) to provide credit facilities for the development of agriculture, fisheries and cottage industries.[1] The Ghana Commercial Bank was established with government support and was intended to restrict its dealings to the Africans. But several years after the formation of the Bank, debates in the Ghanaian Parliament reveal a great dissatisfaction with the working of the Bank. The main lines of criticism were that the ordinance under which it worked was drafted by British experts and was responsible for the development of practices which were clearly not in the interests of the indigenous people. It denied loans to good customers because the managing directors were themselves money lenders. Moreover it was more inclined to provide loans to foreign firms rather than to Ghanaians. There was a very strong feeling that it should amend its procedures and make less restrictive the conditions under which it granted its loans and advances.[2] The Bank has even now been unable to progress much in various spheres even though serious efforts have been made. The banking habit has developed slowly and the Ghana Commercial Bank has not been able to secure a large volume of the growing deposits which every Commercial bank requires as its working capital.

At the end of June 1964, the total of branches of the three commercial banks, Bank of West Africa, Barclays Bank DCO and the Ghana Commercial Bank rose to 172 with twelve new branches being opened. Of the 12, five were in the Ashanti Region, three in the Eastern Region (including Greater Accra) two in the Western Region and one each in the Central and Brong-Ahafo Regions.[3]

The development of commercial bank branches facilitated by improved communications and opening up of new areas has

[1] Letter to the writer from Mr. G. N. Parry, Act. Secretary, Bank of Ghana, dated 14 October, 1964.

[2] *Official Report of Parliamentary Debates Ghana August 24*, 1960 (Quoted by E. E. Jucker Fleetwood).

[3] *Bank of Ghana Annual Report* for year ending June 30, 1964. p. 81. The number of bank branches increased further to 186 in 1965 being distributed among the three as follows: Bank of West Africa—33
Barclays Bank D.C.O—61
Ghana Commercial Bank—92

proceeded in an uninterrupted manner with a brief slowing down in 1962 and has helped to bring banking facilities to new areas and towns and to encourage the growth of the banking habit among a greater proportion of the population. This impressive expansion of bank branches is also a sign of the banks' confidence in the economic future of the country. The trend is illustrated in Table[1] No. 11.

TABLE[1] No. 11

DEVELOPMENT OF COMMERCIAL BANK BRANCHES AND AGENCIES

1959	*1960*	*1961*	*1962*	*1963*	*1964 June*	*1964 August**
93	104	130	139	160	172	185

* Letter to the writer from the Act. Secretary, Bank of Ghana dated 14 October, 1964.

The consolidated balance sheet of the banking institutions during 1959-64 indicates on the assets side a marked increase in the holdings of securities, the bulk of which was Government of Ghana Stocks, loans and advances and commercial bills (mostly cocoa finance). There has been, since December 1960, a continuous rise of treasury bill holdings from £5 million to £30 million in March 1965. On the liabilities side total deposits have been continuously rising as is shown in Table No. 12:

TABLE[2] No. 12

Bank Deposits (£ G'000)

	1959	*1960*	*1961 (Dec)*	*1962 (Dec)*	*1963 (Dec)*	*1964 (June)*
Total ..	32484	38855	43165	58775	67033	73935
Demand ..	21480	26102	29806	41470	45816	49926
Savings ..	8461	10747	10756	12491	15068	16752
Time ..	2543	2006	2603	4814	6149	7257

[1] *Bank of Ghana,* Annual Reports for the financial years 1961, p. 22; 1962, p. 31 and 1964, p. 81.

[2] *Bank of Ghana,* Annual Reports for the financial year 1964, p. 78.

The deposits of the public rose further to £90 million in March 1965. The increase in deposits, three fold since 1959 is explained by three main factors, first, accumulation of idle funds in Ghana as a result of the imposition of exchange control against the sterling area which prevented expatriate trading establishments from transferring out their profits; secondly, import control leading to the running down of the traders' stocks so that their imports lagged behind their sales, the proceeds being held idle in banking accounts; and thirdly, greater payments made to farmers owing to larger cocoa crops finding their way into the banks as deposits with few goods to buy in the market.[1]

An analysis of the loans and advances of the commercial banks in Ghana by different sectors is given below. From the breakdown given in the table it will be observed that up to 1962 the tertiary sector accounted for the highest percentage of bank credit obtained and the primary and secondary sectors accounted for relatively lower percentages. Thus while in 1962 commerce, including cocoa marketing obtained 57.1 per cent of the total

TABLE * No. 13

BREAKDOWN OF LOANS AND ADVANCES BY REPORTED END-USE

	Percentage of Total 1961 Dec.	1962 Dec.	1963 Dec.	1964 June
1. Agriculture, Forestry and fishing ..	4.6	4.2	23.4	22.2
2. Mining ..	1.0	0.9	0.7	1.5
3. Manufacturing ..	3.2	2.3	3.0	4.6
4. Building and construction ..	3.4	7.5	12.2	22.5
5. Electricity, Gas & Water ..	0.1	13.6	3.3	4.2
6. Commerce (including cocoa marketing) ..	37.5	57.1	45.2	24.8
7. Transport, storage and communication ..	..	1.2	1.1	1.2
8. Services ..	2.9	1.9	3.6	5.6
9. Miscellaneous ..	47.3	11.3	7.5	13.4
Total: ..	100.0	100.0	100.0	100.0

* SOURCE: Annual Report. *Bank of Ghana for the year 1964*, p. 70.

[1] *The Bankers' Magazine*, March 1966. Art. entitled 'Recent Trends in Ghana,' p. 189.

advances, agriculture, forestry and fishing received only 4.2 per cent and manufacturing only 2.3 per cent. As the country developed, the shares of the last two increased to 22.2 per cent and 4 per cent respectively at the expense of that of the first which dropped down to 24.8 per cent in 1964 (June). This movement away from the traditional channels of finance and trade however has not affected the composition of the commercial banking institutions which remain as before.

In spite of the increasing separation of the country's economy from its traditional framework of membership of the sterling area, and a shift of trade away from U.K. and U.S.A. to the Eastern block states and the shadow of political upheavals, the banking system has shown remarkable resiliency and has adapted itself to the changing economic and political scene. The economy itself with its well planned infra-structure, cheap supply of electricity and skilled man-power resources shows clear signs of buoyancy.

Chapter Three

Economic and Financial Structure of the Countries

LIBYA

Libya to-day is an independent Sovereign Kingdom with an area of 1,759,540 Sqr. Km., most of the area however being a desert, and a population of nearly 1.6 million and is a member of the sterling area.[1] Before World War II the country had formed a "fourth-shore" for Italy and was subjected to demographic colonisation. Its name was then merely a geographical expression and its people preferred to be known as Cyrenaicans, Tripolitanians and Fezzanese, rather than as Libyans, according to the three territories which composed the country. The attainment of an independent status by Libya after World War II was not marked by an intermediary stage of semi-sovereignty. At the end of the War although Libya was freed from the control of Italy, she was still legally the sovereign power in the country which was one of her former colonies. The political status of Libya could not be decided even when the Peace Treaty with Italy was signed in 1947 because no final decision could be reached regarding the disposal of Italian colonies. The whole question came up before the United Nations in 1949. While Italy had all the time been urging that not only Libya but also her other African colonies should be restored to her in the capacity of an administrator under the United Nations Trustee System, a great deal of interest came to be aroused by what is known as the Bevin—Sforza Plan which received the support of Great Britain, U.S.A. and the Latin American countries. According to the Plan independence was to be granted to Libya after 10 years. During this period Cyrenaica, (Western Part), Fezzan (South Western Section) and Tripolitania (Western Coastal Area) were to be placed under the U.N. Trusteeship, the administrative authorities for the three countries being U.K., France and Italy respectively. But the resolution sponsoring the plan was defeated in the General Assembly by an overwhelming majority through a combination mainly of Arab-Asian and Soviet blocs. When the trusteeship

[1] *The Statesman's Year Book* 1966-67. In April 1963 the Federal form of Government was abolished.

plan fell through, most of the members came to favour independence, some calling for "immediate" independence, but others pressing for a transitional period of 3-5 years. After a prolonged debate over the question, a draft resolution was adopted by a large majority by the General Assembly in November 1949. The main features of the Resolution were:

(1) Constitution of an independent sovereign state of Libya comprising Cyrenaica, Tripolitania and Fezzan as soon as possible and in any case not later than January 1, 1952;
(2) Determination of the constitution for Libya by representatives of the inhabitants of the above three territories;
(3) Appointment of a U.N. Commissioner for Libya by the General Assembly, together with a Council to advise him, for assisting the people in the formulation of a constitution and the establishment of an independent government.

The U.N. Commissioner Mr. Adrian Pelt was appointed on 10th December, 1949. An Advisory Council of Ten was formed soon after. At the first meeting of the National Assembly of sixty members drawn in equal numbers from the three territories, held on November 25, 1950 at Tripoli, two fundamental laws were enacted. One provided for a federal state, without which no surrender of sovereignty could be expected from either Cyrenaica or Fezzan and therefore no unity could be achieved. The other stipulated that the form of government should be monarchical and the throne of Libya should be offered to Amir Idris of Cyrenaica. The constitution drawn up later provided for a democratic form of government which could be said to be on par with any other democracy in the East.[1]

On the eve of independence the Egyptian pound which had been used to pay the British Eighth Army based in Egypt had been in circulation in Cyrenaica since 1942. The amount in circulation was estimated by its Ministry of Finance in 1950 to be between 750,000 and 1,500,000 Egyptian pounds. In Tripolitania the currency in circulation was the Military Authority Lira (MAL) originally issued in exchange for the Italian lira on a one-for-one basis in September, 1943. The British Military Administrative Pound introduced earlier and the Metropolitan Lira were retired and ceased to be legal tender in November 1943.

[1] See Majid Khadduri, *Modern Libya. en passim.*

A branch of Barclays Bank D.C.O. which had been opened in April 1943 was the only banking institution in operation. Some of the former Italian banks were understood to be contemplating to apply for permission to re-open. In the Fezzan area the Algerian franc equal in value to the French metropolitan franc was in circulation. No data are available as to the total amount in circulation there.

At the request of the U.N. Commissioner in Libya, two staff members were sent by the IMF to advise him on the unification of Libyan Currency as a prelude to the attainment of independence. The experts recommended a unified currency system which they thought would be able to provide the necessary financial stability during the period of strains and stresses involved in the economy's growth process in the years lying ahead. The proposals had a definite anti-inflationary bias and may be summarised as follows:

(1) The par value of the currency unit should be 0.497656 grammes of fine gold. The obligation to redeem the currency was to be limited to an undertaking to deliver the currency in which the major portion of the reserve was kept.

(2) The currency unit should be divided into 100 parts instead of 1000 and have a value equal to 4 shillings sterling or U.S. $0.56, the size being convenient to the majority of those who would use it.

(3) The reserves to be maintained for the new currency should be 100 per cent in foreign exchange. This recommendation was linked with their recommendations concerning external financial assistance to Libya. The maintenance of a 100 per cent reserve was called for in the interests of a sound currency, and for inspiring the confidence so desirable in the case of a newly independent developing country. Elaborate arguments were advanced in this connection to support the case of a 100 per cent as against a fractional reserve system. At any rate the system was in line with the 100 per cent reserves maintained by the Currency Boards in the British Colonies. Whatever rigid link the system might maintain between the country's balance of payments and its domestic money supply, it was to be alleviated

through a guarantee of foreign financial aid for stabilization and development both in the public and the private sector.

(4) 75 per cent of the reserves should be held in sterling and/or convertible currencies and/or gold. The balance of 25 per cent might be held in the currencies of the trading partners of Libya, provided that no soft currencies other than sterling were to be held to the extent of more than 10 per cent of the reserve. The Currency Authority should however have the competence to determine from time to time what currencies were eligible for reserve purposes.

(5) The monetary system should be administered by a Currency Authority composed partly of Libyans and partly of foreigners, the latter drawn from British, Egyptian, French and Italian nationalities. The Authority in sharp contrast with some of the Currency Boards/Commissioners in British dependencies was to be legally domiciled in Libya from the start. The new government, when formed, would certainly desire the location of the Currency Authority at home. The public through its officials would also have an opportunity to meet its members.[1]

All these recommendations were subsequently considered at a meeting of experts representing U.K., France, Italy, Egypt, and the U.S. and accepted by them. The only change was that the currency should initially have a 100 per cent backing in sterling but that the Libyan Currency Authority should have the discretion to invest up to 25 per cent of its reserves in currencies other than sterling, subject of course to the consent of the competent authority of the country of each currency. The Provisional Libyan government agreed to all the proposals except that it chose to make the monetary unit, to be called Libyan pound, to be equal in value to the pound sterling and to have it subdivided into 100 piastres and 1000 millièmes. The provisional government opted for the sterling area.[2]

Depicted in classical literature as the "grain bowl" of Europe, Libya through the ages came to be converted in the present

[1] IMF Staff Papers, November 1952. Art. by G. A. Blowers and A. N. Mcleod entitled "Currency Unification in Libya", pp. 453-456.

[2] Ibid, p. 466.

century into a gigantic "dustbowl". As Prof. Benjamin Higgins has observed, it combines within the borders of one country virtually all the obstacles to development to be witnessed in any underdeveloped territory,—geographic, economic, political, sociological and technological.[1] Rainfall is scanty and erratic in most areas while in others it is entirely absent. Without vast extensions of the irrigated area, prospects for rapid agricultural development were not very bright. Prospects of industrialisation were still more limited because of lack of coal or water power or of known mineral deposits ready for exploitation. The supply of domestic capital was scarce owing to the extreme poverty of the people. Most Libyans were not able to save at all. Even when they saved in exceptionally good harvest years, that saving was not in a form favourable to the economic development of the country. Lack of skilled labour and of vigorous entrepreneurship in the pre-war and pre-independence days were the other obvious obstacles to rapid economic growth. The problem of incentives was also there with a social attitude which may be characterised as "the backward sloping supply curve of effort". The people were mostly confined to agriculture of a primitive kind. Large elements of population were nomadic or semi-nomadic. The only important non-agricultural occupations were textiles and handicrafts. The war brought in its train a substantial return of Italians, the advanced sections of the population, to the home country. The postwar wave of anti-semitism drove out the Jews who before the war had been engaged in trade and small enterprises. Thus in both the pre-war and pre-independence days Libyan economy was "deficitary" in the sense that it did not produce enough for the consumption of the people even at the prevailing admittedly low standards and the balance had to be made up by capital and other imports from the ruling countries. It is interesting to observe that Tunisia with an area of less than Tripolitania, one of the three territories comprising Libya, supported a population which was thrice as large as that of Libya.[2]

In 1959 when the World Bank Mission visited the country, they were struck by the existence side by side of a subsistence sector as well as a modern sector. One facet of the dual economy

[1] Benjamin Higgins, *Economic Development, Principles, Problems and Policies*, p. 27.
[2] *Ibid*, p. 34.

was to be seen in the almost primitive rural community which was leading a simple, almost austere life, unaffected by the spread of the twentieth century technology, and dominated chiefly by strong tribal traditions. The other aspect of the economy was to be witnessed principally in the highly sophisticated population, inhabiting the cities of Tripoli and Benghazi with their suburban villas, gaily decorated shopwindows, cinemas, hotels and motor cars. The prosperous agricultural farms managed mostly by foreigners, the government office buildings, the schools, parks, hospitals and the metalled roads constituted the various other facets of this modern economy. There was no doubt however that Libya was in the process of a rapid change. Living standards were rising, demand for imported foods and western consumer durables was increasing, movement of population from the country-side to the cities and towns was quickening the pace of urbanisation. The process of change was undoubtedly hastened by the discovery of oil, the exploration of which commenced in 1955.[1] The impact of the oil discovery on the economy of the country has been far-reaching as will be shown presently. Whatever that may be, it is clear that all these trends together with oil provided a favourable setting for the rapid economic growth of Libya.

On the eve of independence, the national income of the country was very low but it would be difficult to determine the precise level owing to lack of adequate data on production and prices. It was estimated by Dr. Lindbergh at about £15 million sterling in 1950.[2] By 1959 it was estimated to have risen to £L56 million and by 1964 to about £L118 million.[3] But very little of this increase could be attributed to an increase of gross domestic output or internal productivity. Exports had been more or less constant since 1950 with some declines in 1958 and 1959, while the annual population growth was believed to be about 1.2 per cent. Inflationary forces might have been responsible for raising the nominal value of the national income but that again must have been to a minor extent. It was foreign military expenditure, external aid and the recent oil explorations which must have

[1] IBRD Mission, *Economic Development of Libya*, p. 32.
[2] Quoted in the *IBRD Report on Economic Development of Libya*, p. 371.
[3] *Seventh Annual Report of the National Bank of Libya* for the year ending 31 March, 1963, p. 53. Also *Ninth Annual Report*, p. 24.

been mainly responsible for this growth of the national income. Exports of oil were rapidly increasing. Since the beginning of September 1961 until the end of 1964/65 the value of crude petroleum exports reached the figure of £L 116,861,000 in 1963 and £L 216,533,000 in 1964 constituting 98.6 per cent and 99.0 per cent of total exports in the respective years.[1] These oil exports no doubt earned foreign exchange for Libya, and the local expenditure of the oil companies stimulated employment, brought funds to the Libyan Government and generally contributed to the growth of the national economy. Petroleum alone accounted for 30 per cent of the national income. But the oil discovery was not an unmixed blessing for the country's economy whose foundations and structure came to be profoundly affected by it. Concentration of wealth was an important result. The primary beneficiaries were the business community and allied affluent groups. The profits earned in this sector came to be used in financing real estate speculation and the construction industry. It was further responsible for considerabe conspicuous consumption.

The increasing demand for modern suburban homes on the part of the foreign community employed by the oil companies led to the distressing conversion of productive agricultural land and mature orchards into luxury villas, roads and playgrounds. All this, however, was taking place at a time when Libya was importing large quantities of food-stuffs, fruits and vegetables from abroad. Considerable amounts of the foreign exchange earned were not only being used for the imports of these food-stuffs but were also being dissipated in the purchase from abroad of non-essential commodities chiefly consumed by a limited group of affluent people.[2] In view of the extremely undeveloped nature of the Libyan agriculture and low level of indigenous technical and managerial skills it was inevitable that such developments would take place and continue unchecked unless specific policies and programmes were adopted. The upsurge in foreign expenditure particularly of the oil companies, and the continuous budgetary deficits generated strong inflationary forces in the economy. Such forces were calculated to thwart the

[1] *Ninth Annual Report of the Bank of Libya* for the year 1964/65, p. 26.

[2] *Fourth Annual Report, National Bank of Libya* for the year ending March 1960, p. 31.

economic development of Libya unless these were countered by adequate monetary, fiscal and direct controls.[1]

Even before oil had become a significant factor in Libya's economy, it was not exactly a monoculture economy after the pattern of most of the African economies, under discussion. Libya had a relatively more diversified line of exports.[2] Groundnuts, live animals, esparto grass, sponges, fish, olive oil, hides and skins, almonds and castor seeds constituted the principal exports. Minor agricultural exports comprised citrus fruits, potatoes, tobacco and in very good crop years even cereals.[3] An analysis of the composition of the country's domestic exports and imports together with the percentage share of each commodity in them for the years 1954-1958 is given in Table No. 14.

TABLE * No. 14

COMPOSITION OF EXPORTS
LIBYA

Commodity		*Percentage of domestic exports*				
		1954	*1955*	*1956*	*1957*	*1958*
1. Groundnuts	..	16	15	21	18	24
2. Live Animals	..	15	17	19	11	19
3. Scrap metal	..	6	10	13	9	4
4. Esparto	..	17	12	11	7	6
5. Olive oil	..	7	12	2	25	10
6. Wool and animal hair	..	8	8	6	5	3
7. Hides and skins	..	6	5	6	5	5
8. Sponges	..	10	6	5	2	3
9. Others	..	15	15	17	18	26
Total domestic exports	..	100	100	100	100	100

* SOURCE: Govt. of Libya Central Statistics Office (Quoted in the Report of the World Bank Mission Table S. 13. p. 360).

[1] *Inflation in Libya,* Economic Research Dept. National Bank of Libya, 1961, pp. 64-65

[2] *The Banker,* September, 1961. Art. by A. G. Chandavarkar, p. 628.

[3] *IBRD Report,* pp. 136-137.

TABLE[1] No. 15

COMPOSITION OF CIVIL IMPORTS

LIBYA

Percentage of total civil imports

	1954	1955	1956	1957	1958
1. Food, clothing, drink etc.	57	53	49	43	43
2. Coal & coke	2	5	2	2	1
3. Petroleum	5	5	4	6	6
4. Machinery	8	8	10	10	12
5. Transport equipment	7	7	8	12	14
6. Base metals	5	5	7	6	6
7. Building materials	2	4	5	4	3
8. Fertilizers	1	1	1	1	1
9. Other chemicals	2	1	2	3	3
10. Rubber tyres	1	1	1	1	1
11. Other materials	10	10	11	12	10
Total	100	100	100	100	100

The value of the exports in 1958 at £L 4,313,000 was not very high in absolute terms nor in relation to its national income. In the circumstances the economy could not be said to be subject to the usual export induced fluctuations; and there was hardly any problem of containing the built-in instability that arises generally from such a situation.

Recent trends in the exports position, indicating the value of different categories of domestic exports and the significance of each item, are brought out in the table given below. The declining trend of non-oil exports and the corresponding rise of petroleum exports are to be clearly observed. Even exports which had been ordinarily stable in the past like groundnuts, almonds, citrus fruits and fish and fish preparations registered a fall. Groundnuts, however, still continue to be the most important item in relative terms next to petroleum followed by live stock and live stock products. The percentages of total domestic exports constituted by these three items were 35.04, 15.86 and 9.66 in 1962 as compared to 37.01, 23.58 and 13.78 in 1963. But

[1] Govt. of Libya Central Statistics Office Reproduced in the *Economic Development of Libya*. I.B.R.D. Bank Mission, pp. 361-62.

groundnuts dropped by 11.70 per cent, almonds and citrus by 32.97 per cent and fish and fish preparations by 34.6 per cent. All other non-oil items declined while exports of crude petroleum went up by 150 per cent, and constituted 98.56 per cent of total exports in 1963.

TABLE * No. 16

MAIN EXPORTS

	1963 (£L '000) Value	*Percent of total*	*1962 (£L '000) Value*	*Percent of total*	*Percentage change 1963/62*
Domestic exports					
Other than Petroleum					
Goundnuts	634	37.01	718	35.04	—11.70
Live stock & Products	404	23.58	325	15.86	+24.31
Castor oil seeds	236	13.78	198	9.66	+19.19
Almonds and citrus	124	7.24	185	9.03	—32.97
Scrap metal	107	6.25	95	4.64	+11.26
Fish, fresh and processed	72	4.20	110	5.37	—34.55
Esparto	65	3.80	71	3.47	—8.45
Olive oil	..	..	280	13.66	—100.00
Others	71	4.14	67	3.27	+5.97
	1,713	100	2,049	100	
Crude Petroleum	1,17,415	98.56	46,967	95.82	+150.00
Total Domestic Exports	1,19,128	100	49,016	100	+143.04

Table No. 17 gives a picture of the composition of imports in recent years:

TABLE* No. 17

COMPOSITION OF IMPORTS

Percent of total

	1963	*1964*
1. Durable producer goods	33.8	33.7
2. Non-durable consumer goods	26.8	28.1
3. Non-durable producer goods	28.8	27.9
4. Durable consumer goods	10.6	10.3

*SOURCE: *Eighth Annual Report, Bank of Libya* for the year ending 31 March, 1964, p. 32.

The table given above shows the proportion of capital to consumer goods imported. Non-durable consumer goods include food-stuffs like oils, fats, sugar, cereals and their preparations and dairy products. These have by and large tended to increase. The value of the imports of durable consumer goods which cover electrical household appliances, passenger cars, furniture etc. has also increased. At the same time it is observed that imports of producer non-durables and raw materials as well as producer durable goods like non-electrical machinery, instruments and lorries recorded big increases. As a result of the tariff reductions effective from January 1, 1965 the imports are likely to increase more. The reductions were made to secure mainly a twofold objective (1) to arrest the rising cost of living by exempting essential goods from import duties and (2) to quicken the pace of economic development by permitting duty free imports of essential raw materials and industrial plant and agricultural machinery.[1]

The quantum of Libya's imports rose from £24,422,000 in 1958 to £104,380,000 in 1964. It was even an increase of 22.4 per cent over 1963. This increasing trend in the country's imports is to be explained by the uninterrupted rise in income and consumption, expansion of oil activities and last but not least liberal trade and exchange policy.

THE BANKING STRUCTURE OF LIBYA

There would not appear to be any basic difference between the structure and problems of commercial banking in Libya and those of the other emerging countries in Africa studied here. The banking system of the Kingdom consisted wholly of expatriate banks which were branches of foreign banking institutions. At the time of the visit of the World Bank Mission, eight foreign banks were in operation, three had their head offices in Italy, two in Great Britain, and one each in France, Egypt and Jordan. All the banks operated in Tripoli and five had also opened their offices in Benghazi. The process of reorganisation of the Libyan banking system really dates from November 15, 1950 when the Tripolitania Banking Proclamation was promulgated and a Banking Control Board was set up. It was during the

[1] *Ninth Annual Report, Bank of Libya* 1964/65, p. 35.

period 1951-52 that most of the commercial banks functioning in Libya at the present times had commenced their business. In recent years a dominant feature of Libyan banking has been the Libyanization of foreign banks operating in the country. Banco di Sicilia and Societe de Banque offer two interesting cases which have started working since 1964 under the names of Sahara Bank and Societe Africaine de Banque respectively. Two other banks, the British Bank of the Middle East and Bank Misr have also agreed to comply with the requirements of the policy of Libyanization of commercial banking which includes among others Libyan majority capital. The broad objective of this policy is to transform the old banking system into one which is more integrated with the national economy and conforms to the country's over all economic requirements.[1]

The total number of banking offices in Libya as late as 1961 was 27 which gave a banking density of one office for every 40,329. It is of course true that population per office is not an adequate criterion of banking growth. But even then compared with other underdeveloped economies the banking density must be considered fairly high.[2] But most of the offices were located in the two cities of Tripoli and Benghazi, the smaller cities having not more than one office each. The liquid assets of the banks consisted mostly of foreign currency reserves held with head offices abroad.

TABLE No. 18

COMBINED BALANCE SHEET OF PRVATE COMMERCIAL BANKS IN LIBYA.[3]

As at the end of	*Assets (£L'000)*		
	Liquid Assets (cash, balances with National Bank, Foreign, currency, and balance due from banks abroad)		*Credit Extension* (Advances, overdrafts, bil discounted and othl loans).
December 1958	3,127	•	8,374
December 1959	4,981		10,766
	Capital and Reserves	*Liabilities Total Deposits*	*Borrowing from banks abroad etc.*
December 1958	1042	10243	18759
December 1959	1031	13868	25660

[1] See Introduction to the Ninth Annual Report, Bank of Libya 1964/65, p. 7

[2] A. G. Chandavarkar. Art. in *the Banker* Sept. 1961, p. 630 entitled "Banking in Libya".

[3] Statistical Appendix Table S20. *The Economic Devlopment of Libya*, p. 367.

The World Bank Mission reported that only three banks had their capital and reserves in Libya. All banks were controlled from abroad and some of the foreign banks operating in the country had no capital and their reserves were practically zero.

An examination of the pattern of the assets and liabilities of the commercial banks in Libya in 1958/1959 brings out clearly the basic structure of banking in the country.

The liquidity ratio of the commercial banks (ratio of cash and money at call to deposit liabilities in Libya) averaged round about 32 per cent which was much above the legal minimum of 20 per cent. The actual cash deposit ratio stood at 35.9 per cent in December 1959 which appears to be an unusually high ratio.[1] This high degree of liquidity of the banking system indicates that the credit policies of the system were very cautious and conservative. It also reflects the absence of suitable outlets for the safe and profitable employment of the surplus cash resources of the banking system. At one end the risk factor involved served as a deterrent to extension of more loans and advances to the public, at the other end there was no short-term government securities market which could provide an avenue for the employment of the excess resources. In such circumstances it was no wonder that the banks did not make any serious efforts to mobilise local savings.

A second feature of commercial banking in Libya was the predominance of short-term loans and advances, extended usually for a period of 3-12 months. These constituted practically the whole of their earning assets in the absence of government securities which were still not issued. The bank customers would hardly offer any suitable tangible security to serve as collateral for the bank credits. The banks inevitably adopted the policy of providing unsecured credits on the strength of the standing and reputation of the borrowers. In such circumstances bank lending had to be confined to relatively few sectors represented by a small number of bank clientele personally known to the management. This obviously reflects the shortage of suitable assets which could serve as collateral and highlights the need of a close banker-customer relationship.

A third characteristic to be observed is that the sectors to which by far the greater proportions of bank credit were extended were

[1] *Economic Development of Libya,* p. 381.

the tertiary sectors of the economy comprising trade (wholesales) and service industries. As will be observed from the table given below, 42.1 per cent and 41.9 per cent of the total bank loans went in favour of wholesale merchants in 1958 and 1959. 9.4 per cent and 13.8 per cent of the total were in favour of motor vehicles and transport. The share of strictly productive loans was much smaller but not negligible. Agriculture including livestock received 12.1 per cent in 1958, though it dropped to 9.7 per cent in 1959. The construction industry received 4.8 per cent and 3.2 per cent respectively in the two years while all industrial firms put together accounted for 11.3 per cent and 12.5 per cent.

TABLE No 19

ANALYSIS OF CUSTOMERS' LIABILITIES TO PRIVATE BANKS

	*Percentage Distribution** 1958		1959	
Agriculture	12.1		9.7	
Industries:				
Food, Drink & tobacco	3.7		4.5	
Textiles	1.6		1.7	
Soap & oils	1.5		1.1	
Metal products & machinery	1.2		1.7	
Store, cement & bricks	0.9		0.8	
Other	2.4		2.7	
Construction	4.8		3.2	
Wholesale merchants	42.1	52.4	41.9	49.4
Retail merchants	10.3		7.5	
Motor vehicles & transport services	9.4		13.8	
Professional and Private Individuals	1.4		1.9	
Mortgages	2.3		1.6	
Miscellaneous	6.3		7.9	
Total	100.0		100.0	

* Table A6. IBRD Mission, *The Economic Development of Libya.* p. 380.

The distribution of bank credit according to sector has undoubtedly been altered to some extent in recent years owing to the developing economy of the country. But as in the past, general commerce (wholesale and retail) still accounted for the largest share of bank credit at 41.2 per cent in December, 1964. The proportion, however, has been declining steadily since 1958 when it had been more than 52.4 per cent. The continued predominance of credit to general commerce emphasises the importance of distributive activity in the economy. The decline to 34.7 per cent in December 1965 has been made up for by the spectacular growth of the share of bank credit that has gone in favour of the construction industry—the percentage having jumped from 4.8 per cent in 1958 to as high as 16.2 per cent in March 1965. Motor vehicles and transport services, being ancillary to general commerce, naturally accounted for the next largest share and appear to have received even greater attention than before, the percentage having risen to 14 per cent in March, 1965 from 9.8 per cent in 1958. The proportion going to manufacture has increased but it is even now much below that of any one of the three previous sectors. The assistance provided to agriculture, though as before not negligible, has not significantly changed. Thus it may be observed that the tertiary sectors have continued to secure the major portion of bank credit. The position in the more recent times is clearly brought out in Table No. 20.[1]

TABLE No. 20

DISTRIBUTION OF CREDIT ACCORDING TO SECTOR

	(Percentage) 31 Dec. 1963	31 Dec. 1964	31 March 1965
1. General Commerce (wholesale and retail)	40.2	41.2	34.7
2. Construction	10.3	13.1	16.2
3. Manufacture	8.0	7.9	7.8
4. Agriculture	3.4	3.3	2.5
5. Public utilities	2.4	2.2	3.9
6. Motor Vehicles and transport services	15.1	13.5	14.0
7. Hotel entertainment concern	2.1	1.7	1.0
8. Professional and Private Industries	3.2	2.5	3.7
9. Building (Mortgages)	2.4	3.3	4.2
10. Others	12.5	11.2	12.0
Total	100.0	100.0	100.0

[1] SOURCE: *Ninth Annual Report of the Board of Directors, Bank of Libya 1964-65*, p. 27, p. 30.

It is clear from the tables given above that commercial credit extended to finance wholesale and retail business and transport services and purchase of motor vehicles constituted a far greater proportion of total credit extended than that provided to industry and agriculture in 1958 and 1959. This pattern of the distribution of bank credit continued through the years down to 1964 and 1965. There has no doubt been a slight reduction in the share going to wholesale and retail activities which dropped to 41.2 per cent in 1964 and subsequently to 34.7 per cent in 1965 but the overall position remains unchanged. The dominant feature of the distribution of credit is even now the very large slice going to wholesale and retail business and by and large to the tertiary sector. The impact of such credit distribution is obviously inflationary.

As the bulk of credit is not flowing to the productive sectors of industry and agriculture, it cannot be contended that any restriction of credit will adversely affect the economic development of the country.

An interesting trend to be witnessed in the development of commercial banking in Libya in the present times is a definite shift away from the policy of extreme conservatism that had characterised lending activities of the banks a decade ago. The banks have adopted relatively more liberal and expanding credit policies while numerous outlets for more efficient employment of their surplus cash reserves have opened up in the developing economy of the country. That they have been filling a significant role in the financing of the rapidly growing commercial sector is amply demonstrated by the continuous downward trend of their liquidity ratios and increasing trend of their credit-deposit ratios.[1]

Liquid Assets as percent of Deposits*				*Credit-Deposits ratio.*			
1951	57	1961	39	1951	28	1961	67
1952	61	1962	34	1952	34	1962	72
1953	43	1963	28	1953	51	1963	78

*Liquid assets include cash on hand, demand deposits with the Bank of Libya and other banks, and foreign currency on hand and due from banks abroad.

[1] *Seventh Annual Report of National Bank of Libya for the year 1963*, pp. 62-63. Also *Eighth Annual Report, Bank of Libya for the year 1964*, pp. 52-55.

A consolidated Statement of Selected Assets and Liabilities of Commercial Banks (excluding the Commercial Department of the Bank Libya) is represented in Table No. 21:[1]

TABLE No. 21

AT END OF 4TH QUARTER 1964 AND END OF FIRST QUARTER 1965

(£ L'000)
Selected Assets

	Liquid Assets	*Credit Extension*	*Investments*
	Cash on hand, demand deposits with Bank of Libya, other banks in Libya and banks abroad.	(Advances and overdrafts, bills discounted and negotiated and other loans)	(Including time deposits with Banks)
At the end of the 4th quarter, 1964	6,216	23,597	1,026
At the end of the 1st Quarter, 1965	9,472	23,653	2,191

Selected Liabilities
(£L'000)

	Capital and Reserves	Total Deposits including Savings Accounts	Borrowings from Bank of Libya, other banks in Libya, Banks Abroad
At the end of the 4th quarter, 1964	5,623	2,66,44	92
At the end of the 1st quarter, 1965	5,735	3,11,23	47

From the above table it will be found that the percentage of liquid assets to deposits dropped further to 23·33 per cent at the end of the 4th quarter of 1964, though it rose slightly to 30.43 per cent in the first quarter of 1965. The credit-deposits ratio rose as high as 88.56 in the fourth quarter of 1964, though it declined to 76.00 at the end of the first quarter of 1965.[2] Thus the pursuit of expansionary credit policies by the Libyan commercial banks witnessed in the previous years is continued down to the present times.

[1] *Ninth Annual Report, Bank of Libya*, 1964-65, p. 29.
[2] Estimated from the data as given in the above Table.

Chapter Four

Currency Boards as the Precursors of the Central Banks in the African Colonies

The rise of central banking in all these newly independent countries was not an accident: it was the inevitable outcome of the acquisition of political sovereignty and a consciously growing economy. To these countries the central bank was an appropriate symbol of financial independence which was the counterpart of political freedom. The possession of a central bank of its own was as much a question of prestige and status as operating a national airline, constructing a parliamentary building and establishing an embassy. These countries, as shown above, had inherited from the previous political regime a commercial banking system conducted mainly by expatriate banks and had hardly an indigenous banking system of their own. The expatriate banks had been the target of bitter criticisms in that their lending policies led to the concentration of their credit on expatriate primary producing and trading enterprises and they were depriving the economies of the countries concerned of the benefit of their surplus resources by repatriating them to the money markets of their home countries.[1] The establishment of a national central bank with "embryonic powers" for regulating the banking system and fostering the growth of an indigenous money and capital market was considered to be urgently necessary in the interests of their economic well-being. Currency boards were operating as mere administrators of the monetary system. Like central banks they could not formulate a national monetary-credit policy tuned to the requirements of their overall economic policy. The newly independent countries were anxious to utilise the experiences of central banking not only in the traditional but also in the non-traditional spheres of activity. They had a new concept of central banking which was clearly related to the urge of an underdeveloped country to achieve a rapid rate of economic growth. In the emerging countries a national central bank came to be the chosen instrument through which they could quickly reach the goal not only of economic development but also of national fulfilment in every way.

[1] E. Nevin, *Capital Funds for Underdeveloped Countries*, p. 47, p. 50.

The emerging countries did not wait for the development of any clear philosophy of central banking with particular reference to the peculiar characteristics of their economic situation. They were not inhibited by the absence of any crystallisation of thought as to the appropriate role of central banks in economies such as theirs. They could not be deterred by the dominant view in certain quarters that central banks had no place outside the developed money markets and international financial centres; and that if established in countries with an undeveloped banking system they would be an expensive luxury. According to some commentators (e.g. Lord Cobbold)[1] reliance on the central bank in the early stages of economic development could even be dangerous. Foreign advisers brought up in the traditions of classical central banking invited to report on the desirability and practicability of establishing central banks in underdeveloped countries had almost invariably argued that it would be inadvisable to contemplate the establishment of a central bank in the existing stage of the countries' economic and financial structure. Mr. H. S. Tomkins of the Bank of England observed in his Report on the "Hongkong Banking System" that the establishment of a central bank would mean unnecessary expense for the country. Some of these advisers again thought that most of the functions of a central bank could be exercised by currency boards in a much better and less expensive way. Thus Mr. H. C. B. Mynors who was invited to review the case for a central bank in Southern Rhodesia as early as 1948 had recommended that the elaboration of the Currency Board System, rather than the outright establishment of a central bank, would be more appropriate at that stage of the country's economic development. Sir Cecil Trevor, who was requested by the colonial office in 1951 to undertake on behalf of the Gold Coast Government an enquiry into the whole field of banking and "examine the question of setting up a National Bank on commercial lines to finance development projects and act as a reserve bank", reported that the time was not ripe for the formation of a full-fledged Central Bank of Issue and recommended the formation of a semi-government commercial bank which would accept deposits with or without interest, make loans and advances, and issue demand drafts as well as

[1] See Lord Cobbold's Lecture. in the *Journal of the Institute of Bankers*, February, 1963. "Some Thoughts on Central Banking". (Stamp Memorial Lectures).

perform some central banking functions as those of acting as an agent for the government and local authorities, and of purchasing and selling and rediscounting bills and foreign exchange. What was required, according to Sir Cecil, was the nucleus of an institution which would grow and extend, assuming more and more functions as the general economy of the colony developed, making its contribution at every stage but not absorbing up more vital resources of men and material than could be spared. The difficulties, according to him, in forming a full-fledged central bank at that stage consisted in (1) the building up of a currency reserve in gold, which would mean its non-availability for development and would in effect be no more than taking the gold out of the mines merely for the purpose of burying it again in the vaults of the central bank, (2) the absence of such flexibility instruments as a government securities market, a bill market, a stock exchange and a developed banking system and (3) last but not least the non-availability at the time of suitable premises for housing a full-fledged central bank.[1] Mr. J. L. Fisher in his Report on Nigeria also observed that the questions of expense and trained staff were not negligible. The currency was being managed by the currency board with the minimum expense, while a new central bank would immediately require capital for its premises. According to him two transitional stages had to be completed before the transfer of the currency issue to the central bank could be contemplated. The first stage should be the domiciling of the West African Currency Board in West Africa and the second should be the constitution of a Nigerian Currency Board as a separate unit having its own distinctive currency. It is clear that these suggestions about the reform of the currency board were intended to satisfy nationalistic aspirations. After adequate experience in currency doctrine and practice had been gained, the function of the currency board could be transferred to a Bank of Issue which would be able to assume other functions of a central bank in the light of the stage of development of the financial mechanism. He made it clear that it would be inadvisable to have a central bank for Nigeria at that moment, when its financial environment was ill-suited for its proper functioning. It would be a logical step only after the financial mechanism was

[1] Sir Cecil Trevor, *Report on Banking Conditions in the Gold Coast and on the Question of Setting up a National Bank*. Accra 1951, Paras 98-104, 153-55, 169. Also. Ch. XI.

adequately developed. It could then act as a "coping stone to the banking system". What was more urgently needed at that moment was capital for development and the fostering of voluntary savings. "The formation of a development corporation, the establishment of a state sponsored co-operative credit organisation and the building up of a short-term credit market through the issue of treasury bills should precede the establishment of a central bank of Nigeria".*

Most of the opposition to the establishment of central banks in these newly independent colonies as voiced in these Reports of British advisers was based upon a conviction that currency boards were quite adequate for the needs of these colonies at the prevailing stage of their development. Even Mr. J. B. Loynes who had been mainly responsible not only for recommending the establishment of a central bank in Nigeria but also for the design of the Bank is found to have advised Sierra Leone in another Report to set up a "Monetary Institute", rather than a central bank, with hardly more powers than a currency board.

It has so often been contended that the system of monetary arrangement generally known as Currency Boards virtually performed the functions of central banks and effected monetary management with a minimum of expense that it will be worthwhile to examine this contention and bring out the difference between the working of a Currency Board and a central bank. The investigation may best be made by reference to the working of the West African and East African Currency Boards, both originally domiciled in and managed from London. The former covered Gambia, Gold Coast (Ghana), Nigeria and Sierra Leone and the latter Kenya, Tanganyika, Uganda and Zanzibar. There were other currency boards such as the Central African Currency Board (covering Rhodesia and Nyasaland), the Palestine Board (covering Palestine and Trans-Jordan), the British Caribbean Currency Board (covering British Guiana, Trinidad, Tobaga etc.). Although the structures and procedures of these different currency boards exhibited many variations, some serving only a single territory and some locally domiciled but serving several territories, they tended to conform by and large to an underlying pattern. In all colonies and dependencies whether in the sterling

* J. L. Fisher, *Report on the desirability practicability of a Central Bank in Nigeria.* December 15, 1952.

group or in the rupee, ex-silver or dollar group, the same functions of currency management were exercised by a Board of Commissioners of Currency, or a local Commissioner of Currency.

THE WEST AFRICAN CURRENCY BOARD

The first of these currency boards, the West African Currency Board, was set up as a result of the recommendations of a Parliamentary Committee (1912) appointed to enquire into matters affecting the currency of British West African colonies and protectorates. At the time when the committee reported, the local media of circulation were the gold, silver and copper coinage of the U.K., and certain American, Spanish and French gold coins which were all legal tender. Besides these one could witness in the interior the use of couries, "manillas", brass and copper rods and even gold dust as media of exchange. Silver coin could be delivered to any person, merchant or banker in the colony on payment of equivalent face value in London, the cost of delivery being borne by the U.K. Government. This system was highly disadvantageous for the colonies. One of the most important defects was the absence of any obligation on the part of the U.K. Government to buy back the silver coin on its face value or indeed at any value at all. Thus apart from the silver transactions being in effect a one-way traffic, there was another defect in that the seigniorage on the silver coin issued was retained by the U.K. Thus large quantities of silver coin were being bought from the U.K. by the colonies at a price much above their intrinsic value without any assurance of getting back their money.[1] The main recommendations of the Parliamentary Committee referred to above were (1) the minting of a new silver coin in West Africa, (2) the establishment of a Currency Board to manage it, the Board purchasing silver bullion, having it minted, and issuing and redeeming the coinage at its face value, less a small commission either for sterling in London or for gold or British silver coin in West Africa, (3) the accumulation of the profit secured from the seigniorage in a fund for guaranteeing the reconvertibility of the new currency into sterling if so required by circumstances,

[1] *The Economic Journal*, April, 1944, Art. by Sir G. L. M. Clauson entitled "The British Colonial System".

(4) the issue of a West African paper currency on the same principles as those of the coinage.

The West African Currency Board was set up and began to issue the new coinage in 1913.[1] Notes came to be issued later in 1916. It was under obligation to instruct its currency officers in West Africa to issue coin and notes on a £ for £ basis to the local branch of any bank in West Africa on receipt from the head office in London the equivalent amount in sterling plus a small commission of $\frac{1}{2}$ per cent. Conversely it was obliged to pay the equivalent amount to the head office, less the small commission, in London of the local branch of any bank on tendering by the latter of notes and coins to any of its currency officers. The establishment of the Board resulted in the provision in the colony of a depository in which surplus currency could be placed as well as a source from which additional currency could be secured at short notice. The West African monetary arrangement was typical and the monetary systems in the other colonies and dependencies where Currency Boards or local Commissioners of Currency or Boards of Commissioners of Currency were subsequently set up were broadly similar with minor variations. The general investment policy for these bodies was laid down by the Colonial Secretary under which each authority was permitted to invest its funds in British Government or Dominion Government securities and was debarred from investing in the issues by its own Government. With the establishment of central banks in Ghana and Nigeria and subsequently in Sierra Leone, the original scope of the West African Currency Board became considerably reduced in 1964. The history of these different boards and commissioners, however, was not equally fortunate. For instance the East African Currency Board fell into difficulties in its initial stages which could be cleared considerably later.

THE EAST AFRICAN CURRENCY BOARD

Since its establishment in December 1919 the area covered by the East African Currency Board has passed through several phases of evolution till it came to stand on the verge of dissolution in 1965. It seems to have a chequered career marked by

[1] See J. B. Loynes, *The West African Currency Board 1912-1962* for a full history of the Board.

additions to or withdrawals from its territory by constituent governments from time to time. Formed originally to provide for and control the currency of Kenya and Uganda, Tanganyika joined the EACB in 1920, Zanzibar in 1936, and Somaliland (both the Italian and the British Protectorate) Eriteria and Ethiopia during 1942-1943. Ethiopia, however, left the Board in 1945, Italian Somaliland in 1950 and British Somaliland in 1961 on its attainment of independence. Aden had become a member in 1951 when the East African shilling became legal tender there. Aden's accession to the Federation of South Arabia in January 1963 and the replacement of the East African shilling by the South Arabian dinar are later developments. In June 1965, the three East African Governments of Kenya, Tanzania and Uganda declared their intention to establish their own central banks and to issue their own currency. The East African Currency Board in the circumstances is expected to continue its operations up to the period when the new central banks are formed and are ready to take over its responsibilities.

The operations of the EACB followed the same pattern of an automatic currency changer as that of the WACB and other British Currency Boards. Money supply was determined by the shifts in the balance of payments position of the member-countries and as such was outside the purview of the Board's control. There was no question of pursuing independent monetary-credit or balance of payments policies. Following the accepted practice of other boards, EACB did not make any investment in the domestic governments' securities until 1955 when the regulations were amended. During the earlier stages of its operation, however, the EACB was not able to provide a hundred per cent sterling cover for its currency issue because of the difficulties it had to face in replacing the Indian silver rupee and other silver coins of the Indian standard issued by the German Government by its own currency at face value. Unlike the WACB which successfully effected the conversion of British silver coins circulating in Western Africa at their face value, the EACB had to sell the retired coins at their bullion value and sustain a loss.

When the conversion of the former currencies into the EA Shilling was completed in 1925, the Board had to face a total loss of £ EA 1.75 million. The currency cover ratio which was 43.6 per cent only at that time did not reach the 100 per cent mark until

1950 (101.2 per cent). It had fallen as low as 10 per cent in 1932, and had risen to 30.2 per cent only in 1935.[1]

It was in 1955 that the EACB could deviate for the first time from its purely passive role of an automatic money changer when it was empowered by an amendment of Regulations to subscribe for, buy or sell and hold publicly issued securities of the constituent territories, provided that the total value of the securities so held did not exceed £10 million. The original limit for the fiduciary issue prescribed at £10 million was subsequently raised to £ EA 20 million in 1957. In 1959 EACB was permitted to acquire local treasury bills within the above limit of the fiduciary issue. Thus it was enabled to extend both long-term and short-term credit to the member governments which lost no time in availing themselves of the facilities.

EACB is observed to have passed through several stages of reorganisation. The year 1960 witnessed a significant change in its administration and mode of operation, when its seat was shifted from London to East Africa and its head office located at Nairobi. The members, though still appointed by the British Secretary of State for the colonies, were representatives of the constituent territories and the administration of the EACB came to be directed from within the currency area. From this period onwards EACB is observed to be interested in widening the scope of its activities and undertaking operations in the monetary-banking sphere analogous to those of a central bank. A significant extension of its function consisted in providing facilities of seasonal finance for export crops with the twin objective of acting as a promoter of exports as well as a lender of last resort to the banking system. In this connection it sought the necessary authorisation from the Secretary of State to discount and rediscount bills and other appropriate instruments related to the marketing of crops which was granted subject to certain limits. The commercial banks resorted to EACB for the first time in 1961-62 for financial assistance under the new system.

During this period governments of the constituent territories faced with dwindling revenues as a result of depressed economic conditions made increased recourse to the EACB for short-term borrowing. Holdings of treasury bills issued by Kenya, Tanga-

1 Sources: Annual Reports of the East African Currency Board for various years. Quoted in the *IMF Staff Papers*. July, 1966, p. 237.

nyika and Uganda are observed to have significantly increased in the portfolio of EACB. The Board found it necessary to adopt certain principles for providing finance to the various governments. One such principle to be adopted was to allocate as equitable a share as possible of the fiduciary issue to each member government. A second was to insist upon prior consultation with it before any government undertook to issue treasury bills or bonds. It also sought to establish a suitable formula for the equitable distribution of the net income to the different member governments.[1]

Ever since that period EACB has encouraged short-term borrowing by the governments by successive raising of its ceilings for lending, and developed closer relations with the commercial banks in the field of crop financing, rediscounting of treasury bills and settling of clearing accounts. Long-term borrowing by governments has however been discouraged lest the funds needed for short-term accommodation should be locked up and flexibility in monetary policy should be restricted. Attempts have also been made to extend its currency services by establishing new centres in the various parts of the territory comprised under it. A significant step was taken in 1964 when the almost rigid link between the London rates and the local rates for treasury bills was somewhat relaxed. By 1965 EACB is found to have strayed away from the traditional role of a currency board and moved closer in the direction of a central bank particularly in relation to monetary-credit policy. The most remarkable developments in this context, as summarised by a recent commentator, lie in three directions, (1) greater authority to extend credit in place of the original authority to issue and exchange currency only; (2) conscious manipulation of its charges for buying and selling sterling as a policy instrument, and (3) effective insulation of the domestic treasury bill rates from London rates.[2]

It is clear that the EACB in the recent past has moved away from the "accepted responsibilities and tasks of a currency board" and closer to the areas of central banking. This development has been picturesquely characterised by a recent commentator as "a major experiment in central banking without a central bank".[3]

[1] *IMF Staff Papers*, July 1966. Art. entitled "East African Currency Board" by J. W. Kratz, pp. 240-241.

[2] Ibid. p. 249.

[3] *Commonwealth Banking Systems* (1965) Ed. by W. F. Crick, p. 7.

But it would be misleading to overstress the analogy. As a result of its authority for fiduciary issue, it has no doubt powers of credit expansion akin to those of a central bank. But these powers are neither very broad nor double-edged. Apart from moral suasion and the initial control inherent in the legal limit on the fiduciary issue, it had no power to control and restrict credit. It had also no authority to direct the maintenance of minimum reserve ratios by commercial banks nor could it affect the level of their reserves through open market operations. It did not act as a full-fledged banker to the governments nor as a depository of treasury funds. Manipulation of treasury balances as a potential instrument of credit policy was in consequence unavailable, although it could be of limited use in the context of the large deficits governments were incurring.[1] So long, again, as the expatriate banks could replenish their cash resources by making recourse to their head offices in London rather than to the EACB, the scope for monetary policy was obviously limited. In some other areas the EACB's operations however reflected progressive deviations from earlier practices. Variation of the spread between buying and selling rates of sterling referred to above came to be adopted as an instrument of policy to stimulate inward movements of foreign funds or to check the temporary out-flow of funds induced by higher rates in London. Its efforts in providing a preliminary basis for an East African Money Market by preventing local rates from following automatically the movements in the British bank rate constituted another break with past practices. It had prepared for consideration of the governments of the constituent territories a scheme for the creation of an East African Treasury Bill in place of the territorial bills. It had also made proposals for further amendment of its regulations so that it could be equipped with powers for liquidity and credit controls. But the decision taken in June 1965 by Kenya, Tanzania and Uganda to establish their own central banks nipped in the bud the aspirations of the Board to move yet closer to central banking.

Compared with central banks, the most important point to be noticed is that these currency boards had no discretionary authority. Their functions were wholly automatic and passive. They created an automatic link between money supply and the balance

[1] *IMF Staff Papers*, July 1965. Art. by G. S. Dorrance "Instruments of Monetary Policy", p. 277.

of payments. As such, the domestic money and credit situation could not be insulated against the ebb and flow of external trade and payments. With increasing exports, export earnings flowed into the banks and the currency board and there was an automatic rise of currency circulation and bank deposits. An export boom was likely to be followed by an import boom with rising prices, a greater demand for imports, and increased bank lending to finance imports or new enterprises or the holding of stocks. In the other direction a slump in exports might lead to a reduction of bank lending and a slowing down of domestic activity. Any country engaged in foreign trade is subject to such fluctuations but under the mechanism of the currency board the effects were likely to be felt more quickly and fully. Under the currency board mechanism a positive influence could not be exerted on the internal credit conditions and the inevitable consequence was the enforcing of a painful and drastic readjustment. The automatic reaction of the currency board mechanism on the currency circulation and hence on the total money supply was no doubt in practice tempered in most colonies by the use in the lean years of the surplus funds stored up abroad in good times of marketing boards, banks, commercial firms, and governments and the power of the banks to cushion the inflow and outflow of funds. But the financial mechanism in all these countries was undeveloped and internal trade was less organised and less dependent upon the banking system than external trade. If there were an increase in local deposits, the banks might not be able to employ the extra money locally. If there were an increase in currency, part of it would lie idle in banks or disappear in private boards.[1]

A second criticism that could be directed against the currency boards, at any rate against some of them at their earlier stages, was the requirement to maintain a hundred per cent backing in sterling against their currency liabilities with the proviso that an additional reserve amounting to 10 per cent in some cases could be accumulated. Currency boards were under obligation to issue their currency on demand against an equivalent amount of sterling, and at least in the past, not against any other kind of asset; and secondly, to redeem the currency in sterling on demand.

[1] Report by J. B. Loynes on the Establishment of a Nigerian Central Bank, Lagos. 1957, p. 2.

The aim therefore had always been to maintain at all times a full backing in sterling and to build up an additional sterling reserve out of the income from their investments to cope with emergencies. When a country's economy is growing and reaches a certain stage of development, such a policy may indeed be much too restrictive. Some currency boards had no doubt taken powers to maintain a domestic securities backing against their currency issues. But with these exceptions all currency boards worked by and large to the same pattern. There was not only a strong feeling in the colonies that the entire reserve should not be held in cash or foreign securities but that at least a certain portion should be allowed to be held in local government securities. In the postwar years when the demand for development finance came to be very great and the traditional sources of investment became scarce, this feeling gathered considerable force. It now found expression in the criticism that the countries were being deprived of large working balances sterilised in the form of external reserves for their currency which could not be utilised for the financing of domestic capital investment. The criticism came to be buttressed by theoretical arguments in favour of a substantial fiduciary issue which would liberate a part of the foreign exchange backing of the currency and make it available for financing their economic development. A large portion of the external reserves, it was contended, was being practically hoarded by the governments and had the consequence of retarding their economic growth.[1] There was a hard core of the domestic currency circulation which would never be presented for redemption, for this was the irreducible minimum required for carrying on the trade and commerce in the country. This portion of the money supply was the fiduciary issue which could have a security backing and could be a source of savings for the developing economies. Some of the Boards in response to this demand had indeed come to be empowered subsequently to make limited fiduciary issues of currency against local government securities. In addition to the powers of fiduciary issue some Boards were further authorised to issue currency against bills discounted for the banks in respect of crop financing.

The authorisation of credit creation by currency boards with-

[1] *Measures for the Economic Development of Underdeveloped Countries.* United Nations, p. 36. Also E. Nevin, *Capital Funds for Underdeveloped Countries*, pp. 14-15.

out the machinery of a central bank constituted a remarkable development. Some of the facilities for monetary management of the banking system rendered elsewhere by a central bank were thus provided but they were not aimed at forestalling or impeding the development of central banking in a form suitable to new political conditions.[1]

Although the system of currency boards was cheap to run and relatively trouble free and preserved at all times a stable value of the colonies' currency in terms of sterling, it could not provide a national currency after which every independent country aspired as much as its economic betterment. Nor would it have allowed the newly independent territories to pursue an independent monetary policy or speed up the development of a local money and capital market. A central bank would be responsible for the stability and integrity of the country's currency like a currency board. But unlike a currency board a central bank does banking business, though of a specialised character and its banking operations like purchases of securities and grant of loans to governments and banks could expand currency circulation without a corresponding increase in its external backing, and similarly sales of securities and recalling of loans could reduce circulation without loss of such backing. Such operations would thus affect the liquidity of the banking system and thereby influence the amount of bank credit. The central bank would have discretionary powers and would not leave the increase and decrease of money supply in good and bad times to the automatic working of currency boards. The central bank again would be in a position to foster the development of an indigenous banking system and build up the financial infra-structure of the country as no currency board would do. In an underdeveloped economy as that of the emerging countries there were obvious limitations to the spohisticated functions of a central bank operating in the developed money and capital markets of a mature economy. But even then there was plenty of useful work to do for a central bank in the former economies. Central banks could issue and administer a national currency system. They could carry on banking functions for the Government and furnish expert advice and information on general economic problems and technical

[1] Report of the Bank of England, 1962. Art. entitled "Currency and Banking Developments in some Commonwealth Countries".

problems of finance and management of foreign exchange reserves. They could act as a supplementary source of funds for commercial banks for financing the needs of trade, industry and agriculture whose growing credit requirements could not be adequately met with their small deposit resources. They could act as bankers to ordinary banks and undertake the tasks of creating investment outlets of a more liquid nature than loans and advances and provide opportunities for the employment of the excess funds of the banking system during the seasonal lull in the demand for credit.[1] As the key monetary authority the central bank could be an instrument of bank supervision. Thus during the past decade the replacement of currency boards by the creation of central banks has been an interesting institutional development in the colonial countries in the years immediately following their political independence. The assets and liabilities of the West African Currency Board and the Central African Currency Board were taken over by central banks in Nigeria and Ghana, and Rhodesia and Nyasaland respectively, the first two being established on May 15, 1958 and March 1, 1957, and the last earlier in March 1956. The Sudan Currency Board created under the Sudan Currency Act, 1956 as a transitional arrangement was replaced by the Bank of Sudan in 1959. Official British advice was unable to prevail against the pressure of nationalistic African opinion for the establishment of central banks which was also fortified by academic support, though the ground for support was different. While nationalist opinion in favour of a central bank was derived from an undercurrent of feeling that the expatriate banks discriminated against African traders, agriculturists and industrialists,[2] the academic view was that such an institution could promote economic development not indeed by monetary management but by fostering indigenous banking, development finance institutions and a money market.[3]

After independence when pressures for quickening the pace of economic development were intensified in these countries, it is clear currency boards or monetary institutes with the limited powers of central banks would fail to assist the mobilisation of

[1] *South African Journal of Economics*, March 1960. Art. by A. F. Brimmer, entitled "Banking and Finance in the Sudan".

[2] See *Trevor Report* op. cit. para 45.

[3] W. T. Newlyn and D. C. Rowan, *Money and Banking in British Colonial Africa*, pp. 275-276.

resources for development as well as to apply the brakes when inflationary forces tended to retard this rate of growth. When a number of emerging countries established their central banks, the "demonstration effect" was not lost upon others who acquired their independence subsequently. A good case in point is furnished by Sierra Leone which not only modelled its central bank officially opened in August 1964, on the lines of the Nigerian institution but also copied the design of its permises and that on an even grander scale.[1]

The central banks which have superseded the currency boards in the newly independent colonies will undoubtedly have to undertake responsibilities far beyond the maintenance of a high degree of confidence in the national currencies both at home and abroad which currency boards had established for the common currency. They will have to fulfil new functions and face new problems of monetary control. They will have to evolve their international reserve policies and determine the size and composition of their external reserves. They will have to nurse the indigenous banking system and foster development finance institutions. Above all they will have to guide the economic development of their respective countries in the context of their development plans with a reasonable degree of monetary stability. An appraisal of the working of some of the newly established central banks in the emerging countries of Africa which follows will make it clear if the supersession of currency boards by central banks has been justified.

[1] *The Bankers' Magazine*, March 1966, p. 197. Art. by C. V. Brown entitled "Banking in Sierra Leone: A Comparative Survey".

Chapter Five

Structure and Design of the Central Banks

RELATIONSHIP BETWEEN THE CENTRAL BANKS AND THE STATE

THE NEW concept of central banking referred to above which has permeated central banking philosophy to-day in both developed and developing countries has been embodied in the charters of all the central banks, which are the subject matter of our study. This concept is reflected in the provisions in their statutes concerning their relations with the government, and the banking and financial community, the role of monetary reserves, their objectives, functions, and techniques of monetary policy and last but not least their attitude towards economic development.

All the central banks except that of Libya were from the start envisaged to be wholly owned by their respective governments. The authorised capital of the Bank of Sudan amounting to LS $1\frac{1}{2}$ million was wholly provided by the government. In Nigeria, of the authorised capital of £ $1\frac{1}{2}$ million to be subscribed by the government, £ 1,250,000 has been subscribed and paid up. The capital of the Bank of Southern Rhodesia as in the case of its predecessor the Bank of Rhodesia and Nyasaland has been prescribed to be £ 1 million to be held by the government. The capital of the Bank of Ghana, originally fixed at LG 1 million under the 1957 ordinance to be taken up and paid by the government was subsequently raised by the Bank of Ghana Act 1963 to LG 10 million to be taken up by the government from time to time.[1] The entire share capital of the Bank of Morocco amounting to 20,000,000 dirhams is held by the state.[2] The capital of the Central Bank of Tunisia under the provisions of the Law No. 58-110 of 18th October 1958 was fixed at 1 million 2 hundred thousand dinars to be subscribed by the State in the form of real estate, movable property, (securities) and materials acquired by it upto 1 million dinars and in the form of bullion upto

[1] The unit of currency viz. one pound (=2.48828 grams of fine gold) was changed to cedi (=1.03678 grams of fine gold), one ghana pound being equivalent to 2.40 cedis.—The Bank of Ghana Amendment Act, 1965. Sec. 2(1), (2) & (3).

[2] The subscription of the capital of the Bank of Morocco was paid by the state to the extent of 1660 million francs in conformity with the real estate and securities acquired by virtue of a convention between the state and the State Bank of Morocco.

2 hundred thousand dinars.[1] The capital has been fully subscribed by the state as above. In the case of the Libyan Central Bank, when started originally there was however no complete state ownership as in the other newly independent colonies. The authorised capital of the National Bank of Libya, which came into being under a Law of April 26, 1955 and commenced operations in 1957, was laid down at £L 1 million of which £L 500,000 was to be forthwith subscribed and paid by the Government of Libya. Such part of the remaining £L 500,000 might be offered for public subscription as the Board in agreement with government should deem appropriate.[2] Unlike other central banks which are the subject of our study, the National Bank of Libya was not originally envisaged as a wholly state owned institution. Before the Bank commenced its operations in 1957, the government contributed a total of £L 700,000, out of the Libya-American Reconstruction Commission fund, and the remaining £L 300,000 of the authorised capital could be offered for public subscription.[3] The National Bank of Libya was renamed Bank of Libya in 1963 under the Banking Law of the year subscription to its capital of being restricted to that of £L 1 million the Government.[4]

All this state-ownership offers a remarkable contrast to the Reserve Bank of South Africa which, after the nationalisation of the Bank of England and the Reserve Bank of India, enjoyed in the Commonwealth a position of lonely eminence as a pure shareholders' type of a central bank. State ownership has also been a common feature of central banking organisation in the Latin American countries and is in conformity with the modern conception of the relationship between central banks and the State. The relationship between the central bank and the State however has evolved into the present stage after passing through various phases. Before World War I the statutes of central banks had by and large stressed the importance of the control of the central bank by the State. After the orgy of inflation indulged in by most belligerent governments in the war and immediate post-war years, a sharp reaction set in against state control and

[1] See *Textes Organiques Banque Centrale de Tunisie*, p. 31.
[2] Art. 7. *Law No 30 of 1955 Establishing the National Bank of Libya.*
[3] *The Bankers' Magazine, June 1960.* Art. by A. G. Chandavarkar "Central Banking in Libya.
[4] *Law No. 4 of February 5, 1963* Art. 2.

state management. The concept of independence of central banks came to be embodied in the Brussels Conference Resolution of 1920 which was to the effect that "banks, especially Banks of Issue, should be freed from political pressure and should be conducted solely on the lines of prudence". This concept of independence of Banks of Issue was the central feature of the reconstruction schemes initiated by the League of Nations and was enshrined in the statutes of most of the central banks established at the time as in Austria, Hungary, Estonia, Greece etc. The charters of the Banks subsequently established in certain Central American Republics exhibit the operation of the same principle. The banks came to be regarded not so much as 'State Departments' but as "public trusts". From this point of view the concept of a State Bank did not find favour on the ground that its direction would not be unbiassed, continuous and free from political pressure. The past banking history of several South American countries was frequently quoted to justify such fears.

But the imposing facade of complete political independence that central banks in many parts of the world had so assiduously built up crumbled to pieces by the impact of the great Depression. As a commentator has aptly observed, the fate of the independent central banks came to be sealed and the mirage that was fostered so carefully in the 1920's that finance and politics should be kept segregated in troublous times was shattered to pieces.[1]

The post-depression years witnessed an increasing trend towards state-ownership and state control of central banks. This trend has been reflected in the central banking statutes relating to ownership of capital, participation in administration and intervention in monetary policy. The change in the relationships between the central banks and the state is nowhere more evident than in the statutes drawn up during and after World War II. For the first time we came across statutory definitions of the central banks' position vis-a-vis the state. This formalisation of the relations between the two has found expression in the nationalisation of a large number of central banks in the post-war years and is the outcome of complex, political, economic

[1] G. G. Johnson, *The Treasury and Monetary Policy*, 1933-38, p. 6.

and ideological forces.[1] In underdeveloped countries with immature banking systems and the doctrine of state-directed economies having full play, the concept of a private shareholders' bank was an anomaly. In the context of the highly complex economic and financial structures of most civilised countries in the present times and against the background of policies of full employment pursued by them, the old concept of a central bank confining itself to its own business and in a state of isolation from governments and politics had also become unworkable. Monetary and fiscal policies have become integral parts of the overall economic policy of the governments. A central bank cannot obviously pursue a policy that runs counter to the objectives of the national economic policy. Thus the concept has been developed that the central bank, though fairly independent, should act in the closest harmony with the government. While conceding that ultimate responsibility for overall policy rests with the government, modern central bankers would like to stress that the due discharge of their responsibilities would call for a certain measure of independence in their technical operations as well as in their policy thinking.[2] The modern concept of the relation between the central banker and his government has been succinctly stated by Mr. Roosa in course of his Per Jacobsson Foundation Lecture. The central banker's job is not that of a free agent, pursuing an independent course. His task is to adjust himself to the broad aims of economic policy as adopted by his country. At the same time no arm of government is free to determine objectives and pursue them in defiance of the ultimate necessities imposed by monetary discipline. The central banker, however, is privileged to continuously remind those other arms of governmental policy that these requirements of monetary discipline can be disregarded or side-tracked only at the cost of a failure of the policy objectives.[3] The relationship between the central banks in the newly independent countries and their governments is more or less the same as stated by the Governor of the Bank of Rhodesia and Nyasaland in the memorandum to

[1] Art. by M. A. Kriz in the *American Economic Review*, Sept. 1948. "Central Banks and the State To-day".

[2] "Some Thoughts on Central Banking", Speech of Lord Cobbold published in the *Journal of the Institute of Bankers*, London, Feb. 1963.

[3] Robert V. Roosa, "The Place of Monetary Policy in the Economic Policy in the U.S.A." Lecture at the Per Jacobsson Foundation. October 1965, p. 33.

the Radcliffe Committee. The Central Bank enjoys a fair measure of independence in the performance of its responsibilities. The constitutional provisions relating to the appointment of the Governor and the Board of Directors have contributed a great deal towards ensuring this independence. The relationships between the Bank and the Treasury are very close and harmonious. There is a great deal of informal consultation and close working contact between them. On general principles the policies of the Bank are not at variance with those of the government.[1] The Bank of Ghana reports a continuous strengthening of the relations between the Bank and the Central Government. The Ministry of Finance has been assured by the Board of the Bank fullest co-operation in achieving the targets set in the Seven Year Development Plan.[2]

This view of the position of central banks vis-a-vis the government is taken even by the Governor of the South African Reserve Bank, still a pure shareholders' type of central bank, who observed before the Radcliffe Committee that his Bank was satisfied to regard its independence as independence *within* the government rather than *of* the government.

The statutes of the Central Banks of Nigeria, Ghana, and Rhodesia and Nyasaland though of British heritage, in sharp contrast with those of the Bank of England or the Reserve Bank of India do not contain any provision empowering the government to issue directions. In Sudan, however, it has been provided that the Ministry of Finance and of Economics may from time to time give directions to the Board of a general character as to the exercise by the Board of its functions which appear to affect the national interests, and the Board is bound to carry out such directions. The directions will be issued after consultation with the Board.[3] The elaborate procedure for resolving any possible conflict between the Treasury and the Central Bank as is to be witnessed in the case of certain countries in the Commonwealth e.g. Ceylon and Australia is also missing in the case of all those Banks. In Australia if there is a difference of opinion between

[1] Memorandum of the Governor of the Reserve Bank of Rhodesia and Nyasaland and of the Governor of the Reserve Bank of South Africa to the Radcliffe Committee, Vol. I, p. 283. and p. 286.

[2] *Bank of Ghana, Report for the financial years ending June 1961 and June '64*, p. 9 and p. 5.

[3] Art. 20. *The Bank of Sudan Act. 1959.*

the Reserve Bank Board and Government which cannot be resolved by discussion, the Board has to submit its views in a written statement and the government may thereupon overrule the Board and take responsibility for the policy. Thus the Australian law has given a somewhat superior position to the Reserve Bank of Australia as compared with the Bank of England which under the British law is structurally subordinate to Government. There is the important difference that the disagreement between the Australian Reserve Bank and government has to be formally brought before Parliament. While the Statute of the Ceylonese Central Bank has given the Monetary Board full responsibility for the formulation and adoption of monetary policies and measures, it has expressly provided that any difference of opinion between the Board and the Finance Minister as to whether the monetary policy of the Board has been directed to the greatest advantage of the people should be followed by an "endeavour" on the part of both the Board and the Minister "to reach agreement". In case of failure to reach agreement the Finance Minister may inform the Board that government accepts responsibility for the adoption by the Board of a policy in accordance with the opinion of the government and it shall be the Board's duty to carry out the direction. In the case of the Central Banks of French heritage as those of Morocco and Tunisia, there is no legislation providing for government intervention in any form whatsoever in the conduct of their business. Nor is there any provision empowering the government to issue general-policy directives to be complied with by the Banks. In this respect the influence of the heritage is patent. After nationalisation of the Bank of France, its position in relation to public authorities remains unaffected. It retains complete independence in day-to-day management.[1]

The structural organisation of the Banks has been considerably influenced by their heritage. In the case of the Banks having an English heritage such as Nigeria, Ghana, Rhodesia and Sudan, they incline to the Bank of England tradition in the administrative set-up. There is a seven member Board of Directors, responsible for the policy and general administration of the office, and business of the Bank, including the Governor and the Deputy Governor, as in Nigeria [Art. 8(1) and (2)],

[1] *Eight European Central Banks* (BIS), p. 125.

Ghana [Art. 6(1)] originally, and Sudan [Art. 11(1) and (2)] but in addition to them in the original Bank of Rhodesia and Nyasaland now dissolved [Art. 6(1)]. In the case of the new Bank of Rhodesia the composition of the Board is slightly different where in addition to the Governor and Deputy Governor, the Board will consist of not less than 5 and not more than seven members [Art. 6(1)]. In both Nigeria and Rhodesia and Nyasaland the Governor and Deputy Governor are appointed by the Governor General, the former for a term of 5 years and the latter for 7 years. In the case of the new Bank of Southern Rhodesia the Governor of Southern Rhodesia appoints them for a period of 5 years. In Sudan the governor and the deputy-governor and four other directors are appointed by the Council of Ministers and the remaining one by the Minister of Finance to represent him on the Board—all for a five-year term. In Libya the Board consists of a governor and deputy-governor to be appointed by a Royal Decree for a period of five years and five other directors to be appointed by the Council of Ministers for a period of three years. Under the 1965 Amendment Act, the Board of Directors of the Bank of Ghana are to consist of the governor, two deputy-governors, three executive directors and six directors all of whom will be full-time officers. In most but not all cases members of parliament, commercial bankers and salaried government officers have been specifically excluded from the Board of Directors, and persons engaged in or experienced in commerce, industry, agriculture and finance have been included. The administrative organisation of the Banks with a French heritage has been modelled more or less on the lines of the Bank of France and has no Boards of Directors standing between the (General) Council and the administrative organs. Thus in the case of the Bank of Morocco the organs of administration, direction, supervision and control of the Bank are:

(1) The Governor.
(2) The Council.
(3) The Committee of Directors.
(4) The Government Commissioner and
(5) The Auditors (Censors).

Like the Governor of the Bank of France, the Governor of the Bank of Morocco is appointed for an indefinite period, presides over the general council and holds very wide powers regarding the management of the Bank.[1]

The Governor of the Bank of Morocco executes the decisions of the Council and lays down the Agenda for the session. He watches the implementation and observance of the provisions of the regulations of the Bank; proposes to the Council the nomination of officers; deputes the representatives of the Bank to the Council of other Institutions whenever necessary, and can himself represent the Bank with regard to the third parties. The Governor is assisted either by a Vice-Governor or by a Director General. The Vice-Governor represents the Governor in his absence and exercises among others all other functions devolved on him by the Governor. The Director General exercises his function under the immediate authority of the Governor. He is nominated by a decree passed on the proposal of the Governor after consulting the Minister of Finance and the Council. The Council is composed of (1) the Governor, (2) Vice-Governor or Director-General, (3) Presidents or General Directors of semi-government credit institutions, the list of which will be fixed by the Minister of Finance, (4) two representatives respectively of the Minister of Finance and of the Minister of National Economy nominated by the competent ministers, (5) one representative of the Minister of Agriculture nominated on his proposal by the Minister of Finance, (6) two personalities nominated by the Minister of Finance because of the functions they exercise on state account in the economic and financial field. The Council meets at least once in 3 months, as against once a week in the Bank of France, at the instance of the Governor and each time when at least 3 of its members demand its session. But it can deliberate only when an absolute majority of its members are present. It has very wide powers: it lays down rules and regulations for internal discipline, for the organisation of branches, for fixing the remuneration of the Bank's personnel and gives its advice on the nomination of the Governor, the Vice-Governor and the Director General. It lays down characteristics of notes issued by the Bank and decides upon the volume of circulation, the creation and issue of bank notes. The Council in the Bank of Morocco fixes the basic rate of rediscounting operations. Its decisions relating to matters

[1] Cp. *Banque de France*. C. S. Arts. 16-30, decree law of July 30, 1937, Law of September 3, 1940, decree of April 29, 1959.

of rediscounting can only be executed after being approved by the Minister of Finance. It is informed periodically of the credit operations and foreign exchange operations carried out by the Bank. It decides on the investment of funds owned by the Bank consisting of its capital, reserves and depreciation accounts. It considers all questions relating to the general policy of the Bank. Finally it approves the Bank's budget.[1]

The organisational set-up in the case of the Central Bank of Tunisia bears the mark of its French heritage and as such there is a great deal of resemblance with that of the Bank of Morocco. In Tunisia, as in Morocco, the direction, administration and supervision of the central bank has been entrusted to a Governor, a Council of Administration and an Auditor. The Governor is appointed for a period of six years but not for an indefinite period as in Morocco, and cannot be relieved of his duties except by a Decree of the President of the Republic. Like his opposite number in the central bank of Morocco he presides over the meetings of the Council, organises the personnel of the Bank and with the consent of the Council frames the services rules. He is in the same way assisted by a Director General placed directly under him and charged with the supervision of all personnel of the Bank. He is appointed also on the proposal of the Governor by a Presidential Decree. The composition of the Council in the Central Bank of Tunisia is however somewhat different from that in Morocco. Besides the governor who is the chairman, eight members are appointed by a Presidential Decree of whom four are chosen on account of the high functions they exercise in the economic and financial administration of the state or republic or semi-public institutions, specialising in matters of credit or participating in the economic development of the country; and the other four are chosen for their professional experience.

The councillors are nominated for 3 years but their term may be renewed once or several times. They can be relieved of their functions only by a presidential decree. The powers and functions of the council are as wide as those of its counterpart in Morocco. Within the limits of its statutes it wields extensive administrative powers over the central bank. It receives reports of all transactions of the central bank, decides upon the opening or

[1] Ch. IV Art. 43-52. *Statutes of the Bank of Morocco.* 30 June, 1959 as amended on December 30, 1962.

suppression of branches; approve statutes regarding the personnel and determines the creation, issue, withdrawal and exchange of notes; fixes the rate of interest to be earned on the operations of the Bank; advises on the conditions on which the Treasury should borrow on short medium and long-term; invests funds of the Bank according to the provisions of the statutes (Art. 53); draws the annual budget of the Bank; determines the conditions under which the Bank prepares its accounts; and finally approves the draft Annual Report on the working of the Bank.[1]

In the case of the Bank of Ghana as originally established the influence of the heritage on the organisation of the Bank was quite clear in another respect. The complete segregation of note issue and banking functions and the splitting up of the internal organisation into two departments, the Issue and the Banking, was reminiscent of the Bank of England set-up. The Bank of Ghana Act 1963 which replaced the ordinance however removed the separation between the Issue Department and the Banking Department so that resources of the Bank could be more effectively employed.*

The National Bank of Libya like some of the central banks in the newly independent African colonies, which were members of the sterling area, was organised along the lines of the Bank of England into an Issue and a Banking Department. The Issue Department was the legal successor of the Currency Commission whose assets and liabilities it took over on March 31, 1956. The Banking Department was bifurcated into a central and commercial banking department with effect from June 15, 1963 after the passage of the new Law, stressing the peculiar feature of the Libyan institution as a central-cum-commercial bank. The Bank has a Board of Directors consisting of a Governor, a Deputy Governor and six members. The Governor and Deputy Governor are appointed by Royal Decree for a term of 5 years in the first instance.

[1] Arts. 14-25 *Statutes of the Central Bank of Tunisia.*

*Within the framework of the Bank of Ghana Ordinance, 1957 the method of financing cocoa crop that was open to the Bank had resulted in the accumulation of foreign exchange assets in the Issue Department while the funds of the Banking Department were inadequate to meet the credit demand required for cocoa financing.

Chapter Six

Objectives and Functions of the Central Banks

The objectives and functions of these newly established central banks irrespective of their banking heritage conform to a broad uniform pattern and reflect both the traditional and new concepts of central banking. Thus the traditional objectives such as regulation of the issue of notes and coins, assistance in the development and maintenance of a sound monetary, credit and banking system, preservation of the external stability of the national currency and maintenance of external reserves to safeguard the international value of the currency, and acting as banker and financial adviser to the government are written down into the charters of the Banks of Sudan, Nigeria, Ghana and Morocco. The modern attitude of central banks towards full employment and the economic development of the respective countries is not only implicit in the statutes but is explicitly brought out in some of them. Thus in the case of the Bank of Morocco it is expressly laid down that the Bank is to contribute to the expansion of the possibilities of employment and to the raising of the national income. It is further enjoined to bear in mind the needs of the national economy in its task of developing the money and capital markets.[1] The objective of an orderly and balanced economic development of the country is specifically laid down in the charter of the Bank of Sudan in connection with its responsibility for the development of a sound monetary credit and banking system.[2] Among the principal objects of the Bank of Ghana as provided in its charter are (1) regulating and directing the credit and banking system in accordance with the economic policy of the Government and (2) proposing to the Government measures likely to have a favourable effect on the balance of payments, movement of prices, the state of public finances and the general development of the national economy.[3]

There is considerable resemblance in this respect with the objectives of the Central Bank of Tunisia as defined almost in identical language in its statute under which the Bank has been

[1] Art. 5. *Statutes of the Bank of Morocco.* 1959 as amended 30 December 1962.
[2] Art. 5. *The Bank of Sudan Act.* 1959.
[3] Art. 3 (c) and (e) *The Bank of Ghana Act.* 1963.

empowered to propose to the government all measures, which in the opinion of the governor of the council, are of a nature to exercise a favourable action on the balance of payments, on the movement of prices, on public finances and generally on the development of the national economy. The Statutes of the Bank make it obligatory upon it to support the economic policy of the government and enjoin upon its authorities the duty of informing the President about the facts which in their opinion can impair monetary stability of the State.[1] A careful student of African money and finance has observed that a strong affirmation of the central bank's responsibility for monetary stability and maintenance of the value of the currency is missing in the charter of the Tunisian Bank.[2] But in view of the above definition of the objectives of the Bank, the comment is unwarranted. There is one interesting objective of the Bank, which is perhaps unique in the sense that it has not been expressly provided for in the statutes of any other central bank under review. It is "to ensure the centralisation of all banking risks in its headquarters".[3] The central insurance of bankers' risks is provided through its Central Service for Risks, which collect monthly statistics regarding the distribution of credit among different branches of economic activity, the extent of credit granted by all banks to a single customer, the nature of credit distributed etc. All this information not only enables the central bank to intervene vigorously, whenever necessary, for the purpose of strengthening the banking structure but also the lending institutions to appraise, whenever necessary, the degree of solvency of their customers.

The objectives of the Libyan Central Bank were defined in classical terms in the original Act setting up the National Bank of Libya. Thus regulation of the issue of bank notes and coins, maintenance of reserves to preserve monetary stability in Libya and the external value of the national currency, acting as banker to the government and influencing the credit situation to the country's advantage were explicitly stated to be the objects of the National Bank.[4] There was no reference to the modern concept of a central bank's objective of promotion of the national economy and of adoption of measures to control financial or

[1] Annual Report, *Bank of Tunisia* 1958, pp. 58-59.
[2] E. Jucker Fleetwood, *Money and Finance in Africa*, p. 64.
[3] Art. 34(4) *Statutes of the Central Bank of Tunisia.*
[4] Art. 6 *Law No. 30 of 1955 Establishing the National Bank of Libya.*

economic disorders. On the transformation of the National Bank of Libya into the Bank of Libya by a new Bank Law of February 5, 1963, the objectives are no longer tradition-oriented. Thus along with the traditional central banking aims of regulation and issuing of currency, management of the state's reserves of gold and foreign exchange and maintenance of the internal and external stability of the country's currency, the central bank has been enjoined to regulate credit and banking policy and supervise its execution within the framework of the general policy of the state in such manner as would *promote the national economy.* To fulfil this objective the Bank may (1) influence the direction of credit with regard to quantity, quality and cost so that the real requirements of commerce, industry and agriculture are met; (2) take appropriate measures to combat economic and financial disorders, local or general and (3) exercise supervision over banking concerns to ensure their sound financial position.[1]

This trend in the broadening of the scope of central bank objectives and the practice of statutory definition in the case of the newly established central banks offer a sharp contrast to the oldest central bank in Africa, the South African Reserve Bank established in 1920 without any formal statement of purposes in its charter. The Reserve Bank of India, though established much later and in the post-depression years, had its objectives defined in no more than modest classical terms.

It is well known that the scope of the objectives of central banking has been considerably broadened in the statutes of central banks established after the Great Depression. A remarkable contrast in this respect is offered to the definition of objectives to be witnessed in the central banking charters before World War I. The widening of the scope of the objectives was influenced a great deal by the aftermath of the depression and the widespread introduction of a managed currency system and the abandonment of the gold standard, and last but not least by contemporary developments of monetary thought. The adoption of full employment policies by almost all civilised governments and of economic planning in underdeveloped countries in more recent years has further contributed to this trend in the widening of the scope of central banking objectives. The enlargement of the range of responsibilities of the modern state not only over a broader field

[1] Ch. 2. Art. 13 *Banking Law No 4*, February 5, 1963.

of economic policy but also in the social sphere explains the diverse pattern of the defined objectives, some of which are undoubtedly monetary and banking, while others are general economic purposes, and yet others are in tune with social aspirations. How far the scope of the objectives and functions of the central banks has been extended is clearly brought out in the statutes of the Banks established in the Central and South American countries in the immediate post-war and subsequent years. The classical objectives and functions have been happily blended with others in conformity with the changed concept of central banking. A typical example is furnished by the organic law of the Central Bank of Costa Rica which defined its objective to be the promotion of the orderly development of the country's economy with the aim of achieving full employment of the nation's productive resources, attempting to prevent such inflationary or deflationary trends as may arise in the money and credit market. It shall endeavour to maintain external stability of the national currency and to assure its convertibility, and at the same time supervise the proper use of the nation's monetary reserves for the attainment of these essential conditions for general economic stability.*

For the proper fulfilment of its aims, the Bank under the law shall have the following essential functions: (1) the maintenance of the external value and of the convertibility of the national currency; (2) the custody and administration of the nation's monetary resources; (3) the issue of notes and coins in accordance with the real needs of the national economy; (4) the function of adviser, financial agent and bank of the State; (5) the promotion of conditions favourable to the strengthening of liquidity, solvency and proper functioning of the national banking system; (6) the control of the money supply, of exchange rates and of interest rates; (7) the high level direction of bank credit and supervision and co-ordination of the national banking system; (8) the effecting of such lending and borrowing operations as it may carry out under the present law; (9) the custody of the legal reserves of the national banking system and the settlement of the clearing balances between banks; (10) the granting of author-

*Arts. 4 and 5. Organic Law of the Central Bank of Costa Rica 1953 as amended in June 1960. See Hans Aufricht, *Central Banking Legislation*, pp. 583-84.

izations for the functioning of private banks; (11) co-operation with Costa Rican economic organizations for the better attainment of their goals; (12) the assumption of such other functions as in accordance with the essential status of a central bank, it may or should exercise to the benefit of the national economy.

A significant feature of some of these central banking legislations is the drawing of a distinction between the central bank's domestic and international aims. The principal object of the central banks of Paraguay, Guatemala, and the Dominican Republic has been defined to promote the creation and maintenance of the monetary, credit and exchange conditions most favourable to the orderly development of the national economies.[1] This broad definition is given concrete shape in subsequent articles which fix the principal objectives in the domestic and international sphere. In the domestic sphere the Banks are enjoined to adapt the means of payment and credit policy to the legitimate needs of the countries and to the development of productive activities. But they will endeavour to counteract speculative inflationary and deflationary tendencies detrimental to the permanent interests of the countries. This criterion is imposed not only on the Monetary Department but also on the other two Departments as in Paraguay. Secondly, they are required to promote the liquidity, solvency and sound operation of the banking system and obtain an adequate distribution of credit in conformity with the general interests of the national economies. The legislations of Guatemala and Paraguay further recognise the undesirability of complete isolation of central bank policy from the economic and financial policy of the State under the modern conditions of extensive state intervention and have stressed the need of coordination between the various economic and financial policies which influence the monetary and credit market, especially between monetary policy and fiscal policy. Indeed a number of articles refer to these problems and have provided for practical and realistic procedures of collaboration.

These primary domestic objectives of central banking have been correlated to the international factors which shape the economies of the countries in question. The maintenance of the

[1] Law No. 5130 of the Bank of Paraguay 1944 Arts. 3, 4 and 5. Organic Law of the Bank of Guatemala 1946 Arts. 2-4. Organic Law of the Central Bank of the Dominican Republic 1947 Art. 4.

external value and convertibility of the national currency in the monetary law has been laid down as one of the most important aims in the international sphere. Among other international objectives are found the administration of the international monetary reserves of the nation and the system of international transfer for the purpose of protecting the country from undue monetary pressures. In some countries the law in respect of maintenance of the external value of the national currency attempts a compromise between the orthodox theory of the gold standard and the advocates of flexible exchange in its extreme form. In the Central and South American countries the theory of a flexible exchange rate as an instrument of economic development of poor countries has found ardent advocates. An echo of this advocacy is to be observed in the central banking legislations of Costa Rica and Nicaragua. Thus Art. 114 of the Monetary Law of Nicaragua provides—"whenever internal or external circumstances of the economic development so require, the rate of exchange of the Cordoba with gold shall be variable and may be altered by the Administrative Council of the Issue Dept. by agreement with the Executive Power". The essentials of this theory are an upward revaluation of the currency to combat external price rises and a downward revision to neutralize declines in the external price level. But this policy is likely to prove a one-way movement in most of these countries so vitally dependent on international markets. Devaluation would yield abnormal exchange profits while upward revaluation would not only involve the central banks or the Governments in heavy accounting losses but would also be stubbornly opposed by export interests. In such circumstances upward revaluation in the event of a rise in international prices would not be as easily effected as devaluation when these prices fall. This theory does not appear to have been put into practice even in Costa Rica and Nicaragua where the system has been actually incorporated.

The criterion of external stability adopted in the statutes of the central banks of the undeveloped countries does not certainly mean a swing back to the automatism of the old gold standard for it has been further provided that the central banks must administer the international monetary reserves in such a manner as to moderate through an appropriate monetary, banking and credit policy, the detrimental effects of seasonal, cyclical or erratic fluctuations of the balance of payments upon money supply, credit, prices and economic activities in general. In small countries with export trade concentrated in a few categories of products with inelastic demand, the regulation of the circulating media cannot be left to a rigid monetary automatism. The internal effects of fluctuations in the balance of payments which very often do not arise from international cost-price disparities must have to be neutralized. Monetary and credit policy must be used in such a manner as to safeguard or re-establish the international equilibrium of the country and the competitive position of the national products in the domestic and international spheres. The causes of fluctuations in the balance of payments are too numerous to permit a definite and uniform prescription. The type of measures adopted to correct the disequilibria would depend on the factors which are producing the fluctuations. A monetary devaluation would be more advantageous than a drastic internal deflation in some cases. But it is clear neither deflation nor devaluation can provide a lasting remedy. Direct action on costs of production or selective measures aimed at raising the cost of non-essential imports to consumers would be a more satisfactory solution.[1] The modifications in the gold parity of the national currency may be made, as under Art. 14 of the Monetary Law of Guatemala, to correct fundamental and persistent disequilibria in the volume of payments related to internal and external price-cost disparities, to counteract the harmful effects of fluctuations of major amplitude in the gold prices of the articles which must affect the economy of the country, and in application of decisions emanating from international conventions on monetary stabilization to which the country may have subscribed. But these modifications can be decreed only by the Congress under proposals of the Executive Power. In the Dominican Republic the Law does not permit any modification of the value of the peso and the Bank cannot make use of the 10 per cent margin within which the International Monetary Fund Agreement permits members to change their parities.[2]

In sharp contrast with the delimitation of objectives in the domestic and international spheres to be witnessed in the legisla-

[1] R. Triffin, *Monetary and Banking Reform in Paraguay*, p. 81.
[2] H. C. Wallich and R. Triffin, *Monetary and Banking Legislation of the Dominican Republic*, p. 42.

tions of Guatemala, Paraguay and the Dominican Republic, the Central Bank Act of the Philippines (1948) has drawn no distinction between the two types. The law has provided for the following objectives: *

(*a*) To maintain monetary stability in the Philippines;
(*b*) To preserve the international value of the peso and the convertibility of the peso into other freely convertible currencies;
(*c*) To promote a rising level of production, employment and real income in the country.

The monetary law of the Central Bank of Ceylon resembles the Philippines Central Bank in so far as it also does not distinguish between domestic and international aims. The Ceylonese Bank has been charged with the duty of regulating the supply, cost, availability and international exchange of money in such a manner as to attain the following objectives:

(1) the stabilisation of domestic monetary values;
(2) the preservation of the par value of the Ceylon rupee and its free use for current international transactions;
(3) the promotion and maintenance of a high level of production, employment and real income in Ceylon;
(4) the encouragement and promotion of the full development of productive resources of Ceylon.

The central banking law of Honduras which outlines the objective of the Central Bank as the promotion of such monetary-credit conditions as are most favourable to the development of the national economy does not distinguish between domestic and international aims. The State Bank of Pakistan Act, 1956 has not also distinguished between domestic and international objectives nor have they been outlined in detail. The preamble mentions the fostering of the growth of the monetary and credit system for securing monetary stability and further utilisation of the country's productive resources.

The broadening of the objectives of monetary policy has followed closely the development of monetary thought in this respect. Prior to the Keynesian revolution exchange stability and price stability were recognised as traditional objectives of

*Sec. 2. The Central Bank Act, June 15, 1948.

monetary policy, the former enjoying priority over the latter. The goal of exchange stability as an objective of central banking policy had figured prominently in the 1930's in the discussions relating to the establishment of central banks in India and the Dominions. It is well known that foreign influence and foreign advice were mainly responsible for shaping the structure and policies of central banking in these countries. These influential foreign advisers were internationally—shall we say imperially—minded and they envisaged the object of central banks in these countries as keeping in step with the outside world. But within the countries themselves advocates of monetary management were nationally minded and they believed that the object of central banking was to mitigate the effects of booms and slumps, especially those originating from abroad. In other words the objective was "to break step, whenever the pace set by the outside world appeared to be unsuitable".[1]

The second objective of monetary policy, viz. price stability generally regarded as subordinate to the first viz. exchange stability gave rise to a controversy among economists whether stability should be maintained by keeping the general price index horizontal and suffering per capita incomes to move directly with changes in general productivity or by keeping per capita incomes horizontal and suffering the general price index move inversely in a similar correspondence.[2] A third objective of monetary policy was introduced in the post Keynesian days in the form of maintenance of full employment, more commonly characterised to-day as economic stability. Since the middle of the 1950's a fourth objective has been added to the previous list by several economists: it is adequate economic growth.[3]

The significant development of thought in regard to the scope of objectives of monetary policy that has taken place in recent years can be appreciated by comparing the ideas and attitudes of the Macmillan Committee of 1929 regarding these objectives with those of the Radcliffe Committee reporting in 1959. Profound changes are noticed at once. When the Macmillan Committee elaborated the major objectives of monetary policy,

[1] A. F. W. Plumptre, *Central Banking in the British Dominions*, pp. 422-23.

[2] Art. by F. D. Graham entitled "Objective of Monetary Policy" in the *American Economic Review*, March 1940, supplement, pp. 6-3.

[3] H. G. Johnson, Art. entitled "Monetary Theory and Policy" in the *American Economic Review*, June 1962.

it gave priority to "foreign exchange stability" over "avoidance of credit cycles" and "stability of the price level". Only later "stability of output and employment at a high level" was explicitly stated to be an important aim of monetary policy. While stability of the external value of the country's money has remained a major objective, the most radical change of thought is related to the heightened awareness of the government's responsibilities for maintaining a high and stable level of employment as well as for fostering economic growth and the general raising of the living standard.

It is also of particular significance that the broad consistency of the various objectives was taken for granted by the Macmillan Committee. The possibility of a conflict between the different objectives is however frankly recognised by the Radcliffe Committee. In listing the objectives of monetary measures the Committe has acknowledged that there are possibilities of serious conflict among them. A moment's reflection will show the patent conflict and incompatibilities at any rate among some of them. Thus the stabilisation of domestic monetary values may prove to be incompatible at times with the maintenance of the par value of the national currencies; the promotion of the full development of productive resources of the country may also be inconsistent with the preservation of domestic monetary stability. Many governments and central banks have not hesitated to promote economic development at the cost of monetary stability. Such conflicts are unavoidable but in practice may not prove to be so vexatious as it may appear. The problem is essentially one of striking the right balance between multiple objectives. Those who are entrusted with the responsibility for determining central bank policies should always weigh the various objectives against one another and decide from time to time upon the priority which can be given to particular objectives and the degree to which some of them can be attained or have to be sacrificed altogether. Any attempt to push too far one objective at the cost of another may cause intolerable strain to the body politic and may even disrupt society.[1] Although the Radcliffe Committee recognised frankly the possibility of a conflict of objectives, there has been a tendency in the U.S.A. to evade the issue altogether either by denying this possibility or by insisting on an elimina-

[1] Report of the Radcliffe Committee, paras. 69-70.

tion of the conflicts by some means other than the abandonment of any particular objective. The issue again is sometimes sought to be evaded by expressing the belief that policies aimed at increasing the efficiency and competitiveness of the economy will eliminate the possibility of conflict between high employment, price stability and adequate growth.[1]

POWERS AND FUNCTIONS OF THE CENTRAL BANKS

An important question that has faced the framers of central banking legislation in the developing economies relates to the scope and coverage of the powers and business of the banks in their respective countries. Should the powers and business of the newly established central banks be restricted to the operations which the prevailing economic and financial environment permits them to carry out in the immediate future? Or should the statutes from the very beginning give the central banks a lasting form and endow them with a wider range of responsibilities? To our mind it would not have been appropriate to impose a narrow framework which they were likely to outgrow very soon. Legislating for a long period ahead and providing for a broad framework so that they could be given more elbow-room for manoeuvring in respect of their reserves and operations has been clearly an act of wisdom. Like their prototypes in the Latin American countries, the central banks in the newly independent African colonies have been endowed with functions and responsibilities which may appear to have hardly any relevance to the realities of the existing monetary-banking environment in the respective countries. But the formal powers given to these new central banks are not necessarily less important because all of them cannot be exercised at the moment. Nor should these central banks be judged by the effectiveness with which they perform the conventional functions of monetary control familiar in the advanced countries. Their primary concern is to maintain a sound currency system and assist in promoting the development of the country's economy by fostering the growth of the necessary financial infrastructure. The wide powers and responsibilities provided in the statutes will give the central banks an opportunity to make experiments, to introduce innovations and

[1] Report of the Commission on Currency and Credit, U.S.A., p. 227.

re-adapt their methods continuously, so that they may find their feet. They would then be enabled to build for the future and fulfil their role in the economy of their respective countries. How extensive is the coverage of the powers and business of the newly established central banks is brought out in the following analysis.[1] Broadly speaking the operations authorised by the statutes may be classified under three broad categories, (1) gold and foreign exchange operations which are of a nature to increase the note issue, (2) credit operations in relation to ordinary banks, and (3) banking and fiscal operations in relation to the government. It will be observed that under each of these three heads the scope of the functions is as wide as that of the older established banks in the advanced countries. There may be minor differences in detail, but by and large the powers and functions conform to a standard pattern. Under (1) the central banks may buy, hold, transfer or otherwise deal in gold coins, or bullion or other precious metals like silver, platinum etc. at home and abroad; acquire, hold or transfer foreign exchange, purchase and sell external currency and treasury bills and other securities issued or guaranteed by foreign governments or international financial institutions; open and maintain accounts and appoint agents abroad and act as agents and correspondents for foreign banks, governments and international institutions. They shall from time to time determine the rates at which they will buy specified foreign currencies, and carry out as agents such functions and duties relating to control of foreign exchange transactions as may be authorised by any law.

Under (2) the Banks may undertake the following credit operations such as purchase, sale, discount and rediscount from banks (*i*) bills of exchange or promissory notes arising out of bonafide commercial, industrial and agricultural operations subject to the usual conditions of maturity and endorsement; (*ii*) treasury bills of the government publicly offered for sale and maturing within a prescribed period; grant to banks loans, advances and overdrafts for limited periods against the collateral

[1] See Sec 29 of the Central Bank of Nigeria Act. 1958 (As amended 1962); Secs. 23-30 Bank of Ghana Act, 1963; Secs. 33-63 Bank of Sudan Act, 1959; Sec 9 Reserve Bank of Southern Rhodesia Act, 1964, Arts. 33-40 Bank of Tunisia Act, 1958, Arts. 26-40 Statutes of the Bank of Morocco 1959 and Art. 24 Law No. 30 of 1955 establishing the National Bank of Libya and Arts. 13-15, *Law No. 4 February 5 1963, Bank of Libya.*

of treasury bills, against promissory notes secured by the pledge with the Banks of gold coin or bullion, government securities of a certain minimum maturity, bills of exchange and promissory notes as are eligible for purchase, discount or rediscount by the Bank upto a certain percentage of their nominal value and finally warehouse warrants or their equivalent (securing possession of goods) in respect of staple commodities etc. duly insured. In the case of the Banks of French heritage, Morocco and Tunisia, special provisions are observed which authorise them to discount commercial bills representing medium term credit (maximum duration being 5 years). These bills must have been drawn with the exclusive object of development of means of production, equipment and construction of residential buildings and financing of exports and imports.

An important feature of the statutes of some Banks is their authorisation to subscribe to the capital of and loans issued by financial institutions or enterprises set up with the approval of or under the authority of the government for the purpose of promoting the economic development of the respective countries or participation in or initiation of which is generally in the interest of the national economy or promotes the Bank's objectives (Sudan and Nigeria).[1]

Under (3) the Banks have been appointed the sole bankers and fiscal agents of their Governments as well as Government Boards and Local Government Bodies. They receive and disburse government moneys and keep accounts thereof without remuneration for such services. They are entrusted with the issue and management of government loans publicly issued. They can grant temporary advances to the government subject to certain restrictions upon size and length of the period. They can charge interest on such advances at rates they may determine as in Sudan or as may be determined by the Board in consultation with the Minister of Finance as in Ghana.[2] The Banks may also purchase and sell securities issued by their respective governments which have been publicly offered for sale subject to certain restrictions on maturity and amount. For instance, the maturity of government securities that may be

[1] Art. 64 *the Bank of Sudan Act 1959*, Art. 29 (i) *Central Bank of Nigeria Act, 1958.*

[2] Art. 57 *the Bank of Sudan Act 1959.* Art 37 (1)-(4) *Bank of Ghana Act 1963.*

purchased or sold by the Bank of Libya has been prescribed at a maximum of 15 years. Originally there was also a ceiling on the amount of such securities that the central bank could hold viz., not more than four times its paid up capital and reserve funds. The ceiling, however, was removed when the Law was amended in 1963. In some cases, as in Ghana, the Bank after consulting the Finance Minister may issue its own securities and buy or sell them.[1]

Besides the above long list of operations, the Banks have been authorised to perform any kind of banking business which is not specifically prohibited under the Statutes or which is not inconsistent with their character as central banks. The banks have been prohibited specifically from the following kinds of business:

(1) Drawing or accepting bills otherwise than on demand;
(2) Engaging in trade or participating directly in the ownership of any agricultural, commercial, industrial or other enterprises save as provided in the statutes;
(3) Making unsecured loans or advances except as provided in the law;
(4) Purchasing or retaining ownership of real estate except so far as is necessary for the conduct of the business;
(5) Paying interest on deposits (Nigeria);
(6) Purchasing the shares of any corporation or company, including the shares of any banking company (Nigeria).

[1] Art. 35 (3) *The Bank of Ghana Act 1963.*

Chapter Seven

The Central Banks and Their Monetary Reserves

The traditional concept of the role of monetary reserves was the preservation of the overall liquidity of central banks. This concept was embodied in the statutes of most central banks from the 19th century down to the outbreak of the Great Depression and found expression in the prescription of a minimum ratio of reserves to note issues and sight liabilities. The concept of the role of monetary reserves of central banks, however, came to be radically altered as a result of the impact of World War I and the Depression upon monetary policies and monetary institutions.

With the complete disappearance of gold coins from circulation, it was no longer necessary to hold reserves for the conversion of notes and deposits into gold for domestic purposes. International flows of private capital could not be relied upon any more as a source of cushioning for imbalances in a country's current account payments. On the contrary some of these movements served to aggravate the impact of current account disequilibria. Official loans and grants which came to be substituted in their place could not be depended upon as a normal source of financing the short-term current account deficits. In the circumstances the old concept of the function of central bank reserves as preserving the overall liquidity of the banks came to be abandoned, and an altogether new concept, that of financing the short run deficits in the country's balance of payments came to be adopted. New criteria for the measurement of the adequacy of monetary reserves, entirely foreign to nineteenth century and pre-depression ideas, came to figure in both academic analysis and legal prescriptions. It was Lord Keynes who for the first time among academic economists drew pointed attention in his *Treatise on Money* to the need for a new criterion for determining the adequacy of monetary reserves by relating them to the possible range of fluctuations of a country's balance of payments —the probable magnitude of the external drain. Current discussions since then have tended to stress the ratio of a country's overall reserves to annual imports or sales of foreign exchange as a suitable criterion, however rough and approximate, for measurement of reserve adequacy. A distinction has also been drawn between the 'cover' and 'international currency' functions of central bank reserves relating the strength of central banks to the adequacy of 'international' rather than 'cover' reserves. The latter helps to "support" national currency and credit structures. The former provides the international currency which is needed as a "buffer stock" to meet discrepancies in the country's international balance of payments. The gold and foreign exchange, which the law requires the central bank of a country to hold as "cover" against its domestic currency, is obviously unavailable at the same time for use as international currency. For the settlement of its foreign indebtedness, only the excess over and above the legal cover will be available for use. In the event of emergencies, therefore, legal minimum reserves are useless and for all practical purposes immobilised and frozen. The effect of legal reserve requirements, it has been rightly observed, has been to withhold a certain amount of gold and foreign exchange from the "international currency" function and to set it aside for an altogether different use, namely, the "cover function".[1] Whenever central banks are asked by law to maintain high cover ratios, their position is not necessarily strengthened. Except in the case of a major cataclysm like that of a war, the public are practically indifferent to the question of the cover of bank notes: while in the event of such an upheaval even a cent per cent cover would not be able to sustain confidence in the notes. A legal "backing" of gold and foreign exchange adds little to the strength of a note currency in ordinary times.

Moreover, in an attempt to build up the large cover reserve, the central bank is often unable to provide an adequate reserve of international currency. It has already been noted that the surplus above the legal cover is the amount available for meeting a deficit in the country's balance of international payments. In practice the whole of this surplus even is not frequently available. A "cushion" so to speak is generally provided by the central banks above the legal minimum lest the law should have to be infringed. With a reserve of 40 per cent, for instance, the cushion may be another 5 or 7 per cent. This cushion will tend to be virtually as immobilised as the legal minimum itself. It is the surplus reserve, therefore, which strengthens the position of the central banks, but the surplus reserves of central banks in the pre-

[1] *International Currency Experience (Language of Nations)*, p. 95.

depression period were, as Keynes put it, "uncomfortably small". The entire amount of gold held as a statutory reserve and even a portion of the surplus held as a "cushion" were a dead asset and, in the picturesque language of a commentator might vanish into thin air or lie at the bottom of the sea without any consequence, provided no one knew. However paradoxical it may appear, the more strictly and conservatively the gold reserves of a central bank are sought to be regulated by law, the weaker does it grow.[1] In other words, the soundness of the position of a central bank depends not so much on its "cover" reserve as on that portion of its reserve, which performs the international currency function. Contemporary central banking legislation has abandoned the old concept of a minimum reserve ratio rigidly tied down to domestic note issues and/or sight obligations and substituted for it the concept of a "critical" level of reserves related to balance of payments needs. The motive behind the minimum legal reserve requirements was to curb the power of central banks to overexpand credit. Experience in many countries showed that the legal cover provisions were never sacrosanct and were liable to liberalization or even complete waiving whenever monetary authorities found themselves hampered by the existing law to make further expansions in money supply considered necessary or unavoidable in times of a crisis. Further the maintenance of high reserve ratios in many Latin American countries did not provide a safeguard against the threat of an internal monetary inflation. A rigid observance of the legal reserve ratio, again, would have the effect of defeating the very purpose for which these reserves are maintained viz. to correct temporary deficits in the countries' balance of payments. The central bank may even be prevented under the system from discharging its responsibilities as a lender of last resort. The new concept was explicitly recognised in the central banking legislations of Paraguay and many other Latin American countries, and new criteria of central bank management such as rates of annual increase in the money supply and average annual sales of foreign exchange were prescribed. Thus the rules of monetary policy call upon the Central Bank of the Dominican Republic to send a detailed report to the executive power whenever the money supply increases by more than 15 per cent in a period of 12 months

[1] J. M. Keynes. *A Treatise on Money* Vol. II, p. 271.

pointing out the causes of expansion and suggesting what further economic and fiscal measures may be undertaken, and require it to refrain from further expansion of credit whenever the foreign exchange holdings of the banking system are reduced by more than 25 per cent in a period of 12 months.[1] Similarly in the case of the Bank of Guatemala whenever the money supply increases or decreases by more than 15 per cent within a period of 12 months, the Monetary Board shall transmit to the executive power a detailed report showing the internal and external factors causing such expansion or contraction and its repercussions on monetary, exchange and credit conditions and on the level of employment, national production and economic activities in general and suggest the legal, administrative, fiscal and economic measures to be adopted to combat such disturbances.[2]

Such bench marks in the form of a certain rate of annual increase in the money supply or average annual sales of exchange are no doubt arbitrary and artificial. But some such mechanical ratios, some such quantitative clear-cut criteria are necessary to draw forcibly the attention of the monetary authorities to the growing monetary instability in the economy.

It must, however, be observed that neither legal cover ratios relating gold and foreign exchange reserves to the note issues nor the refined ratios relating them to the balance of payments needs are an adequate substitute for the sound judgment of the central bank. The inadequacy of such ratios has been recognised by eliminating them altogether in the central banking legislations of Australia, Philippines, Ceylon and Korea. In Ceylon for instance the Central Bank has been enjoined to maintain among its assets an international reserve "adequate" to meet any foreseeable deficits in the international balance of payments. In judging the adequacy of the international reserve the Bank's Monetary Board shall be guided by estimates of the prospective receipts and payments of foreign exchange by Ceylon; by the volume and maturity of the Central Bank's own liabilities in foreign currencies; and in so far they are known or can be estimated by the volume and maturity of the foreign exchange assets and liabilities of the government and of banking institu-

[1] Arts. 66-68. Organic Law of the Central Bank of the Dominiocan Republic, 1947.

[2] Art. 97. Law of the Bank of Guatemala, 1945.

tions and other persons in Ceylon. The composition of the international reserve has been defined by law; but there has been no attempt to limit narrowly the types of securities of foreign governments which the Ceylonese Central Bank may hold. At the same time it may be observed that the Monetary Board has been directed to hold at least a nuclear reserve in gold or currencies freely convertible into gold directly or indirectly.[1] Under the provisions of the Act establishing the Bank of Korea (1950) the Bank has the exclusive right to issue currency but it is not to maintain a minimum ratio of gold and foreign exchange against its note issue and deposit liabilities.[2] Burma presents a peculiar case where the international reserve maintained by the Bank of Burma, though established as late as 1952, has to amount to not less than 25 per cent of the Bank's liability on account of deposits and currency in circulation, and is not related to probable deficits in its balance of payments.[3] In the final analysis, the main purpose of the central banks' reserve is not domestic but international. These reserves are intended to provide the means for meeting temporary deficits in the country's balance of payments as well as to inspire confidence in its foreign exchange position.

The statutes of the central banks in the African countries, however, have not found it feasible to do away with legal reserve ratios altogether. The volume of gold and foreign exchange reserve in almost every case has been rigidly linked with the note issue. Thus in Morocco the Bank is required to hold a reserve of gold or of foreign exchange convertible into gold amounting to at least one-ninth of the total note circulation. The percentage may be increased to a maximum of one-third on the proposal by the Ministry of Finance, if requested by the Council (Art. 21). The Bank of Sudan is required to maintain at all times a reserve of gold and external assets amounting to at least 25 per cent of the aggregate volume of the currency in circulation and other sight liabilities of the Bank [Art. 32(2)]. The percentage in Nigeria is fixed at 40 per cent of the total demand liabilities of the Bank (Art. 25). In both these countries the composition of the reserve has been elaborately prescribed, and should include gold coin or bullion, bills of exchange and promissory notes denominated in

[1] Monetary Law Act No. 58 of 1949 as amended by Monetary Law Act No. 33 of 1954 Arts. 65-66. (See Hans Aufricht, *Central Banking Legislation* p. 305).
[2] *Central Banking in South and East Aisa* Ed. by G. Davies, p. 92.
[3] Art. 35. *The Union Bank of Burma Act, 1952.*

foreign currency, treasury bills issued by any foreign government, and securities issued by or guaranteed by any foreign government. In Sudan while there is no stipulation regarding the maturity of the bills of exchange or the treasury bills and no restriction as to the amount of securities issued by foreign governments which may be held by the Bank, the Nigerian statute provides a maximum maturity of 90 days for bills of exchange and 184 days for treasury bills and of five years for not more than two-thirds of the foreign government securities held. The holdings of such securities by the Central Bank in Nigeria again are limited to 30 per cent of the total amount of external assets [Art. 25(*c*) and (*d*)]. The Nigerian statute further expressly provides that the treasury bills and securities should be those of governments whose currency is sterling or freely convertible into gold or sterling; but the Sudanese charter is flexible in this respect and the origin of the bills has been left to be determined from time to time by the Bank [Art. 32(1)].* In the Rhodesian Bank born on the dissolution of the previous Bank for Rhodesia and Nyasaland the value of the reserve has been fixed at not less than 25 per cent of the Bank's liabilities. As regards the composition of the reserve unlike the other Banks a great deal of discretion, even much greater than that in Sudan, seems to have been left with its authorities. It is simply provided that the reserve should consist of gold, sterling or foreign assets convertible into gold or sterling [Art. 17(1) and (2)]. In both respects it has closely followed the original Bank of the Federation [Art. 18(1) and (2)].

Under the ordinance of 1957 the Bank of Ghana was empowered to issue notes and coin against an equivalent amount of sterling for immediate delivery in London. The assets of the Issue Department should include gold coin and bullion, sterling notes and bank balances, treasury bills of the United Kingdom of a maturity not longer than 93 days, sterling securities of or guaranteed by the Government of the United Kingdom maturing within 5 years (up to not more than 50 per cent of the total assets of the Issue Department), bills of exchange bearing at least two good signatures and drawn on and payable at any place in the United Kingdom, and treasury bills of the Government of Ghana deno-

*A number of convertible and externally convertible currencies were determined by the Board of Directors as eligible for inclusion in the statutory reserve of external assets, but the bulk of the assets have continued to be held in sterling (Annual Report, 1960, p. 14).

minated in pounds and maturing within 93 days and other securities of the government of a maturity of not more than 20 years, provided the amount of the treasury bills and government securities held did not exceed 12 million pounds of which again not more than 6 million pounds should be in securities having a maturity of not more than 2 years.[1] On the eve of the establishment of the Central Bank the Ghana pound was in effect backed by 100 per cent in sterling. The ordinance of 1957 made provision for a fiduciary issue for the first time of a small amount which was less than 50 per cent of the seasonal minimum circulation figure. But the fiduciary provisions were significant in that they offered the possibility of creating the real beginnings of a money and securities market in Ghana and afforded the opportunity of employing the fiduciary issue profitably in the interests of the country's economic development.[2]

The provisions relating to the composition of the currency reserves were radically altered with the amalgamation of the Issue and Banking departments by the Bank of Ghana Act, 1963.[3] The restrictions relating to the holding of only sterling notes, treasury bills and securities of the U.K. Government and bills of exchange payable in U.K. have now been removed. Notes whether sterling or not, treasury bills of the government of any convertible currency country and bills of exchange drawn on any place outside Ghana can now be held in the currency reserve. This change has rendered the law in this respect more flexible and brought it up to the same lines as those of the Bank of Nigeria and other Banks. It has been further provided that the aggregate holding of treasury bills and securities of the Ghana Government should not at any time exceed 40 per cent of the currency in circulation which percentage could be varied by the Government between 40 per cent and 60 per cent. The provision of an absolute amount has been replaced by a percentage under the 1963 Act. In December 1963, gold accounted for 3.7 per cent of the currency in circulation; foreign exchange assets 59.2 per cent (76.8 per cent in 1962); Ghana Government treasury bills and securities, 10.0 per cent (19.5 per cent in 1962); internal bills for cocoa finance 27.1 per cent. In June 1964 the percentages were as follows: Gold

[1] The Bank of Ghana Ordinance, 1957. Sec. 28 (1) and (2).
[2] *Bank of Ghana,* Report for the Financial year ended 30 June 1958, p. 2.
[3] *Bank of Ghana Act,* 1963. Sec 15 (1) (2), (3) & (4).

—4.1, Foreign Exchange—65.4, Ghana Treasury Bills—9.2, Cocoa Bills—21.3, as shown in the table No. 22:[1]

TATBLE No. 22

CURRENCY COVER: BANK OF GHANA (%)

	1962	*1963*	*1964 (June)*	*1962*	*1963*	*1964 (June)*
Gold	3.7	3.7	4.1			
Foreign assets	76.8	59.2	65.4	Value of the total external reserve (in percentages)		
Ghana Treasury Bills	19.5	10.0	9.2	80.5	62.9	69.5
Cocoa Bills	..	27.1	21.3			

Although the charters of these newly established central banks have not made any attempt to correlate the volume of the reserve to the fluctuations in the volume of payments and have adopted the outmoded minimum legal reserve formula by linking it to the volume of the note issue, there has been considerable discussion in the countries as to the appropriate criteria to be adopted for determining the adequacy of foreign exchange reserves. The controversy arose in connection with the maintenance of a 100 per cent backing for the note issue in Ghana, which was subjected to the criticism that it was sterilising a substantial portion of the national reserves which could otherwise be more usefully utilised for financing their plans of economic development. The point which was keenly debated in this connection however did not concern the question of cutting off the link between the note issue and the reserve but the adequacy of foreign exchange coverage in the perspective of the growing economy of the country and the consequent prospective increase in money supply. When the initial 100 per cent foreign exchange backing for the currency in circulation in Ghana came to be subsequently reduced, the debate turned on the question of the new percentage to be maintained. In Nigeria the value of the total external reserve was 57.75 per cent in 1963 and it rose to 59.55 per cent in 1964. But it was much higher in 1962 at 87.75 per cent. In some quarters it was pointed out that the level of Nigeria's total external reserves at 87.75 per cent in 1962 would, unchanged, be valued at

Annual Reports of the Bank of Ghana for the years 1962-64.

about 40 per cent in the near future in the context of the rapid rate of the country's growth and increasing monetisation and therefore was not unduly high. The adequacy of minimum reserves was sought to be judged by adopting the standard of a specified number of months' worth of imports. Thus the Annual Reports of the Bank of Nigeria refer to the relation between the total external assets (including those of the central bank and official banking institutions) and the number of months' imports at the end of every year. It is found that the total external assets which were equal to about 8 months' imports at the end of 1962 became more or less equal to $5\frac{1}{2}$ months' imports in December, 1963.[1]

The crucial point to remember in adopting a year or any other period's imports as the yardstick for the measurement of an adequate external reserve is that it is the free reserves—the excess or margin above the statutory minimum required as a currency backing—which would give the central bank the desired strength and manoeuvrability in the event of an adverse turn in the country's balance of payments. If the minimum reserves of foreign exchange held are the equivalent of four months' worth of imports, as is the official policy in Nigeria, that portion of the reserve which is required for the purpose of a legal note cover would not be available for meeting a probable deficit in the country's balance of payments. Taking account of the needs for the currency backing, it may be found that the reserve is of not more than two months' worth which would obviously be inadequate. It is interesting to observe in this connection that Nigeria's external reserves fell from £211 million at the end of 1959 to £63 million in 1964. Indeed the position regarding the external assets of almost all these countries has worsened during the last few years. With increasing imports as a result of the quickening of the pace of economic growth and dwindling foreign exchange reserves the size of the free reserves will tend to be still more inadequate. There is a growing realisation on the part of the authorities of the Bank that the statutory provision relating to the note cover sets an absolute limit on the amount of the Bank's external reserves which can be utilised in meeting adverse movements in Nigeria's international transactions. Even

[1] *Annual Report & Statement of Accounts 1964*. Bank of Nigeria, p. 10. Also E. E. Jucker Fleet Wood, *Money and Finance in Africa*, p. 89.

if the 40 per cent legal cover ratio were to be abolished, the Bank of Nigeria's slender foreign exchange reserve would admittedly be still inadequate for financing balance of payments deficits indefinitely.

The provisions relating to the currency cover of the National Bank of Libya, as it was named originally, may be examined usefully in this connection. The assets of the Issue Department were to consist of (*a*) sterling balances, (*b*) sterling treasury bills of the United Kingdom, (*c*) sterling securities of or guaranteed by the U.K., (*d*) securities issued or guaranteed by other governments and (*e*) foreign exchange balances other than the pound sterling. It was however provided that not more than 70 per cent of the total assets should be held in terms of (*c*) viz., sterling securities, the maturities of such securities to be held being limited to a maximum of five years. Not more than 25 per cent of the total assets, again, should be held in terms of (*d*) and (*e*).[1] The assets of the Issue Department should be available for meeting the liabilities of the Department and should be equal to the total of bank notes and coin for the time being in circulation. It may be observed that in this hundred per cent currency cover there was no provision for the inclusion of gold as external reserve. The entire reserve was to be held in foreign securities, treasury bills and exchange balances, sterling and non-sterling, the proportion of the non-sterling assets being limited to 25 per cent of the total. The declared policy of the Currenny Commission to keep at least 40 per cent of the assets invested in bank balances and treasury bills maturing within 90 days was continued by the Bank during the first year of its operation. But such a high degree of liquidity was not called for in the security cover of an expanding currency in a developing economy. Indeed it was not even legally called for.[2]

Whatever justification the I.M.F. advisers might have in recommending a 100 per cent currency reserve system for the Libyan Currency Commission proposed by them, it is doubtful whether the validity of their arguments remained unaffected after the inauguration of the central bank and in the context of the country's developing economy. In consonance with the growing

[1] Arts. 28-29. Law No 30 of 1955 Establishing the National Bank of Libya.

[2] *First Annual Report, National Bank of Libya* for the year ending March 31, 1957 (Tripoli) p. 9. Also App. 3.

population, increasing economic activity, and monetisation of the subsistence sector, the developing economy of the country called for a gradually expanding money supply. With the hundred per cent reserve it would have been difficult for the central bank to ensure a rate of growth of money supply consistent with the over-all economic policy of the country. The central bank of Libya itself was finding the 100 per cent reserve system to be an impediment in the way of its regulation of the amount or rate of note issue and indeed in the way of its assumption of the full responsibilities of a central bank.[1] The World Bank Mission also found that the fundamental reason why the National Bank was not in a position to regulate the money supply lay in the prevailing 100 per cent currency reserve system.[2] It was virtually an automatic sterling exchange standard system where the volume of national currency could not be determined at the discretion of the central bank at all but was instead automatically regulated by the public's preference for and its capacity to tender or hold approved foreign exchange or national currency.

The defects of the system were realized in the course of the next few years and the provisions relating to the note cover were amended when the Banking Law No. 4 of February 5, 1963 was promulgated. The object of the new Law, as will be observed later, was to enable the central bank of the country to fulfil the functions of a true central bank in a more effective manner. The most important features of the change in the legal cover provisions related to the authorisation of the Bank of Libya, as it now came to be known, to include in the currency cover bullion and gold coins and securities and treasury bills issued by the Libyan government. Notes and coins in circulation were henceforth to be covered by (1) gold bullion, gold coins or foreign "convertible" currencies up to 25 per cent of the total assets of the Issue Department; (2) treasury bills issued by foreign governments whose currencies were convertible; (3) securities issued or guaranteed by such governments having a maturity of not more than 5 years up to a maximum of 65 per cent of the assets of the Issue Department provided that foreign securities of longer maturities up to 15 years could be held up to 15 per cent of the total assets; and (4) securities including treasury bills issued and guaranteed by

[1] *Fourth Report of the National Bank of Libya*. 31 March 1960, p. 51.
[2] IBRD Mission Report, pp. 378-379.

the Libyan government of not more than 15 years maturity up to 10 per cent of the total assets.[1]

The inclusion of Libyan government treasury bills and securities for the first time would enable the central bank to exercise the power of creating credit for financing the country's economic development. Under the previous law not more than 25 per cent of the total assets could be held in non-sterling securities. The change in the Banking Law brought about a considerable diversification of the assets of the Issue Department. It is observed from the balance sheet of the Bank dated 31 March, 1964 that gold bullion to the value of £L 2,032,257 figured for the first time among the assets of the Issue Department. All other assets were invested in "convertible" foreign currencies. In order that gold and balances in convertible currencies could be kept within the newly prescribed limit of 25 per cent of total assets, a reduction had to be effected in the amount of balances held with foreign banks by as much as 69.9 per cent which dropped from £L 9,697,173 to £L 2,921,404. This change called for other consequential changes leading to an increase of foreign treasury bills from £L 1,040,613 on 31 March, 1963 to £L 3,006,448 i.e. by 188.9 per cent. Holdings of securities also increased from £L 6,162,196 on 31 March 1963 to £L 12,329,891 i.e. by 108.2 per cent. For the purposes of comparison the balance sheets relating to the Issue Department before and after the passage of the new Bank Law are reproduced below.[2] It would be noticed that although the Bank was authorised to hold securities and treasury bills issued or guaranteed by the Libyan government, these were conspicuous by their absence.

ISSUE DEPARTMENT BALANCE SHEETS

(In Libyan Pounds)

31.3.1963		31.3.1964
..	Gold Bullion	2,032,257
9,697,173	Balances in convertible currencies	2,921,404
1,040,631	Foreign treasury bills	3,006,448
5,387,155	Foreign securities maturing within 5 years	9,520,315
775,041	Foreign securities maturing between 5 and 15 years	2,809,576

[1] Art. 31. *Banking Law of February 5, 1963.*

[2] *Eighth Annual Report, Bank of Libya, 1964.* Balance sheets of the Bank of Libya.

It has already been observed that the maintenance of a hundred per cent currency reserve involves a sterilisation of foreign exchange reserve which could otherwise have been profitably employed in financing the developing economy of the emerging countries. The shortcomings of this system might not have been acutely felt in the early stages of the central banks' operation in some countries because of the flow of foreign aid. The release of foreign exchange brought about by an abandonment or amendment of the 100 per cent reserve might not have released in some cases a substantial amount of foreign exchange, for the prevailing currency circulation at the time was considerably below the annual value of imports and foreign aid. But it is clear that under this system "cost less" creation of money was precluded in a manner as to retard capital formation at a fast rate in these underdeveloped countries. Inflation has no relation to a 100 per cent or a fractional reserve system. But deflation cannot be guarded against or mitigated because of the inability of the central bank under the 100 per cent reserve system to create additional purchasing power. In the primary producing countries it may be argued that there is not much scope for monetary-fiscal policy for raising the real income of the people. But even there in the event of droughts and declines in export prices, central banks would be powerless to create the necessary money supply for financing public work projects by way of domestic relief work. In the earlier years of newly found independence and immature financial economies, there might have been a case for a 100 per cent currency reserve for adding prestige to the national currency and inspiring confidence in it. But as a commentator has observed in the case of the Libyan system, the overriding considerations of a discretionary monetary policy in the context of the developing economy of the countries obviate the necessity of such a system merely for the purpose of giving a status to the currencies.[1]

The maintenance of the foreign reserve ratio at so high a level as 100 per cent or near is a relic of the Currency Board System, and has been the outcome of a very cautious financial policy followed by the authorities. They remained unshaken by the strong demand for the creation of a large fiduciary issue as a

[1] *The Bankers' Magazine June 1960*. Art. entitled "Central Banking in Libya" by A. G. Chandavarkar, Economic Adviser to the National Bank of Libya.

source of development finance. Such a policy could have been perhaps justified during the period when there was no lack of finance for assisting economic development. But in the present times the reserves are very much needed in the interests of development. A drastic reduction of the legal cover ratio or even the snapping of the link between the reserve and the volume of note issue is called for to-day. India has already taken the lead by divorcing her foreign exchange reserve from the volume of note issue and thereby "scrapping" the currency reserve.

There was another factor which might have been responsible for the legal prescription of a minimum reserve ratio. The framers of the statutes of these new central banks drew lessons from the experience of the war and postwar years when a large number of belligerent countries had used their central banks as an engine of inflationary finance to meet their extraordinary expenditures. Not only was it believed that such legal prescriptions would prevent the central banks, owned as they were entirely by the governments of the country, from extending to them unlimited credits but these would also inspire confidence in the new currency both at home and abroad. This anxiety is reflected in the statutory provisions relating to imposition of ceilings on the volume of central bank credit that may be furnished to the governments. The control over the operations of the Banks exerted by foreign exchange reserve requirements is thus sought to be reinforced by restrictions on the power of the Banks to lend to their governments by purchasing government securities. In expanding their liabilities and domestic assets, they will have to take into account not only the need to maintain legal external reserve but will also have to ensure that the holding of government securities, the purchase of which is one of the ways in which their domestic assets could be increased, is kept within the legal limit. These two requirements taken together were designed to prevent the Banks from becoming a source of inflationary finance, irrespective of the needs of external balance or the volume of the national currency.

Thus in Nigeria the total amount of temporary advances that the central bank can make to the government has been limited to twelve and one-half per cent of the estimated recurrent budget revenue. Such advances again have to be repaid by the end of the financial year [Art. 34(2) and (3)]. In Ghana such advances may be made up to 10 per cent and in certain cases up to 15 per cent of the estimated budget revenue and are repayable within three months of the relevant financial year. [Sec. 37(1) (2) (3). The Bank of Ghana Act, 1963]. In the case of the Bank of Sudan the limit to the outstanding advances to the government has been fixed at 15 per cent of the estimated revenue. The advances have to be repaid within 6 months following the end of the financial year (Art. 57). The Sudanese Bank has further been prohibited from holding government securities exceeding in value one half of its total paid in capital and general reserve fund (Art. 58). The new Bank of Rhodesia has been prohibited by its statute from lending or advancing moneys to, or directly purchasing treasury bills or notes from the government to an extent which may make the total amount outstanding at any time to exceed 20 per cent of the estimated revenues. Such advances have to be repaid within three months of the termination of the financial year [Art. 9 (2)(*a*)]. As in the case of other banks a maximum limit has been prescribed to its investments in government securities of a longer maturity than six months. Such investments must not exceed the capital and general reserve Fund plus 20 per cent of its liabilities to the public [Art. 9(2)(*b*)]. It is interesting to note that the provisions in the new Bank Act have followed closely those laid down in the charter of the original Federal Central Bank [Art. 10(*d*) and (*g*)]. Similarly the financial accommodation that the central banks of Morocco and Tunisia have been authorised to provide to the State has been limited in amount as well as duration. Both the Banks are authorised to grant the Treasury in the form of cash facilities/overdrafts the necessary accommodation to meet the normal execution of public expenses, but the total duration of such advances should not exceed 240 days in a calendar year, whether consecutive or not. While the total accommodation that can be provided in this form has been limited to 10 per cent of the ordinary budget revenue in a year in the case of Morocco, it is 5 per cent in the case of Tunisia.[1]

Under the provisions of the old Law, the National Bank of Libya had not been subjected to any ceiling on its advances to

[1] Art. 49. *Statutes of the Central Bank of Tunisia,* Art. 35 (3) *Statutes of the Bank of Morecco.*

the government. But the new Law of 1963 provided that the Bank of Libya, as it now came to be called, could extend temporary advances to the government to cover temporary deficits in the budget revenue, subject to a ceiling of 10 per cent of the total estimated revenue and repayable by the end of the fiscal year under mutually agreed conditions.[1] This departure is in line with contemporary central banking legislation elsewhere.

Statutory limits on the net amount of central bank advances to their governments bearing a prescribed percentage to their average actual receipts have not been unknown and are to be found in the case of earlier Banks, as in Cuba [Art. 52(*b*)] and in the Phillipines (Art. V, Sec. 95).

It is interesting to observe in this connection a strong official bias in favour of the traditional gold backing for note issues in a highly advanced country like U.S.A. The minds of the monetary authorities there have been exercised in recent years over the question of relaxation of the existing gold reserve requirements. Such relaxation might take place in three different ways: first, by reducing the present overall Federal Reserve ratio of 25 per cent against both note and deposit liabilities; secondly, by reducing or abolishing the ratio against Federal Reserve Bank deposits only and retaining that against Federal Reserve notes; and thirdly, by dropping the reserve requirements altogether against both notes and deposits. Theoretically speaking, owing to the fundamental change that has taken place in the function of gold in the monetary system to-day and particularly because the private use of gold as a store of value has been practically discontinued in the U.S.A., there is a good prima facie case for abolition of the gold reserve requirements—both against notes and deposits. But the "symbolic tie" with gold, according to the Chairman of the Federal Reserve himself, should be preserved with reference to the notes. The retention of the traditional gold backing for the Federal Reserve notes would be re-assuring to those who see in the gold cover requirement an element of strength. The value of any currency is so closely related to the confidence of the people that this advantage should not be ignored. Instead of resolving for ever the problem of whether a gold cover serves a useful purpose or not and eliminating altogether the possibility of Congress having to take further action

[1] Arts. 14-20, *Banking Law, February 5, 1963.*

later, the traditional cover requirements, he argues, could be simply readjusted to meet the present and foreseeable future needs. From this point of view the purpose would be served by reducing the gold cover ratio against notes only from 25 per cent to say 15 per cent and by removing the almost "arbitrary" reserve requirement of maintaining a gold certificate reserve against deposits altogether. The resulting release of gold is considered to be fairly adequate to cope with the present problem of a deficit in the country's balance of payments. At the same time the unique position of the dollar in international commerce and finance would not be impaired and the ability to make good the country's pledge to maintain the gold parity of the dollar at $35 an ounce would not be doubted.[1]

[1] See Statement of W. M. Martin, Chairman of the Federal Reserve System before the Senate Committee on Banking and Commerce, Feb. 2, 1965. *Federal Reserve Bulletin*, February 1965, pp. 226.

Chapter Eight

Twin Role of the Central Banks in the Emerging Countries

It has been a platitude to observe that central banks in underdeveloped countries have a twin role to perform, that of a regulator as well as that of a promoter. A central bank has been regarded in underdeveloped countries as an engine of economic growth. In the circumstances the promotional or developmental aspect of the central bank's role has come to be considered as more significant than that of the regulatory aspect in an underdeveloped economy. But there is no inherent contradiction between the two roles. In fact the two may be co-ordinated with each other or one may even be superimposed upon the other. The statutes of most of the central banks under discussion have explicitly defined the banks' functions as including among others the task for assisting in the development of the countries' economy. Where there is no explicit statutory obligation to help in the task of economic development, a careful study of the statutes will show that the central banks have been implicitly enjoined to be pre-occupied with the development problems of the country. Now the question is what principles should the central banks follow and what instruments should they adopt in their efforts to implement the injunction in their charters, express or implied, to foster the countries' economic growth and at the same time maintain a reasonable degree of monetary stability.

Although the regulatory role of the central banks in such developing economies is not very significant, it may be observed that their relationship with the commercial banks and the contents of their policy to these banks have been meticulously and elaborately defined by law. The central banks' first obligation in all the countries under review is maintenance of the internal and external value of the currency. To preserve the internal and external stability of the national currency, the central bank will inevitably have to act as a controller of the monetary situation. In controlling the monetary situation the aim will be to stimulate and not to hamper economic growth. It is of interest to observe that these central banks have been equipped by their statutes with most of the traditional and non-traditional weapons of monetary control that may be found in the armoury of a modern central bank. In the existing conditions of the money and capital markets in the independent colonies most of the operations which the central banks have been authorised to perform would have to be kept in abeyance not only at present but for the foreseeable future. For, the technical conditions for the employment of most of the control devices are non-existent. A question often raised is why the tools of these central banks should not be restricted only to those which they can wield today or in the immediate future. In our opinion it would not have been appropriate to restrict at the start the kit of tools which the banks would soon find to be inadequate, as the economy develops. The framers of the statutes were quite justified in equipping the central banks with the wide range of sophisticated weapons available to modern central banks. They have acted prudently and imaginatively in legislating for a long period ahead and in providing for an ample supply of ammunition which could be adapted to the requirements of a rapidly changing situation. There is a precedent in the case of the central banks established earlier in Latin America where the statutes had armed them with instruments of credit control equal and even superior in variety and flexibility to those to be found in the armoury of the more mature central banks functioning in the developed countries of Western Europe and North America.

REGULATORY ROLE OF THE CENTRAL BANKS

The statutes of the African Banks are relatively more brief and flexible as compared to those of their counterparts elsewhere. The Central Banks of Ghana and Nigeria have 58 and 52 clauses respectively while the newest among them, the Reserve Bank of Rhodesia, has only 28 Articles; while some of the earlier banks established elsewhere like Cuba and the Philippines have 138 and 142 respectively. There has been no intention to "legislate" monetary policy as in the case of many of their counterparts in Latin American countries.[1] Only broad powers have been granted in the sphere of monetary control. There has been no attempt to provide special powers or arm them with a variety of non-traditional complex instruments of control. A study of the

[1] *Federal Reserve Bank of New York Monthly Review* October 1960. Art, entitled "New Central Banks".

practices developed by these central banks, as revealed in their Annual Reports, clearly demonstrates that they have preferred to place major reliance upon techniques of credit control as developed in the older countries, the countries of their heritage, rather than evolving untried or new-fangled gadgets. Thus discount rate policy, fixation of commercial banks' reserve requirements and moral suasion have been the principal control weapons they have used. They have, however, suitably adjusted the traditional weapons to meet the special needs of their credit situation and have often given a selective undertone to the traditional instruments. The Sudanese Bank has been expressly authorised by its statutes to establish differential rates of discount for different classes of transactions and maturities (Art. 42). But provisions fixing an elaborate structure of rates to be charged by them in the same manner as is specified in the laws of the earlier central banks elsewhere are conspicuous by their absence. Again the Bank of Sudan has been empowered to exercise direct control over the cost and availability of credit by imposing ceilings on the aggregate of loans, advances and discounts outstanding at each bank as well as upon the size of individual loans by requiring that all applications for loans above a specified amount must be submitted by the banks to the central bank for approval [Art. 45(1) (*a*) (*b*) (*c*)]. Directional control of credit was actually used in the Sudan as a transitional measure before discounting of bills was introduced. The central banks in the countries which were formerly French colonies, the Bank of Morocco and the Central Bank of Tunisia have placed considerable reliance upon this instrument for the purpose of altering the structure of credit through variable ceilings on the over-all volume of credit. The Bank of Tunisia also has in the same way relied not only upon qualitative control over distribution of credit but also over the volume, cost and availability of credit. The power to exercise direct control over the cost and availability of credit, however, has not been expressly granted to all the African banks. It has been rather exceptional for the central banks of Sudan, Morocco and Tunisia, the latter being explicitly endowed with the responsibility of acting on the cost of credit with a view to encouraging investment and reducing the financial expenses of business. All the new banks will certainly be able to exercise "moral suasion" though there is no explicit statutory provision as in

Malaysia empowering the central bank to "recommend" credit policy to the commercial banks.

OPEN MARKET OPERATIONS

In spite of the narrow, rudimentary money and capital markets in these countries, the Banks have invariably been authorised to conduct open market operations and given wide powers to buy and sell most of the assets they could discount or accept as collateral. The gadget incorporated in the central banking statutes of several underdeveloped countries like Ceylon, the Philippines, Paraguay, Guatemala, Korea etc. to reinforce their open market operations by issuing their own obligations is however missing in the case of most of the Banks under discussion here. It is interesting to observe in this connection that the central bank of Ghana in marked contrast has been empowered to issue its own obligations guaranteed by the government. Thus the Bank of Ghana may after consultation with the Minister of Finance issue securities of its own, prescribe conditions therefor and sell or purchase them.[1] The newly established Reserve Bank of (Southern) Rhodesia has also been empowered to buy, sell and discount bills, notes or other obligations issued by itself.[2] This power had not been granted to the original Bank of Rhodesia and Nyasaland. The device enables a central bank in an underdeveloped money market not only to protect itself against the possibility of the ammunition being exhausted at a time when a restrictive credit policy is needed but also to expand the market itself. It may however be observed that the prevalence of narrow security markets in the emerging countries does not by itself militate against the conduct of open market operations as a policy instrument by the central banks in underdeveloped economies. The narrowness of the security market may not be the inevitable result of the country's underdeveloped economy but may indeed be brought about by the adoption of mistaken policies by the government with regard to its own securities. A careful student of the securities market in Pakistan has shown how government policy has contributed to the narrowness of the market and even destroyed an embryonic market. The country's

[1] *The Bank of Ghana Act, 1963*. Art. 35 (3).
[2] *The Reserve Bank of Rhodesia Act, 1964*. Art. 9 (1) (IV).

stage of economic development was not the basic factor contributing to the immaturity of the market. Whenever a new government issue was to be planned, the State Bank suggested a "quota" which it practically insisted upon every bank to carry. Thus banks were often holding such low yielding securities much in excess of their liquidity requirements. The banking system in Pakistan was holding to maturity most of the marketable government debt in its portfolio. The balance was held by insurance companies; and non-bank investors held very little. The banks were practically forced to hold this large amount of debt. They were afraid to sell the unwanted surplus lest the State Bank should be offended.[1] Admittedly security markets in these countries are always relatively narrower than those of financially developed economies. As a consequence the scope of traditional open market operations is obviously restricted. Open market sales of government securities even in small amounts serve to dislocate the market and raise interest rates but may not very much affect the availability of money and credit in the economy. But as Mr. Porter has observed that does not rule out the possibility of useful and effective open market operations of a non-traditional kind. Instead of carrying on open market operations in terms of quantities of government securities, the central bank may conduct them by quoting their prices. The technique of this kind of non-traditional open market operations should consist, not in varying the volume of securities to be sold or purchased, but in varying the prices and hence the yields at which the central bank would buy and sell unlimited amounts of government securities. The commercial banks could thereby be induced to hold securities in any desired quantity and in any desired pattern of maturity distribution. Whenever necessary, prices for buying and selling could be altered afterwards so as to induce purchases or sales as the case may be by the public. Through this means not only the structure of yields on monetary assets and hence the relative profitability of bank lending could be manipulated but the reserves of the banking system also could be affected by stimulating purchases or sales of government securities. It is quite likely that banks would be induced to hold securities in amounts exceeding what would be required to maintain their minimum

[1] R. C. Porter, *The Volume of Bank Credit in Pakistan,* Monograph No 10 March 1963, p. 18.

liquidity ratios so that they could avert capital losses or might earn higher interest rates. This technique would then enable the central bank to launch a three-pronged attack on the quantity of credit and money through the traditional methods of the bank rate and the variable reserve ratio as well as open market operations in their non-traditional form instead of wielding a weak bank rate instrument.[1]

One line of criticism that may be levelled against the technique of quoting different prices on government securities by the central bank relates to the burden of interest costs. The interest rates on the securities would have to increase otherwise the central bank would be turned into a position of selling too few and buying too many at the prices quoted by it. But on theoretical grounds the rates of interest need not rise considerably. With the creation of a market for government securities at all times, even though at uncertain prices, some non-bank buyers are likely to be induced into the market. As the holding of securities of a given amount would not then be confined to the banking system alone, rates would not be likely to rise sharply. If the central bank continues to hold a larger percentage of the government debt, as is the practice with the Reserve Bank of India, there would not probably be any marked increase in the interest rates. The rise in interest rates however would of course not be zero; and as a consequence the burden of servicing the public debt may be slightly increased. Much of the increase would be in the nature of a book debt going from one pocket of the government to another. Even if there were an actual increase in the burden, that would indeed be a small price to pay for the high marginal return in terms of the potential for monetary policy.[2]

THE VARIABLE RESERVE RATIO

A tool of monetary policy which has been explicitly provided to the Banks with a British heritage is the variable reserve ratio either with reference to the cash reserve or the liquidity assets as a whole. The range or upper limit of the permissible variations

[1] *Economic Development and Cultural Change*, October, 1965 Art. by R. C. Porter entitled "Narrow Markets and Monetary Policy".

[2] *Ibid.*, pp. 48-50

is usually prescribed.* The Bank of Morocco and the Bank of Tunisia patterned after the French system have not written down into their charters prescriptions of reserve requirements but the statutes appear to be sufficiently flexible for their establishment. The Sudanese Bank has been empowered to request the ordinary banks to maintain reserve balances with it in the form of deposits or in any other form determined by the Bank bearing a specified ratio to their demand and time liabilities with a maximum of 20 per cent. Within this specified maximum the Bank may from time to time alter the required reserve ratio and establish different ratios for sight and time liabilities [Art. 44(1) (3) & (4)]. The Nigerian statute prescribes a minimum amount of specified *liquid assets* to be held with the central bank and expressed as a percentage of the demand liabilities together with a percentage of the time liabilities of each bank arising out of its time and savings deposits [Art. 40 (1) (2) & (3)]. Similarly under the Bank of Ghana Act, 1963, the Ghanaian central bank has been empowered to prescribe that banking institutions shall hold liquid assets of a specific amount and composition and may fix such amount either as a certain percentage of all its deposit liabilities or in any other manner. It may also fix different percentages for different classes of deposits or assets [Art. 29(1)]. The Libyan Banking Law of February 5, 1963 empowered the Bank of Libya to fix the proportion and kind of liquid assets to be maintained by the banks.[1] In the case of the new Rhodesian Bank the provisions relating to variation of reserve requirements are relatively more complex and three kinds of ratios have been prescribed which may be varied by the central bank. First, the minimum reserve balance to be maintained by every commercial bank shall be equal to percentages, which the Bank shall determine and may from time to time amend, of the time and demand liabilities to the public. Secondly, the Bank may require ordinary banks to increase the reserve balances maintained with it by an amount representing a certain percentage of the advances and bills discounted. And thirdly, with the permission of the Ministry of Finance the Bank may vary the percentage prescribed for the

*In the case of a large number of newly established central banks like those of Lebanon, Somalia, Jamaica, Cyprus, Uganda and the Congo, reliance for purposes of credit control is plaed upon variations in commercial bank reserve requirements.

[2] Art. 36 *Banking Law, February 5, 1963.*

minimum holding of liquid assets provided the variation does not reduce the percentage to less than 25 per cent.[1]

It is interesting to observe that in all the cases except Ghana provision has been made to notify commercial banks reasonably in advance of the date on which the increased percentages are to become effective. This is missing in India and Ghana where there is no period of grace for compliance with the directive; and the prescription may be made by notice to the banks and published in the 'Gazette' simultaneously. But such notice is in line with the central banking laws in the Philippines, Ceylon, Cuba, Malaysia, etc. and is intended to avoid the shock effect that might otherwise result and provoke a credit panic. The period of grace is not less than ten and not more than 21 days in Nigeria. In the case of the newly established Rhodesian Bank, no specific period has been mentioned but it has been provided that "reasonable" notice of the date on which the amendment of the percentage will take effect has to be given [Art. 22(3)]. This reminds one of the Korean Bank where "appropriate advance notice" has to be given (Art. 62). In Sudan however *due* notice has to be given to the banks in the case of the first requisition only. To minimise the "announcement effect" provision of a minimum grace period has often been coupled with another in many of the elder banks: the increase in percentages is to be required in a gradual and progressive manner. As in the case of Libya, not only a notice of at least 15 days, except in emergencies, has to be given before directing a change in the ratio, but the percentage has to be varied in a gradual manner.[2] It has been further provided in the case of some of these banks that high marginal reserve requirements, that is, high minimum reserve requirements should be applied against future increases in deposits rather than against total deposits. The objective here is to prevent the discriminatory effect that the application of the variable reserve ratio in the conventional form is likely to produce on different categories of banks. The absence of these provisions in the charters of the African Banks discussed here is rather remarkable and is a departure from current trends in central banking legislation.

[1] *The Reserve Bank of Rhodesia Act. 1964.* Art. 22 (1)-(7).

[2] Sec. 104. *The Phillipines Central Bank Act.* Sec 66 *Law of the Central Bank of Guatemala.*

Mr. J. Aschheim has given an excellent analysis of the theoretical arguments underlining the choice between the variable reserve ratio and open market operations. It is not necessary to go over the same ground again. It will be sufficient to observe here that there is an "asymmetry" between restrictive open market operations and raising of reserve requirements as well as between expansionary open market operations and reduction of reserve requirements, though the asymmetry may not be equally pronounced in all cases. Under conditions of commercial banks being fully loaned up and persistent excess demand for credit, the application of the variable reserve ratio would be likely to cause a switch from govrenment securities into advances much greater than open market operations. As a consequence, compared with the latter, there will be a relatively greater rise in the yields of government securities and consequently a greater fall in their prices. It is what Mr. Aschheim has called the "income and liquidity effect" of directing a rise in reserve ratios which induces the banks to sell government securities and use the proceeds to increase their loans. At the other extreme in the absence of excess reserves and persistent demand for bank credit the variable reserve ratio may also induce the banks to shift away from government securities and in favour of private loans much more than under open market operations, though not to the same extent as in the former case. It is only when the banks are enjoying excess reserves, even though the demand for credit may be excessive, the raising of reserve ratios does not produce the "income effect" or the "liquidity effect" referred to above and thus causes no switch over from governments to private loans. As a consequence a rise in the interest rates on government securities and a fall in their prices do not take place.[1]

It is with the objective of circumventing the limitations to open market policy arising from the absence of a broad and active capital market, that the instrument of the variable reserve ratio or its variant changing liquidity ratios has been sought to be introduced into the armoury of central banks in the underdeveloped countries. Although there is, broadly speaking, a good prima facie case for the employment of the variable reserve ratio in some form or other in underdeveloped money and capital

[1] J. Aschheim, *Techniques of Monetary Control*, p. 42. Also Art. in the *Economic Journal*. December, 1959.

markets, a great deal will depend upon the reserve ratio policy of the commercial banks and the frequency with which changes in reserve requirements may be called for. In a system where minimum reserve ratios are frequently altered the banks may attempt to frustrate the effects of central bank action by anticipating the changes and maintaining round the year reserve balances much in excess of the statutory requirements. The spread between the required minimum balance and actual holdings will be sought to be widened or narrowed in adjustment of anticipated increase or reduction of the minimum. Under a regime of variable reserve ratios, therefore, the banks will inevitably tend to maintain actual ratios at a higher level than the statutory minimum and develop flexible reserve ratio practices.[1] It is clear from the above analysis that the use of the weapon has to be restricted to dealing with crisis or near-crisis situations.

LIQUIDITY RATIOS OF THE AFRICAN BANKS

The prescribed composition of the liquid assets is broadly similar in Nigeria, Ghana and Rhodesia with minor variations. The "specified" liquid assets are to be composed of:

(1) notes and coin which are legal tender in the territory
(2) balances at the central bank
(3) net balances at any other commercial bank
(4) money at call (with an acceptance house or discount house in Rhodesia)
(5) treasury bills issued by the government (the maturity of which in Nigeria must not exceed 93 days)
(6) inland bills of exchange and promissory notes (rediscountable with the central bank and in such maximum proportions as may be determined by it from time to time)
(7) local registered securities issued and guaranteed by the government or municipality listed in the Stock Exchange and having a final maturity of not more than six years (Rhodesia)

[1] *IMF. Staff Papers. July, 1965.* p. 276. Art. entitled "Instruments of Monetary Policy in Countries Without Highly Developed Capital Markets" by G. S. Dorrance, p. 276.

(8) treasury bills issued by the government of a country in an approved monetary area and having a maturity within 184 days (Nigeria).

The African Banks are found to be maintaining liquidity ratios much above the "specified" minimum. The following table brings out the liquidity ratios of the commercial banks in three different countries. It will be found that in some cases there is evidence of excess liquidity.

TABLE* No. 23

LIQUIDITY RATIOS

Nigeria			*Rhodesia and Nyasaland*			*Ghana*		
1961	April	32.9	*1961*	April	28.8	*1960*	March	64.2
	Sept.	35.1		Sept.	40.0		Sept.	48.1
	Dec.	43.1		Dec.	34.2		Dec.	44.5
1962	April	33.8	*1962*	April	29.2	*1961*	March	42.9
	Sept.	27.3		Sept.	41.4		Sept.	32.7
	Dec.	29.1		Dec.	36.2		Dec.	32.2
1963	April	32.1	*1963*	March	32.4	*1962*	March	46.9
	Sept.	31.1		Sept.	37.0		Sept.	61.3
	Dec.	31.0		Dec.	34.3		Dec.	46.3
1964	April	32.1	*1964*	April	28.4	*1963*	March	46.7
	Sept.	29.6		Sept.	40.2		Sept.	32.3
	Dec.	31.1		Dec.	35.1		Dec.	26.5
1965	April	30.6				*1964*	March	41.4
	Sept.	32.6						
	Dec.	34.4						

It will be observed from the above table that the liquidity ratios are not stable but have varied over a fairly wide range. Unstable liquidity reserve ratio practices will blunt the edge of both open market operations and the variable reserve ratio. Some banking laws differentiate the ratio according to the type of the bank or the financial intermediary. In Rhodesia the Bank may fix one percentage for commercial banks and another for acceptance

**Central Bank of Nigeria*, Economic and Financial Review. Dec. 1965, p. 33. June 1966, p. 41; *Bank of Rhodesia and Nyasaland*, Annual Reports for the years 1961, 1962 & 1964, p. 35, p. 38, p. 58. *Bank of Ghana:* Annual Reports, 1962, p. 29. 1964, p. 75 (Table LVII).

houses when it directs an inccrease in the reserve balances in relation to the advances and bills discounted [Art. 22(4)]. In Nigeria, however, it is specifically prescribed that no bank shall be required to maintain a higher percentage than another. The Australian central bank was deliberately empowered to discriminate between individual banks with regard to the call to "special accounts" so that it might be enabled to compensate for the different liquidity policies of the individual banks. It was bitterly resented by the trading banks; and in actual practice it was never used. A proposal has sometimes been made that in directing variation of liquidity ratios, different percentages may be required for expatriate and indigenous institutions. It will be discriminatory between the two categories of banks and even more so between banks of the same category. Individual expatriate banks may not be more liquid than their indigenous counterparts, although as a whole the former may be more liquid. The solution lies in applying the variation in the cash reserve ratio to *future* increases of deposits, and not to the total deposits at any one time. In many central banks established earlier in underdeveloped countries the variable reserve ratio was employed in this form to avoid discrimination between indigenous banks themselves who might possess different amounts of excess reserves. It would cause no hardship to indigenous banks in a less liquid position. At the same time no advantage will be provided to the expatriate banks enjoying a relatively higher degree of liquidity.

"NEW ORTHODOX" METHOD OF MONETARY CONTROL

A reference may be made in this connection to the debate that has centered round the question whether the object of central banking control should be the cash ratio or the liquidity ratio. The Radcliffe Committee found little to choose between the two but was inclined towards a straightforward power to raise the 30 per cent liquidity ratio which the British banks conventionally held to some higher percentage. The case for the control of liquidity was based by the Committee on the assumption that liquid assets had become the effective base of bank credit. The Bank of England's concern was the maintenance of reasonable stability in the treasury bill rates. As it believed that the market for treasury bills was rather narrow, it was prepared to deal freely between cash and treasury bills. Treasury bills could therefore be converted into cash without disturbing the market rates of discount on them. If the Bank of England had tried to restrain bank lending by limiting the creation of cash, it could not be sure of the stability of the treasury bill rate. The assumption was that there was a strong positive causal correlationship between the supply of treasury bills and the supply of bank deposits. Hence the "fulcrum" for the operations of the central bank was not the cash base but the manipulation of supply of treasury bills. The manipulation could be effected through (1) funding and unfunding and (2) their retirement out of the proceeds of the budget surplus or their further issuance so that a budget deficit could be financed. This is the so called "new orthodox" method of monetary control. This theory was written down into the Radcliffe Report and figured in the memorandum of the Bank of England before the Committee. The basic thesis that the supply of treasury bills is causally related to bank deposits is to be found in the recent writings of three well-known commentators of the British system,—Sayers, King and Dacey. But recent developments in the British money market have led other commentators to dispute the efficacy of the "new orthodox" method.

The structure of bank liquidity has undergone remarkable changes since the Committee wrote their Report. As one observer has remarked, "the assumed constants of the mid-1950's have changed into the crucial variables of to-day". From the table given below it will be found that over the five years 1959-1964 the total market supply of treasury bills dropped by 24 per cent. Treasury bill holdings of clearing banks declined by 44 per cent, Commercial bill holdings increased from 1.9 per cent of gross deposits to 5.6 per cent. The total liquid assets rose by £126 million. The Bank of England has had to accept much wider fluctuations in short term rates owing to difficulties "in funding". In the context of the present market conditions the case for the control of the cash base rather than the liquidity basis in the British system appears to be rather strong.

Attempts have been made through empirical testing to refute the hypothesis implying a strong positive correlation between deposits and the stock of bills. The advocates of the "new

TABLE[1] No. 24

CHANGED STRUCTURE OF BRITISH BANKS' LIQUIDITY

	April, 1959	*April, 1965*
	Percentage of gross deposits	
Cash Money at Call	7.1	10.4
Treasury Bills	13.9	5.1
Other Bills	1.9	5.6
Liquid Assets	31.2	29.5

orthodox" method have based their analysis on the assumption that all treasury bills are held within the banking system. If this assumption were correct, the reduction in their supply would have inevitably reduced the supply for the banking sector which would then have to contract to re-establish its minimum liquidity ratio of 30 per cent. But the assumption is not correct. There are "other tenderers" and the public hold substantial quantities of the bills. Thus control of the supply of cash, rather than that of the supply of bills, is both necessary and sufficient to provide control over bank deposits.[2]

IMPORT PRE-DEPOSIT REQUIREMENT AS A TOOL OF MONETARY POLICY

Some commentators have questioned the efficacy of the liquidity ratio as an instrument of monetary management in export-oriented dependent economies like Ghana, Nigeria etc. Mr. Olakanpo has argued that changes in liquidity ratio would hardly have an effect on the behaviour of the banking system because the demand for bank credit is relatively small in such economies. In such countries the balance of payments is a crucial factor influencing the level of money income and the liquidity of the economy. In such circumstances the mere replacement of currency boards by central banks will not by itself weaken the automatic link between money income and balance of payments. In such countries, he has argued, the technique of import pre-

[1] *The Economist*, British Banking 1965. June 19, 1965, p. VIII.

[2] *The Economic Journal*, December, 1964, p. 932. Art. entitled "The Inadequacy of 'New Orthodox' Methods of Monetary Control" by R. L. Crouch.

deposit requirements could be a more useful and more effective monetary measure for influencing the level of money income and the liquidity of the economy. In an export boom the weapon may be employed with the twin objective of maintaining a higher level of external assets and preventing domestic inflation through a secondary rise in money incomes. On the one hand by increasing the cost of imports, their volume may be reduced and slender foreign exchange resources may be conserved. On the other hand, a part of the rise in money income resulting from the export boom may be "syphoned off" and frozen so to speak in the central bank. The stronger the propensity of the importer to obtain funds for the advance deposit requirements, the greater will be the curb on the increase in money supply. The check to the rise in money supply brought about by import pre-deposit requirements will tend to restrict the availability of credit for it will have an impact on the lending capacity of the banking system. The restricted availability of bank credit will have a restraining effect on money income. There would also be the balance of payments effect which is closely related to the former arising from the "diffused difficulty" in obtaining the necessary funds to finance the advance deposit requirements. There will be the "interest burden" and a long waiting period for accumulating the funds.[1]

There is nothing original in Mr. Olakanpo's proposal that central banks in these African countries should adopt the technique of advance deposit requirements for imports as a tool of monetary policy. The use of this device has been widespread in the underdeveloped countries of Latin America such as Bolivia, Chile, Paraguay, Ecuador etc. where the amount of the advance deposit has varied over a range of 5 per cent to 500 per cent of the import value depending upon the "essentiality" of the goods. The present writer had advocated on many occasions the use of this instrument of monetary control in the context of the prevailing inflationary conditions in India. The usual practice is for the deposits to be held in the central bank in a special account for a definite period, to be released thereafter to the importer. Although the original purpose was to discourage imports, it has also served as a tool of monetary policy, similar

[1] *Economica* November 1961, pp. 401-406. Art. by J. O. W. Olakanpo entitled "Monetary Management in Dependent Economies".

to open market operations or shifts of fiscal or public funds between the commercial banks and the central bank. To produce the desired monetary effect the deposits will have to remain sterilised with the central bank for the desired period. If the regulations establishing advance deposits do not provide for this and permit such deposits to be held by private banks, so that lending capacity remains unimpaired, no use can be made of advance deposits as a tool of monetary policy. The banking system again as in Argentina (and in India) must be prevented from granting loans to their customers for the purpose of meeting the advance deposit requirements. The restrictive effect will obviously be temporary and will continue so long as the advance deposits are being accumulated with the central bank and are actually lying immobilised there. With the release of the deposits, net monetary expansion will follow. There is the great problem again involved in choosing the proper time of repayment.

The effectiveness of the device will obviously depend on the amount of reserves which the banks lose in making payment of advance deposits and the amount of excess reserves enjoyed by them before the imposition of the deposit requirement. These are the limitations to the successful functioning of open market operations and are equally applicable to advance deposits held in the central bank. But the technique of advance deposits may be used selectively by requiring different percentages of deposits for different categories of imports (essential and non-essential) and thus assist in re-shaping the whole structure of imports so as to conform by and large to the requirements of the national plan of economic development. Selective use of advance deposits in this form as an instrument of monetary control is not inhibited by difficulties faced by traditional selective credit control measures which arise out of the banking system's attempts at evasion. With respect to the balance of payments problem such use of advance deposits may produce effects which resemble in some respects those of multiple exchange rates. From this point of view, again, it is superior to devaluation. For advance deposits affect only payments for imports and if necessary, only payments for certain undesired categories of imports, whereas devaluation affects all kinds of international payments. The technique is also more flexible, for changes in the amounts of advance deposits can be introduced much more easily than changes in exchange rates. But it is clear that advance deposits unlike devaluation or multiple exchange rate systems cannot be employed as a device for promoting domestic exports.[1]

The experiences of countries like Indonesia, Nicaragua and Paraguay which employed advance deposit requirements to counteract the expansionary effect of continued increases in central bank assets demonstrate that the restrictive effects of these requirements were only temporary. The advance deposits which were to be maintained with the central banks had to be raised from time to time so that the expansion effect of continued increases in central bank assets could be compensated. Such continuous raising of advance deposit percentages had the inevitable adverse effect on output and employment in the industries using imported materials and equipment. Central banks had to reduce as a consequence the advance deposit ratios shortly after they had been increased. The central bank of Indonesia was even obliged to liberalise its rediscounting to offset the adverse effects.[2]

The device at best is a temporary stop-gap arrangement. It cannot be continued indefinitely and will have to be terminated sooner rather than later. To maintain the desired stabilisation effects, a package of anti-inflationary monetary-fiscal measures will have to be adopted to counter the expansionary effects after repayment. There is also the fear that the government may come to regard the accumulated funds as a treasure chest and may be tempted to dip into it from time to time. In such circumstances the intended stabilising effect will not be realised.[3] It is clear that the use of this tool of monetary policy as advocated by Mr. Olakanpo will not "of itself alter the situation". The instrument cannot be put into use without a central bank functioning in the country. His argument against the replacement of currency boards by central banks thus loses its force.

Generally the advance deposit is required at the time when the importer applies for an import licence or exchange permit

[1] Art. by Jorge Marshall entitled "Advance deposits on Imports" in the *IMF Staff Papers* Vol. VI. No. 2 April, 1958, p. 243.

[2] "Central Bank Policies and Inflation". Art. in the *IMF Staff Papers*, Oct. 1959, 283.

[3] *IMF. Staff Papers* Vol. 8, 1960. Art. entitled "Advance Deposit Requirements for Imports." by E. A. Birnbaum and M. Quereshi, p. 115-122.

or within a specified period after the grant of the permit or issue of the licence. Thus the adoption of this device presupposes the existence of a rigorous framework of import licensing and exchange control. In the developing countries the system of import and exchange control is already there and is likely to continue for a long time during the developmental stage. In the circumstances the technical condition for the operation of the instrument is satisfied. But the question is how far the device will be in the interests of an accelerated rate of economic development, the need for imports of capital goods being very urgent. In the context of a continuously rising barrier of import duties and surcharges and a restrictive monetary policy its operation may prove to be somewhat burdensome and even unnecessary. In recent times the technique was adopted in India* but it had to be abandoned almost immediately after its adoption because of stiff opposition from trade interests and also because the import duties were increased in the form of a surcharge on them. All these factors being taken into careful consideration, the observation made above that the instrument may be adopted only as a temporary emergency measure is reinforced. There is the danger that the authorities will grow complacent and fail to cope with the fundamental issue. The consequence will be the perpetuation of the malady in the economy.[1] In the circumstances the Banks' major reliance should be placed upon the traditional instruments of credit control.

THE BANK RATE INSTRUMENT

The charges of discriminatory treatment cannot be levelled against the traditional monetary instrument of the Bank rate. A great virtue of this instrument is its generality. To say that the Bank rate has general effects is not to deny that it may have directional effects under certain circumstances. But the directional slant is not deliberately given to it. What we intend to mean is that pressures exerted by the Bank rate normally and

*See *Reserve Bank of India Bulletin*, April, 1965, p. 1021. A Notification issued by the Reserve Bank of India required with effect from July, 1965 the maintenance by importers of advance deposits with banks, all of which were to be invested in treasury bills, equal to 25% of the value of imports. The Notification was subsequently cancelled.

[1] E. F. Jucker Fleetwood, *Money and Finance in Africa*, p. 140.

by and large impinge equally upon all economic units in similar liquidity position. They also do not impair inter-unit competition or adjustments. The central banks functioning in the newly independent African countries soon found out that the rediscounting instrument could be a much simpler method of controlling the banking system. All the banks under review have been expressly armed with this weapon. The technical condition of the ideal functioning of a short loan market was undoubtedly not fulfilled. But the countries had been familiar with the bills of exchange or trade bills for a long time. These had been introduced at a very early stage for financing foreign trade. The provisions relating to the discount rate policy of the African central banks are much less elaborate and more flexible than those outlined in the charters of the earlier central banks in other underdeveloped countries. There are few specific references in the statutes to the rates that may be charged on discounts and advances. The elaborate structure of rates and complex rules to be witnessed in this respect in many earlier central bank statutes are absent here. The only specific reference to be found in this connection is the provision in the Nigerian, Libyan and Ghanian laws that the interest charge for making advances against the following collateral shall be at least one per cent above the Bank's minimum rediscount rate: (1) gold coin or bullion, (2) government securities of not more than 25 years' maturity, 10 years in the case of Libya, (3) bills of exchange and promissory notes eligible for purchase, discount or rediscount, (4) warehouse warrants. The Sudanese bank, as already observed, has been authorised to establish differential discount rates for various classes of transactions or maturities.

The range of eligibility of papers for central bank credit, the period for which credit may be extended and the maximum amount of government securities that can be held as well as their maturity have been clearly defined by law and offer the central banks ample opportunities to make their credit policy effective and prepare the way for establishing a flexible interest rate. To be eligible for purchase or rediscount by the central bank inland bills of exchange and promissory notes drawn for commercial transactions must have a maximum maturity of 90 days in the Sudan, Ghana and Nigeria, 180 days in Libya, and 90 days in Tunisia but extensible up to 180 days, and 120 days in Morocco.

But the Rhodesian Bank has been given the fullest discretion about it as no statutory maturity has been laid down. Paper for financing seasonal agricultural operations may have a maturity of 270 days in the Sudanese Bank and 180 days in Nigeria and Libya. The central banks in Morocco and Tunisia, following the French tradition, have been empowered to extend medium term credit for five years for certain specific purposes.

DISCOUNT RATE POLICY IN THE DEVELOPING ECONOMIES

It will be worth while at this stage to distinguish the significance and operation of the central bank's discount rate in the developing countries from that in the developed financial centres, particularly those centres where the Bank of England pattern of central banking has been adopted. While under the British system the monetary authority functions as the lender of last resort, providing short-term liquid funds to the money market at a "penalty" rate in emergencies, in the underdeveloped countries the central bank has often to function as a provider of working funds to the entire economic system. Borrowing from the central bank does not necessarily take place in emergencies only; it may be a continuous day-to-day process, operating through the medium of discounts and advances. In some cases central banks' operations are not restricted to the banking sector alone but the banks are permitted by their charters to extend them to the entire private sector, particularly in the areas where the ordinary banking facilities are not well developed. Indeed in a few cases the central banks are the largest commercial banks. The right to borrow continuously from the central bank has undoubtedly some advantages, not only for the banking system operating in an underdeveloped financial market but also for the central bank itself. While the commercial banks are enabled to economise on their cash reserves and increase their earning power by expanding the volume of their loans and advances, the contacts that develop among the various parts of the banking system facilitate the enforcement of its policy by the central bank.[1]

The discount rate policy of the central banks in the developing countries, again, as observed earlier, appears to be marked by selective overtones. A variety of paper, agricultural, industrial

[1] R. S. Sayers, *Modern Banking* (6th Ed). 1964, p. 297.

and commercial, is eligible for discount; but it is observed that a certain pattern of priority in terms of the National Economic Plan is assigned to different types of paper. Differential rates are often charged according to the kind of paper discounted or provided as collateral, with the objective of stimulating or discouraging, as the case may be, the flow of credit along designated channels and in special directions. But in the sophisticated money markets of the developed countries, the discount rate is related to the domestic conditions of actual and potential demand and supply of money and is influenced by the balance of payments position and international movements of short term capital. Thus while in the developed countries, central banks quote a single rate, a multiplicity of rates is to be witnessed in most underdeveloped countries.

With the help of multiple and discriminatory rates, central banks' monetary policy in the developing economies works more as an instrument for the allocation of credit among the different sectors rather than as a weapon for controlling the volume of credit. The monetary authorities in these countries are inclined to believe that through selective policies they can assist the process of economic development by affecting the general level of prices and production and the pattern of investment. As an example of quoting a multiplicity of rates, the Central Bank of Tunisia in our study which quotes different rates for short-term, medium term and exporters' credit and has as many as seven rates may be particularly mentioned. The Bank of Sudan, another institution studied here, has been authorised under Art. 42 of its statute to establish differential rates for various classes of transactions and maturities. Central banks in several other underdeveloped countries also are observed to adopt multiple discount rates policy. In Costa Rica and Colombia, central banks are found to be quoting ten rates, in the Philippines, Venezuela and Ecuador, nine rates and in Paraguay three.[1] Through the instrumentality of preferential rates the flow of credit is sought to be directed in favour of sectors having high potentialities for growth, and away from the undesired categories. It follows that in the case of these underdeveloped countries changes in discount rates are effected not with a view to alter the interest rate structure but

[1] *IMF Staff Papers* Vol. XIII No. 1. March 1966 Art. entitled "Central Bank Discount Rates" by Rodrigo Jaramillo, p. 118.

to influence the allocation of credit among the different branches of the economy. It must be observed, however, that in many underdeveloped countries the central bank's discount rate policy does not conform to the standard pattern as outlined above. Central banks in Ghana in our study as well as in countries like Malaysia, Jamaica, Jordan and Peru do not appear to be functioning as continuous and important sources of credit for the banking system. In the case of many countries central banks again have sought to control the volume of credit, as distinct from its direction through the manipulation of the discount rate. At the same time it must be observed that in many developing economies the discount rate is by and large inoperative owing to the excess liquidity of the commercial banking system. In such countries the discount rate has no significance for the monetary banking system. The nature of the market itself excludes any recourse to the traditional discount rate weapon. In Somalia, for instance, the National Bank has not been able to use this familiar weapon of control because the commercial banks do not to a significant extent rediscount with the central bank. The latter therefore had to fall back upon moral suasion and launched an appeal in 1965 to the banks not to finance import transactions beyond a certain limit. The response was quite satisfactory.[1]

In sharp contrast with the British practice where the Bank of England will never refuse to lend, quantitative ceilings are imposed as a rule on the amount of borrowing from the central bank and often a steeply rising schedule of penalties payable on amounts borrowed in excess of the limits laid down is prescribed. The cases in point are India, Pakistan, Japan and Tunisia. While a relatively high degree of frequency of changes in discount rates is to be observed in the developed financial system, rate changes are infrequent in the underdeveloped economies. But changes in the discount rate are not so infrequent in developing economies as is generally believed. In the case of at least three countries covered in our study, Tunisia, Ghana and Rhodesia and Nyasaland, discount rates have been subject to frequent alterations almost in the same manner as is to be witnessed in the more advanced monetary systems. The following table indicates the frequency of rate changes in the case of some of these countries.

[1] *The Bankers' Magazine*, May 1966, p. 356. Art. by M. Buonomo entitled "Banking in Somalia".

TABLE No. 25

Ghana				*Rhodesia & Nyasaland*			
March	1960	..	$4\frac{13}{16}$%	August	1957	..	$4\frac{1}{2}$%
June	1960	..	$5\frac{13}{16}$%	August	1960	..	5%
December	1960	..	4%	June	1961	..	$5\frac{1}{2}$%
July	1961	..	$4\frac{1}{2}$%	May	1962	..	5%
				Since	1962	..	$4\frac{1}{2}$%

The central bank of Tunisia is also observed to have changed its rates for short-term and medium-term credit in 1959 and again in 1960.

MONETARY-CREDIT POLICY OF THE BANK OF SUDAN

How the traditional technique of the discount rate weapon which is available to all the central banks has been employed as a method of control over the banking system and as a measure of ensuring a flexible supply of credit to the national economy as well as enabling the central bank to evolve into a lender of last resort is well illustrated by reference to the monetary-credit policy of the Bank of Sudan. The main objective of the Bank of Sudan's credit policy has been twofold: first, to restrict the excessive liquidity of the commercial banks resulting from the high level of balances on cotton boards' accounts; and secondly, to ensure the ability of the banking system to meet all legitimate demand for credit on the part of the exporters and to facilitate as far as possible the genuine additional requirements that might be placed on them as the result of the increasing tempo of economic activity.[1]

From the commencement of its operations the Bank of Sudan realised that the desired objective would not be fulfilled, if discount arrangements were limited to the traditional instrument of credit viz. to commercial bills. The use of commercial bills was relatively restricted in Sudan and these bills formed a small portion of the assets of the banks. The prevailing method of granting credit was in the form of advances and overdrafts. The central bank advances in the circumstances took the form of

[1] *Bank of Sudan*. Annual Report for the year 1962, p. 33.

advances, within ceilings determined from time to time, against the collateral of cotton stored in the port of Sudan, which was obviously an unwieldy system. Treasury bills or securities issued by foreign governments were not held by most commercial banks in Sudan. This method of acting as a lender of last resort was clearly not satisfactory as it was inevitably discriminatory against all banks which could not pledge foreign securities. Thus the Bank of Sudan found it necessary to evolve other methods of lending to the banks and the natural development was along the lines of the classical method of arranging for discounting bills of exchange and promissory notes and for making loans and advances against the collateral of such bills.[1] So within the terms of Art. 41 of the Bank of Sudan Act, a scheme was formulated by the Bank under which the Bank would accept for discount from banks bills of exchange and promissory notes, drawn or issued for commercial, industrial or agricultural purposes and would grant loans against their collateral.. As early as April 1961 a scheme was initiated under which discount facilities were to be extended to bills and promissory notes made by exporters of Sudan's produce. Its success in the field of export movements prompted the Bank to extend the same type of discount facilities in November 1961 to acceptances or promissory notes of the commercial banks' customers, employed in industrial business, issued against advances received for financing the purchase and keeping in stock of raw materials and semi-finished products needed for manufacturing.[2] Steps were also taken by the Bank to embark at a later stage in the discount of "cultivation bills" i.e. bills and notes accepted or issued by the ordinary banks' customers against advances for growing and harvesting crops, beginning with cotton.[3] There was also some directional or selective control in the shape of restrictions on bank advances, in the categories of advances for financing of "imports, retail trade in imported goods, personal advances". The adoption of the technique of rediscounting enabled the Bank to exercise its control over the cost and availability of bank credit, making selective or directional control unnecessary.

Towards the end of 1963 the Bank of Sudan had to adopt a

[1] *Bank of Sudan*. Annual Report for the year 1960, p. 28.

[2] This method has some resemblance to the Bill Market Scheme introduced by the Reserve Bank of India in 1952.

[3] *Bank of Sudan*. Annual Report for the year 1961, p. 26.

more restrictive policy towards the expansion of bank credit to the private sector. The activities of the sector had for some time been adding to the pressure on the foreign exchange reserves. The excessive liquidity of the banks during 1960-61, it has already been observed, was mainly due to the banking arrangements of the cotton boards. The availability to the banks of the large public funds of the Sudan Gezira Board and the provision of the Boards' moneys at much lower rates of interest compared with the lending rate of the Bank of Sudan were a source of instability in the credit situation. The system was calculated to impair the effectiveness of any official monetary policy to be adopted in the national interest. The excessive liquidity of the banks provided an incentive to employ the funds at their disposal profitably and caused some unnecessary advances. The banks also were not prompt in collecting export proceeds and there was considerable delay in surrendering the foreign exchange receipts to the Bank of Sudan.

Banks making full use of central bank facilities were refused increases in advances when a marked decline in their liquid resources occurred. A more selective control was also employed with regard to bills offered for rediscount or as collateral against advances. Additional measures were introduced in early 1964 to prevent any further expansion of advances and it was decided that all deposits of the Sudan Gezira Board should be transferred from the commercial banks to the Bank of Sudan. The Board's current accounts with the banks were closed on 1st April, 1964. Proceeds from the sale of cotton thereafter were to be paid directly to the credit of the Board's account with the Bank of Sudan. A few months later the process of transferring the Board's time deposit accounts was completed.[1] As the credit situation continued to exert pressures on the foreign exchange reserves, the Bank had to reinforce with additional measures the restrictive credit policy begun in the previous year. The restrictive measures had the effect of reducing the volume of advances for financing imports and thereby provided some protection to the foreign exchange reserves through a curtailment of the flow of imports. A review of the situation early in 1965 indicated that no relaxation of the existing restrictions was called for but at the same time there

[1] *Bank of Sudan*, Annual Report for year ending 31st December, 1964, pp. 39-40.

was no case for intensifying the credit squeeze. The level of commercial banks' advances to their customers no doubt fell during the year by LS 9.6 million. But the whole extent of the fall cannot be attributed to the restrictive measures alone. Out of the reduction of LS 9.6 million in advances, LS 6.6 million related to advances for financing exports. But this fall was not the outcome of the central bank's credit policy, for the central bank had always encouraged the financing of exports. The fall in advances for the export of cotton and other crops must be attributed to other factors.[1]

The government's need to borrow from the Central Bank had not arisen till 1965, although it had been experiencing cash deficits since the inauguration of the Ten Year Plan of Economic and Social Development in 1961-62. The reason was that the government had ample balances with the central bank. Until 1964-65 the only item in the balance sheet of the Bank of Sudan involving credit granted to the government was non-transferable treasury bills. It was for the first time in the last quarter of 1964 that the Bank agreed to grant temporary advances to the government. Since the end of March 1965, temporary advances have not only appeared as a regular item in the return of the Bank but have shown an increasing trend. Interest at 4½ per cent p.a. is being charged on the balance of indebtedness in excess of LS 5 million.[2]

The area covered by the discount facility of the Bank became wide enough to embrace practically all cases of legitimate needs which banks might have with regard to the refinancing of their liquid assets in the central bank. The introduction of discount facilities gave an equal opportunity in times of need to all banks with respect to their access to central bank-credit. Whenever it appeared to the Bank that the banking system was enjoying a high degree of liquidity, such liquidity was sought to be countered by controlling the volume of the so called restricted category of advances. But such restrictions were again relaxed when import policy was liberalised and excess liquidity had disappeared. With the withdrawal of the Gezira Board's deposits from the banking system and the resulting decline in its liquidity, credit facilities were extended to the banks which needed them for financing

[1] *Bank of Sudan*, Annual Report for year ending 31 December 1965, p. 39.
[2] *Ibid.*, p. 50.

exports of cotton and other crops. It was no part of the Bank's policy to obstruct or discourage the provision of export finance. It is interesting to observe that since the adoption by the Bank of Sudan of the new form of credit policy, by far the greater proportion of total credits extended by it to the banking system has taken the form of discounted bills and advances against the collateral of bills. As the dependence of the commercial banks on central bank credit increased, the Bank of Sudan did not find any difficulty in implementing and maintaining its restrictive credit policy without recourse to other monetary weapons.[1] The increased percentage of discounted bills and advances against the collateral of bills is brought out in the following table, which indicates the proportion of total credits granted by the Bank in the three forms.[2]

	Percentage				
	Dec. '61	*Dec. '62*	*Dec. '63*	*Dec., 64*	*Dec. '65*
Credit against foreign securities	21%	4%	9%	13%	×
Credit against cotton warehoused in Sudan ..	22%	11%	11%	26%	8%
Credit against Bills discounted	57%	85%	80%	61%	92%

It will be observed that by the end of 1965 there was no credit outstanding against collateral of foreign securities. This form of credit though permissible under the statute had always been regarded by the Bank as a transitional measure which would be necessary only in the early stages of the Bank's activities till it could develop the technique of extending credit in the form of discount of bills and advances against the collateral of bills. Credit against the collateral of domestic assets was considered by the Bank to be preferable to credit against the collateral of foreign securities. The former method should enable the Bank to have a more searching look into the activities of the ordinary banks and provide a direct link between central bank credit and

[1] *Bank of Sudan*. Annual Report for the year, 1960, p. 27.
[2] *Bank of Sudan*. Annual Reports for the year, 1962, p. 34, 1964, p. 41, 1965, p. 41.

changes in the volume of those categories of advances which are subject to seasonal fluctuations. The commercial banks were accordingly informed that the central bank credit facilities in the form of advances against the collateral of foreign securities would not be ordinarily available from August 1, 1965.[1]

MONETARY-CREDIT POLICY OF THE BANK OF NIGERIA

In Nigeria although the central bank from the very start was armed not only with the traditional discount rate weapon but also with open market operations and variation of liquid asset ratios, it had to place its major reliance in recent years on a selective control measure based on moral suasion. In the earlier years of its operation in the absence of a relatively developed banking system and of a money or securities market there was hardly any scope for monetary policy and the Central Bank had made no attempt to use monetary techniques. The Bank had directed its efforts towards the creation of a suitable financial infrastructure. It was the very high ratio of loans and advances to deposits throughout the years 1961, 1962 and 1963, rather than the factor of excess liquidity, which called for the exercise of a policy of monetary restraint in recent years. The average liquidity ratio of the banking system was 28.5 per cent in 1961, 32.5 per cent in 1962 and 31 per cent in 1963. Judged by British banking standards the ratio was not low, although there had been a deterioration in 1963 compared to 1962. But the advances-deposits ratio was 78.0 per cent, 88.6 per cent and 93.3 per cent in 1961, 1962 and 1963. Indeed in the year 1963 it fluctuated between 83.5 per cent and 94.6 per cent as against 73.5 per cent and 90.3 per cent in 1962.[2] The increasing pressure on the reserves of the banking system was obvious. During the past ten years aggregate deposits had risen by only 140 per cent while aggregate bank advances increased by 641 per cent—the liquidity of the banking system had been considerably strained.[3] Indeed bank credit had been expanding during the period 1961-64 at a very fast rate. Credit extended to the public sector had risen from £14.4 million in 1961 to £32.2 million in 1964 while that to the

[1] *Bank of Sudan*. Annual Report for 1965, p. 40.
[2] *Central Bank of Nigeria. Annual Report and Statement of Accounts*. 1963, p. 26.
[3] *The Bankers' Magazine*. January 1956, p. 23. Art. by O. Olakanpo, entitled "Banking in Nigeira".

private sector had increased from £58.7 million to £137.1 million. Owing to a decision of the Cocoa Producers' Alliance to withhold Nigerian Cocoa from the world market, the members of the produce financing Consortium declined to finance the Nigeria Marketing Board and the Central Bank had to step in to fill the vacuum by making advances direct to the Board. These central bank loans served to reinforce the credit creating potential of the banking system. In addition the reserves of the banking system built up in the expectation of cocoa financing must have been directed to expand credit in other directions. The net effect of all these developments was to accelerate the expansion of money supply and intensify the inflationary pressures. This excessive monetary expansion resulted in the continued high rate of importation and a widening balance of payments deficit and drain of foreign exchange resources. The external reserves declined from £159 million in 1961 to £77 million in 1964. The total of reserves at the end of 1964 fell below the minimum level of four months' imports, a level endorsed by official policy.[1] The central bank drew the attention of the National Economic Council to the potential threat to the economic future of the country posed by this remarkable rate of monetary expansions, the increase of money supply between 1961-1964 being of the order of 30 per cent. In considering possible measures to contain this rate of expansion, the central bank was obviously faced with the dilemma of restricting private spending and encouraging capital formation. The problem was rendered mere complex by the policy of deficit financing followed by the government. In the circumstances in the year 1964 a new stage in monetary management was reached when the passive monetary policy in vogue since the days of the West African Currency Board had to be superseded by a more conscious effort on the part of the monetary authority. The Bank had to fall back primarily upon moral suasion and some other regulatory measures. In October, 1964 a letter was addressed by the Governor of the Central Bank to the commercial banks, placing a 15 per cent ceiling on the rate of expansion in the aggregate of each bank's loans and advances. The banks were requested not only to limit the rate of increase of aggregate advances but there was a directive specifically to

[1] *The Bankers' Magazine*. March 1956. Art. by O. Olakanpo, entitled "Banking Problems in Nigeria", p. 183.

exercise restraint in the granting of loans and advances for financing consumption expenditures, such as loans for non-essential imports, advances to hire purchase companies and individuals.[1] The regulatory measures simultaneously adopted included a change in the proportion of commercial bank liquid assets held overseas which could count as part of specified liquid assets to satisfy the liquidity ratio requirements. This proportion was reduced from 7½ per cent to 3 per cent of total bank deposit liabilities. To buttress its restrictive policy the central bank also raised its minimum rediscount rate from 4 per cent to 5 per cent in December, 1964. The commercial banks took the cue and followed immediately by raising their lending and deposit rates by one half of one percentage point.[2] Thus the Nigerian Bank made what may be called "a package deal approach" on the lines of the Bank of England and of the Reserve Bank of India. It is interesting to note that the bank rate weapon was an important component of the package. In the package deal of the Indian Reserve Bank, however, the bank rate was significantly a missing component until recently. It came to be included as an essential ingredient of the package of measures adopted by the Reserve Bank only in September, 1964.[3]

As there was no prospect of a sudden improvement in the situation, the continuation of the central bank's restrictive monetary policy was considered to be desirable. Although there was a reduction in the level of bank credit to the private sector, the banking system's credit to the public sector increased, offsetting to some extent the contractionist pressure of private sector credit on the money supply. At the end of March 1965, the external assets of Nigeria fell to £75.2 million from £81.3 million at the end of 1964. Attention of the government was drawn by the central bank to the persistent threat of a balance of payments crisis and the adoption of appropriate fiscal measures was advised. Drastic measures to arrest a further decline in the balance of payments position were adopted in August 1965. Such measures included higher customs tariffs on non-essential imports, ban on imports from certain countries, prohibition of pre-payment to

[1] *Economic and Financial Review*, Bank of Nigeria, July 1965, 1956, p. 4.

[2] *Bank of Nigeria*. Annual Report for the year 1964, pp. 13-15.

[3] Speech of the Governor of the Reserve Bank of India at the Dinner Meeting of the Calcutta Bankers' Association, March 29, 1965.—*Reserve Bank of Indian Bulletin* April 1965, pp. 480-81.

overseas customers for imports etc. The central bank on its part offered every inducement to commercial banks to rechannel their advances within the framework of the 15 per cent ceiling from the less essential to the productive sectors, including primary exports. At the same time they were discouraged from borrowing short from overseas to finance the needs of the private sector for longterm capital. In cases where banks desired additional resources from abroad and rediscount facilities with the central bank, it was made clear that such resources should not be utilised for purposes contrary to the central bank's policy of restraint on consumer spending.

An evaluation of the effectiveness of these monetary-fiscal measures should be made in the perspective of their aims and objectives and in relation to their impact upon aggregate savings, consumer demand and commercial bank operations. Available statistical material indicates a reduction in the rate of importation of consumer goods, a growth of import substitution and a reduced rate of expansion of bank credit and total money supply during the subsequent months of the year (1965). Aggregate growth of private voluntary savings is reflected in an increase of time and savings deposits with commercial banks by 23.2 per cent as against 21.4 per cent in 1964. Money supply increased in 1965 by 3.1 per cent compared to 16.0 per cent in 1964, while total commercial bank credit outstanding at the end of 1965 increased by 8.4 per cent only as against an increase of 37.5 per cent at the close of 1964. Although imports of consumer goods did not decline in absolute terms, the rate of increase fell in 1965, such imports comprising 44 per cent of the total imports in 1965 as against 53.5 per cent in 1963 and 46.2 per cent in 1964. As regards the impact of the policies of the monetary authorities on the behaviour of the domestic price level, it may be observed that by and large the price situation did not show any alarming signs of instability. The annual price increase in the three years to 1964 averaged a little over 2 per cent. The rate of increase in 1965 over 1964 amounting to 4 per cent was not unwarranted by the rate of growth of Nigerian economy. The gross domestic product at 1957 prices increased by more than 5 per cent during 1965.

The experience of the central bank of Nigeria as that of the central banks in other developing economies in Africa points to the difficulty of employing a policy of credit restraint in the face of mounting government deficits. While the banks are endeavouring to restrict credit to the private sector, credit to the public sector in its potentially inflationary form continued to be on the increase. This increase was inevitable as the result of the adoption of policies of economic development. There is clearly the need of greater co-operation between the central banks and the governments in the area of policy so that stable conditions can be maintained in the economy. Pending the maturity of the financial structure of the countries to a degree which will permit effective employment of the traditional tools of central banking control, the main reliance may have to be placed on fiscal measures for achieving economic stability. But there *is* a case for pursuing selective credit control in favour of the productive sectors of the economy at least for the foreseeable future. The Central Bank of Nigeria subscribes to this policy, as is clear from its operations since its inception.[1]

MONETARY POLICY OF THE BANK OF MOROCCO

Although the Bank of Morocco has been provided by its Statutes with the bank rate weapon, moral suasion and selective control involving directional control of credit seem to be its major instruments of control. Under Art. 13 of its Statute, the Bank has been made responsible for watching the application of the legal and regulatory powers pertaining to the banking profession as well as to the organisation of money and capital markets. The banks of Morocco are organised into a Committee. The Central Bank with the aid of the institutional means available rather than by regulation is in a position to make the Committee use its statutory power in the direction needed to pursue a coherent credit policy. A new system was introduced in 1960 under which each bank was given an upper limit to its rediscounting facilities at the Bank of Morocco relating to commercial bills and other credit instruments.

In its anxiety to prevent excessive creation of credit by the banking system, the Bank of Morocco has adopted the technique of imposing a ceiling on the amount of rediscounts presented by a banking institution. Within the ceiling certain forms of credit

[1] *Central Bank of Nigeria*. Annual Report for the year 1965, p. 13.

again require previous approval. The maintenance of a volume of credit compatible with the development of transactions in trade and commerce and stability of money has been its particular concern. The Bank has special interest in the lines of credit employed for developing means of production in the country. It has been the Bank's policy to ensure that sound institutions always obtain their credit requirements for normal business.[1]

An interesting feature of the Bank of Morocco as also of Tunisia is its authorisation to rediscount commercial bills representing medium-term credit. The bills may have a maximum maturity of 5 years from the date of presentation to the bank and must have for their exclusive object the development of the means of production, transport, equipment, construction of residential buildings and the financing of certain exports and imports.[2] This rediscounting is closely connected with the directional control of credit and is aimed at adequate distribution of available resources in the spheres mentioned above. It may be interesting to observe here the influence of the heritage. The statutory powers relating to selective credit control are reminiscent of the Bank of France which is empowered to apply both quantitative and selective controls. The power and authority of the Bank of France as the central bank has been enhanced by reinforcing its traditional armoury with new weapons of selective control:[3]

(1) Ordinary banks have to submit to the scrutiny of the central bank any credits that they may wish to be able to mobilise by rediscounting; and the central bank will be free to apply to them whatever criteria it thinks fit.
(2) Hire purchase regulation.
(3) Rediscount ceilings.
(4) Floors (planchers) for treasury bill holdings.
(5) Directives issued to banks.

In the light of the reconstruction to be undertaken and the export drive that would have to be promoted after the War (II) the General Council of the Bank in 1944 had agreed in principle

[1] *Structure Et Distribution Du Credit Au Maroc.* A special mimeographed Note kindly furnished by the Bank of Morocco to the present writer.
[2] Art. 31. Statuts De La Banque Du Maroc, p. 28.
[3] *Eight European Central Banks* (BIS Study), pp. 157-161. Art. 59. Statute of the Bank of France.

to mobilise medium term credits. The maximum life of mobilisable credits would be 18 months, 2 years or 5 years depending on the purpose. The 5 year period would be granted only for credits designed to facilitate development of the productive equipment of an enterprise, the financing of certain export transactions guaranteed by the government and real property construction.[1] The statutes of the Bank of Morocco, it is clear, have relied on the Bank of France's charter to a considerable extent in respect of mobilisation of medium-term credits. The influence of the French tradition regarding grant of medium-term credit is discernible in the statutes of the central banks in other countries organised under French auspices before their independence e.g. the Equatorial African Central Bank and the West African Central Bank.[2]

MONETARY POLICY OF THE BANK OF TUNISIA

The monetary-credit policies developed and followed by the Central Bank of Tunisia during the earlier years of its operation had the objective of stabilising the new currency and utilising the distribution of credit as a means of promoting economic development. With this end in view the necessary measures were adopted in both the domestic and the external field.

In the sphere of domestic monetary-credit policy the central mission of the central bank was what has been defined by the statutes as exercising control over the circulation of money and distribution of credit. Different methods were employed by the Bank to fulfil effectively this statutory obligation.

The control over the distribution of credit called for a supervision over the quality and use of credit granted as well as over the quantity of these credits and their influence on the behaviour of money supply.

(*a*) *Qualitative control over distribution of credit*

As regards qualitative control over the distribution of credit, the central bank was able to equip itself with a knowledge of all credit operations of importance by means of the *agreements with respect to rediscounting operations and previous authorisations.*

[1] Art. 59 (c). *Banque De France.*

[2] *Federal Reserve Bank of New York, Monthly Review* July 1964, p. 133, p. 135. The Central Banks of Algeria and Malagasi may also extend medium term credit of five years for similar purposes.

The banks must, if they wanted to ensure an appeal for accommodation to the central bank, obtain from the latter an agreement of rediscount for loans comprising an amount between 10,000 dinars to 75,000 dinars. In practice the banks which are anxious to increase the mobilisable part of their assets and thus improve their liquidity seek almost invariably the previous consent of the central bank before lending to this extent. The central bank examines the loans in question and gives its consent subject to conditions which appear to it to be necessary for producing a favourable effect on the enterprise to be financed or on the distribution of credit in a general way. Loans above 75,000 dinars must have the previous authorisation of the central bank before they may be granted by the banks. They have to inform the central institution whether they propose to "nourish" the credit themselves or intend to carry them to its rediscounting facilities. The central bank intervenes in the same way as before and thus exercises its control. Whatever may be the amount, no medium term credit, however, can be passed on to the central bank without its previous consent. As these "investment" loans are likely to have profound repercussions on the behaviour of money and on the development of the economy, the central bank pays particular attention to it. Whenever such a loan is considered to have the potentiality of increasing output, it is accepted by the central bank and its grant by the ordinary bank is facilitated.

On the qualitative plane the central bank has a positive policy for improving the distribution of credit. Its Central Service for Risks is a method of informing every bank monthly as to the amount of credit granted to a single borrower by all banks. The lending institutions are in this way enabled to judge whenever necessary the extent of the solvency of their clients. This quick and regular exchange of information between the banks and the central bank makes possible a healthy growth of credit. Thanks to the system of centralisation of risks the central bank can collect monthly information regarding the nature of credit distributed by all banks and their distribution among different branches of economic activity. It is thus possible for the central bank to know the fields where its intervention would be most useful. According to the authorities of the central bank, this examination of the nature and quality of the credit granted by the banks is the best way of following the conduct of a bank and of watching the essential harmony between its resources and its investments. Ever since its creation the central bank had to intervene vigorously in this respect with a view to strengthening the banking sector which had been all this time in a state of distressful negligence.

(b) Control over the Volume of Credit

As regards control of the volume of credit, the central bank watches equally carefully the quantum of credit distribution. It is always busy adjusting as far as possible the volume of credit granted according to the importance of production so that the volume may be adequate for financing productive activity which must not be restricted for want of credit. Any other policy, the Bank believes, would lead to an inflationary situation with its damaging consequences on economic and social plans and with the unfortunate repercussions on the behaviour of the national economy. The central bank had adopted several methods to achieve this equilibrium between the volume of credit and the level of production and economic activity.

In order to have a complete knowledge of the general growth of monetary resources and their counter-parts, the central bank processes and centralises all information regarding the activities of the Tunisian banks. These banks have co-operated with the central institution without any reserve. In the past only fragmentary data relating to developments in the monetary situation were available. Since the creation of the central bank the availability of complete and homogeneous statistics makes it possible for the Bank of Issue to exercise continuous supervision which is very useful for the growth of the monetary sphere. The monthly data together with the accounts of the central bank are published regularly and they make it possible for the authorities and planners of enterprises to have an exact understanding of the situation. There is no doubt that this method has tended to strengthen confidence in the national economy both at home and abroad. With the help of such statistical material the central bank can adapt its policy to the economic conditions in general.

It is in this way that the central bank fixes, after taking account of the resources of a particular bank and the importance of its intervention in financing economic activity, the extent to which that bank may appeal to the central bank for accommodation. This overall limitation on the volume of total credit that may be granted by every bank is superimposed on the scrutiny by the central bank of the quality of each credit granted by that bank. In this way it becomes possible for the central bank to achieve a two-fold objective—that of providing sound loans and ensuring at the same time a total volume of credit adapted to the general economic conditions. As a result of this policy, the central bank has been able to ensure the normal financing of the developing economy without straining monetary stability.

(*c*) *Action on the Cost of Credit*

The central bank has the responsibility of acting on the cost of credit with a view to encouraging investment and reducing the financial expenses of enterprises. The abundance of monetary resources worked in favour of a cheap monetary policy in this connection. The situation not being inflationary, there was no risk of an excessive demand for credit with a reduction in its cost. The dual necessity of promoting the expansion of economic activity and of maintaining the parity of the dinar by checking cost increases through a reduction of the financial charges of enterprises worked in favour of a cheap monetary policy. In this way the central bank was able to bring about a progressive reduction in its rediscount rate.

The bank rate was fixed to start with at a relatively high level because of the free flow of capital between France and Tunisia at that stage. If the Tunisian rate had been markedly below the French rate, there would have begun an exodus of capital to France. In the circumstances the existence of much too wide a disparity between the rates could not be allowed to continue. The devaluation of the French franc and the maintenance of the parity of the dinar had however as their consequence the regulation of capital transfers from Tunisia. Since then it has been possible to have rates different from those in France. Subsequent developments have shown the wisdom of non-devaluation of the dinar at that time. The result of non-devaluation was an increase of the foreign exchange reserves of Tunisia and a growth of bank deposits. As a consequence of these developments the central bank was able to reduce its rates for the first time in 1959 by 1 per cent for medium term loans and by 0.25 per cent for short-term loans. A second reduction in rates took place on February 1, 1960. This reduction is more important because the rate for medium credit was slashed from 5 per cent to 3 per cent and that on short-term credit from 3.25 per cent and 4 per cent respectively for rediscounting commercial and financial bills to 3 per cent. Finally, another important measure adopted was the fixation of the rediscounting rate of the central bank for exporters at 2 per cent only. Such has been the enterprising action taken by the central bank for fulfilling the mission of regulator of credit which has been entrusted to it by its statute.[1]

Coming to later stages of the evolution of monetary-credit policy of the Bank, it is observed that the total volume of money which had increased by 27.37 million dinars between 1962-63 remained stable in 1964. At the end of this year the total money supply amounted to 133.33 million dinars which was practically equal to 132.954 million dinars at the end of the immediately preceding year. But the components of the money supply changed somewhat in that currency (fiduciary money) increased by 1.4 per cent while bank money ("scriptural" money) declined by 0.2 per cent. Demand deposits declined by 7 per cent while deposits at the Postal Savings Banks (Centre of Postal Cheques) went up by 7.3 per cent.[2]

The notable increase in production witnessed in 1964 had therefore been financed by an increase in the velocity of circulation and had been facilitated by an activisation (utilisation) of unemployed deposits of certain banks through channels of the money market. This better utilisation of both demand and term deposits enabled the banking system to support a larger amount of credit expansion which increased from 108.175 million dinars in December 1963 to 133.586 million dinars in December 1964. This was an increase of 25.163 million dinars as against that of 21.163 million dinars in the previous year.

The accommodation to the state also went up to 80.973 million dinars in December 1964 from 76.295 million dinars at the end of 1963 and 51.545 million dinars at the end of 1962 respectively.

On the whole the total credit extended to both the private and public sectors increased by 30.089 million dinars in 1964 against an increase of 45.913 million dinars in 1963. Although the expansion of bank credit and accommodation to the state were relatively smaller than in 1963, the impact on the external equilibrium was more pronounced in 1964. It provoked a signi-

[1] *Rapport Annuel*, Central Bank of Tunisia, 1958-59, p. 53.
[2] *La Evolution Monetaire, Rapport Annuel*, 1964, pp. 73-76.

ficant reduction of the claims of Tunisia on foreign countries at a time of payment deficits during three consecutive years in the past. Thus although the expansion of credit and the national debt in 1964 had been less important than in 1963, its effects on the equilibrium of external trade level were more serious and accentuated. The external assets of the country were markedly depleted.

The inauguration of the Triennial Plan necessitated the expansion of expenditure in the public sector. The state had to make recourse to deficit financing for financing the Plan projects. At the same time the delays in the granting and use of foreign credit made it necessary for financing, with local resources, projects for which external assistance would not be obtained. All this caused a serious pressure on the external balance of the country.

The most important difficulty faced in redressing the situation consisted in making the Tunisian export prices competitive. These had already suffered as a result of the French and Moroccan devaluations of 1958 and 1960 respectively, France being the chief buyer and Morocco the chief competitor. The decision to devalue the dinar by 20 per cent had to be taken on 28th September 1964, resulting in a revaluation of the dollar and other foreign currencies in terms of the dinar by 25 per cent and a drop of the gold parity from 2.11588 grams to 1.69271 grams. Tunisia obtained from the IMF the right to draw a stand-by credit and initiated a plan for stabilisation comprising a package of monetary, fiscal and economic controls aimed at re-establishing the economy on a sound basis. Along with devaluation the central bank had to take various policy measures to maintain money supply in line with the development of internal production.

Monetary-credit policy of the central bank in 1964 had two essential objectives.[1] The first was the reinforcement of the control measures with a view to the canalisation of bank deposits along desired lines of investment. To prevent the proliferation of bank credit that might be generated by the fast expansion of deposits, the central bank had already raised in August 1964 the minimum holding of treasury bills from 25 per cent to 30 per cent. With the same objective of pursuing a restrictive credit

[1] *Rapport Annuel*, Central Bank of Tunisia, 1964, p. 83.

policy the central bank instituted by a circular on 28th September 1964 a compulsory reserve in the form of an inalienable deposit with itself amounting to 10 per cent of all increases in bank deposits. It is clear that the Central Bank's policy instruments in the shape of a secondary reserve ratio and marginal reserve requirements compare in this respect to those of the older central banks in the sophisticated money and capital markets of the world.

At the same time with a view to change the attitude of the banks with regard to the employment of their funds and induce them to undertake the financing of projects of general interest, particularly the financing of investments having a priority in the industrialisation policy of the country, the same regulation of August 1964 raised the ratio of the investment in medium term private bills from the initial ratio of 5 per cent to 10 per cent. This measure assured a better distribution of medium term credit among the different banking establishments and forced the banks, whatever might have been their initial function, to channel short-term funds towards productive investments. The second objective was to intensify the policy of selective credit control. A more vigorous adoption of selective credit control policy is also observed. With the objective of ensuring that the banks pursue a policy of selective credit and observe its directives on this question, the central bank had imposed a ceiling on bank advances that could be made without its previous authorisation. Beyond this ceiling any demand for bank accommodation had to be submitted for the sanction of the central bank. It is observed that in August 1964 the minimum amount of credits subject to Prior Approval and to the Rediscount Approval of the central bank was reduced from 75,000 dinars to 50,000 dinars and from 10,000 dinars to 5,000 dinars respectively. All medium term loans must henceforth obtain a rediscount approval from the central bank.[1]

MONETARY POLICY OF THE BANK OF RHODESIA AND NYASALAND

The history of the Bank of Rhodesia and Nyasaland from its inception in 1956 to its dissolution in 1964 is a record of an all-

[1] Report of the *Societe Tunisienne D'Banque* for the fiscal year 1964, June 1965, p. 22.

out effort to formulate a national monetary policy suited to the peculiar conditions of its financial and economic structure. The local money and capital markets were relatively more developed than those in any other territory under discussion. But they were not so mature as in the industrially advanced countries. The stock exchange was also in operation but it was admittedly narrow. In such circumstances open market operations on a scale large enough to achieve the desired objective were not possible. By raising the reserve ratios the commercial banks could be embarrassed and even made to lose their earning power. But it was doubtful whether such a measure would have forced them to restrict their lending. The banks with their head offices in London could always obtain the required liquid funds from the London money market and thwart the restrictive policy of the central bank. There was also the danger of alienating the banks whose co-operation the new central bank would have liked to cultivate. The use of this drastic weapon could not therefore be contemplated except in times of serious crises. The Governor of the Bank in the course of his memorandum before the Radcliffe Committee had placed the greatest emphasis on securing the voluntary co-operation of the banks and other financial institutions. Although the Bank was equipped, in addition to the Bank rate weapon, with such instruments as determining statutory deposits and minimum liquid assets ratio, in actual practice the Bank placed considerable reliance on the technique of moral suasion. Through the method of informal discussions held regularly with the commercial banks, followed, if necessary, by formal requests, it was able to persuade the commercial banks to fall in line with its own policy of monetary restraint. When a difficult balance of payments position arose owing to a severe fall in copper prices, within a short period of the commencement of the Bank's operations in 1956, they did reduce their advances and bill financing at the "request" of the Bank. A "request" was again made to the banks in January 1958 in general terms, as an integral part of a general policy of "credit squeeze". The banks readily responded as before.[1] In spite of its relatively diversified economic structure the Federation was still a primary producing country. According to the Governor of the Bank a policy of moral suasion—"credit squeeze" as he put it—

[1] *Bank of Rhodesia and Nyasaland*, Annual Report for 1964.

had much to commend it for such a country.[1] In extreme circumstances the Bank was empowered to issue a directive to the ordinary banks with the prior approval of the Minister but the power had never been used.[2]

As regards the Bank rate, the monetary authorities considered that through changes in the rate, the central bank could exert an influence on other rates and affect thereby the level of credit throughout the entire financial system. Changes in the Bank rate have indeed taken place from time to time with a view to exert some pressure on the monetary situation. The Bank for the first time quoted its rate in August 1957 at 4½ per cent. It was raised subsequently to 5 per cent in August 1960 and further to 5½ per cent in June, 1961. But in May, 1962 the rate was reduced to 5 per cent and it had the effect of a general lowering of interest rates.[3] The 1964 Report of the Bank, the last to be issued before its dissolution, tells us that the Bank rate remained unaltered throughout the year at 4½ per cent to which it was reduced earlier. The general pattern of interest rates continued unchanged. The minimum reserve ratio maintained by the commercial banks also remained unaltered at 3 per cent of time and 6 per cent of demand deposits. No change was also called for in the liquidity ratios which the banking institutions were required to maintain under the Banking Act. The year, it may be observed, witnessed a marked expansion in the demand for credit. The resulting sharp increase in advances of the banking system was reflected in the decline in the liquidity ratio and the rise in the ratio of advances to total deposits of the combined banks, as will be evident from the table on page 150.

As a result of the expansion in advances the liquidity ratio fell to 28.3 per cent in February, 1964 and continued at about that level. By August, 1964, the position was restored and the liquidity ratio rose to 38.5 per cent which compared favourably with 38.3 per cent a year ago. The sharp fluctuations over the season in the liquidity position of the banks could be absorbed by them owing to the support received from their head offices in

[1] Memorandum submitted by the Governor of the Bank of Rhodesia and Nyasaland. *Radcliffe Committee*. Vol. I., p. 284.

[2] Art by R. I. Grant Suttie, Economist of the Bank in the *Commonwealth Banking Systems*, p. 341.

[3] *Annual Reports of the Bank of Rhodesia and Nyasaland for 1961 and 1962*, p. 3. *Annual Report for 1964*, p. 3.

TABLE [1] No. 26

RHODESIA AND NYASALAND

	Commercial Banks								
	Liquidity Ratio					*Advances/Deposits Ratio*			
	1962	*1963*		*1964*		*1962*	*1963*		*1964*
March	27.7	32.4	January	31.1	March	57.3	56.6	January	57.5
June	33.2	36.2	February	28.3	June	50.5	48.1	February	59.4
September	41.4	37.0	March	28.5	September	45.5	49.2	March	59.4
December	36.2	34.4	April	28.4	December	49.7	52.1	April	58.6

[1] *Annual Reports of the Bank of Rhodesia and Nyasaland for 1962 and 1964*, p. 38 and p. 58.

London. Because of the close connection of the three territories comprising the monetary area covered by the Bank the level of the Bank rate in U.K. was an important, but by no means the sole factor in determining the Bank's own discount rate. In fixing its discount rate the Bank was primarily guided by the local situation, particularly because the local market was largely insulated from that of the U.K. owing to the operation of exchange control. Thus when the U.K. Bank rate was successively raised from 4 per cent to 5 per cent and further to 7 per cent in 1964, the Bank decided not to revise its rate accordingly.

Although changes in the Bank rate influenced the level of other interest rates and affected the level of credits in the financial system, it would be misleading to suggest that the Bank rate would be the same effective instrument of control here as in the more sophisticated money markets of the world. The Bank had to rely more on moral suasion reinforced by the powers to fix statutory minimum balances and liquidity ratios. The year 1962 witnessed an interesting development in the expansion of the Bank's operations in the money market with a view to prevent undue disturbances in the short-term interest rates. The sharp variations in the Bank holdings of treasury bills indicate the extent of these operations. The following table brings out the extent of the variations of the treasury bill holdings of the Bank:

TABLE No. 27

(*£ thousand*)

1961		*1962*	
March	2,145	March	4,270
April	6,470	July	1,365
May	390	October	9,105

Although the money market was narrow, it was consistently active. In a small market wide fluctuations in the supply of money and the demand for bills are inevitable. Purchases and sales of treasury bills by the Bank had to be undertaken with a view to even out these fluctuations. The result of the Bank's intervention in the open market may be said to have been satisfactory.[1] The Bank did not engage in open market operations in the generally accepted technical sense. But when money was

[1] *Annual Report for the year 1962. Bank of Rhodesia and Nyasaland*, p. 3.

in short supply, the Bank relieved stringency by buying bills from the market. When the supply of securities in the market was not sufficient to enable it to absorb all the funds on offer, treasury bills were released to the discount houses.[1]

MONETARY POLICY OF THE BANK OF GHANA

The Bank of Ghana provides a good instance of a central bank in an underdeveloped country endeavouring from a very early stage of its development to determine an interest rate structure independently of the market rates of interest prevailing in other centres. As early as June 1961 within a few years of its establishment the Bank of Ghana took an important policy decision. Up to that time central bank rates, and in fact the whole structure of interest rates in the country had moved in unison with the rates abroad. Thus rates of the local commercial banks, particularly their lending rates, had in the past moved in the same direction as the Bank rate in London. Neither the bank rate of the central bank of Ghana nor the rates of the commercial banks could be regarded as reflecting the internal economic situation. Now the Bank of Ghana decided to adopt a policy of determining the interest rate structure by fixing the rate for local treasury bills independently of the market rates of interest prevailing abroad. The previous policy of rigidly following the London rate has thus been amended and in its place a rate structure has been sought to be established which reflects more the trends in the domestic market rather than those in foreign markets. The commercial banks readily co-operated with the central bank in its new policy and announced their intention to de-link their lending and deposit rates from such rates operating abroad. At the same time they agreed to review their rate structure from time to time in the perspective of current economic conditions in the country.[2]

From the end of December 1960, up to January 1961 the Bank of Ghana rediscount rate for treasury bills had been maintained at 4 per cent. From February to June 1961 the rediscount rate was raised to $4\frac{1}{16}$ per cent. In consonance with the important policy decision referred to above, the rate was increased by

[1] *The Bankers' Magazine*, December, 1962, p. 406.
[2] *Annual Report of the Bank of Ghana for the year 1961*, p. 22.

$\frac{1}{16}$ per cent to $4\frac{1}{2}$ per cent in July 1961. The Bank rate is reported in June 1964 to have been maintained since then at the same rate of $4\frac{1}{2}$ per cent.

A review of subsequent developments does not, however, indicate any close relationship between the rediscount rate of the central bank and other rates in Ghana nor any relationship between the central bank rates and the actual demand for credit. Thus the increase of nearly a half per cent in the Bank of Ghana rediscount rate (from $4\frac{1}{16}$ per cent to $4\frac{1}{2}$ per cent) seems to have produced little impact on the borrowing rates of the banking system. The deposit rates of the commercial banks were hardly affected and remained practically unchanged. Their main lending rates even went down. The rate of discount for commercial bills fell from $7\frac{1}{2}$ per cent at the beginning of 1961 to 7 per cent by the middle of the year; while the interest rate on loans secured by immovable property and government securities declined from $7\frac{1}{2}$ per cent to 7 per cent. It is indeed difficult to explain the movement of the lending rates of the commercial banks in a direction contrary to that of the central bank. Possibly the rates had already been too high and called for certain downward readjustments. Possibly the exchange control directive, prohibiting the maintenance of more than a maximum of half a million pounds abroad, necessitated reduction in their lending rates for the employment of their surplus funds in the domestic market.[1]

An appraisal of the monetary policy of the Bank of Ghana may be attempted against the background of the monetary developments that took place in the country in recent years. Along with the other countries which are the subject of our study, money supply in Ghana had registered a rapid increase in the recent past, though the rate of increase may be said to have considerably slowed down in the last month of 1963, with a lower rate of expansion in 1963 than in 1962. Between the end of 1962 and the end of 1963 the public's financial assets, (the average annual volume of which is the best yardstick for estimating the impact of monetary expansion on demand during a certain period), defined as money supply plus less liquid assets of the public with the banking system, rose by 9.3 per cent compared with 14.5 per cent between the end of 1961 and that

[1] *Annual Report for the year 1962, Bank of Ghana*, p. 30.

of 1962, the increase in money supply being 5.8 per cent as against 11.8 per cent and that in less liquid assets being 25.3 per cent as compared with 28.7 per cent in the previous period. The rising trend of monetary expansion could be observed continuing during the period from December 1963 to June 1964 when the public's financial assets rose by 6.9 per cent and money supply by 1.7 per cent. This rise was in sharp contrast to the normal trend of a decline of 3.8 per cent and 10.2 per cent in the public's financial assets in the previous corresponding periods of 1962-63 and 1961-62 and that of money supply by 7.9 per cent and 16.0 per cent respectively. The main factor responsible for this great monetary expansion was extension of bank credit to the public as well as the private sector, the principal driving force being sometimes the extension of credit to the government and sometimes to the private sector. Thus during the first three quarters of 1963 the principal factor in the monetary expansion was increased borrowing by the government from the banking system to close the ever widening gap between its revenue and expenditure; while in the last quarter of 1963, credit to the private sector was the predominant factor. Sometimes again both the factors exerted their influence simultaneously as was observed during the first six months of 1964. In 1963 net government liabilities to the banking institutions amounted to 61.0 per cent of the average of its liabilities to the banking system and in the first half of 1964 it rose to 77.8 per cent. Fluctuations in the foreign exchange assets of the Bank of Ghana also produced a contractionary or expansionary effect as they tended to decline or increase. Indeed until recent years the foreign exchange assets of the central bank had been the main force behind the expansion of money supply. But the influence of that factor seems to have declined in the present times, while that of bank credit has significantly increased.

The issue of compensatory stocks to some public bodies in the last quarter of 1963 in exchange for their foreign securities and the sale of the latter to the central bank had the effect of swelling up the government balances with the Bank of Ghana and reducing its net liabilities to the Bank. The foreign exchange assets of the Bank increased at the same time by the amount of the foreign securities transferred to it as the result of the transaction. But the net change in the level of money supply was nil.

There were only changes in the sources of money supply which were compensatory.[1] The reduction in the government debt was matched by a corresponding rise in the foreign exchange assets of the central bank.

A reference has to be made in this connection to the change in the composition of government debt which according to conventional banking standards should have reduced the liquidity of the commercial banks and as a consequence curbed their power of creating additional credit. As a result of the funding of the floating debt of the government to the extent of £G 10 million into a medium term loan in August 1964, the liquid assets of the banking system were drastically reduced. The liquidity ratio declined sharply from 52.4 per cent in July 1964 to 30.0 per cent and remained between 32.7 per cent and 26.5 per cent until the end of the year. But at the time there was no legal obligation on the banks to maintain fixed liquidity and cash ratios. The practice was to maintain voluntarily whatever ratios suited them. The consequent fall in the liquid assets ratio did not exert any restrictive effect on the expansion of bank credit to the private sector. This is borne out by the fact that bank credit reached a peak of £G 41.8 million by the end of 1963.

The expansion of bank credit from the middle of 1963 to that of 1964 was not wholly due to seasonal factors. A change in the method of financing the cocoa crop was responsible for accelerating the rate of increase. Under the previous methods of financing the crop, there took place an accumulation of foreign exchange assets by the Bank in the form of sterling bills and securities used as currency cover assets by the Issue Department. The funds of the Banking Department were, however, insufficient to cope with this tremendous demand for credit. Within the framework of the Bank of Ghana Ordinance of 1957, these were the only methods available for financing the crop. A new method came to be adopted in the 1963-64 season with the removal of the separation of the Issue Department from the Banking Department under the Bank of Ghana Act, 1963. The cocoa crop came to be financed by internal bills drawn on the Cocoa Marketing Company now domiciled in Accra. These bills were first discounted by the commercial banks and later rediscounted

[1] See *Annual Report of the Bank of Ghana for the year ended in June 30, 1964*, pp. 46-48.

by them with the Bank of Ghana. Thus the Bank's contribution to cocoa financing in the 1963-64 season came to be reflected in an expansion of credit to the public.

In the developing economy of the country, an increase in the supply of money was undoubtedly called for by the increasing monetisation of the hitherto non-commercialised sector, the rising proportion of cash balances held by firms and households as a result of increased money incomes and the growth of the gross national product. But the rate of expansion of money supply was faster than the growth of the economy. While gross national product increased by 1.2 per cent in 1963, money supply rose by the average of 12.5 per cent. While it would be misleading to suggest that money supply and Gross National Product should necessarily move at a uniform rate, it must be observed that a pronounced disparity between the growth rates of these two magnitudes indicates a serious imbalance between effective demand and availabilities in the economy. The inevitable consequence was a rise in the level of prices. Compared to the end of 1961, the wholesale prices were higher by 12 per cent at the corresponding period of 1963. Between the end of 1963 and April 1964, the increase was of the order of 6.2 per cent. The highest increase in prices took place in local food which registered an increase of 24 per cent in the first quarter of 1964. Central banking control of the banking system had not been exercised in the past because the influence which the system could exert on the supply of money through credit expansion was not considerable. Foreign exchange assets had accounted for as much as 88.9 per cent of money supply in 1958. But the proportion had been declining since then and by the end of 1963 had accounted for only 34.2 per cent. Instead of external assets, it was bank credit to the government and the public which now constituted the main driving force of the expansion of money supply. A remarkable change in the monetary structure had taken place during the past few years of the country's developing economy. The cash component of the money supply had declined from 63.8 per cent in 1958 to 49.2 per cent in June 1964. The system was now considered ripe enough for the application of central banking control over the banking institutions. A battery of control measures came to be adopted by the Bank of Ghana to check the inflationary growth of money supply. The battery included both quantitative and selective control measures and comprised the imposition of (1) a minimum cash ratio, (2) a minimum liquidity ratio, (3) a special deposit account ratio, (4) a minimum reserve ratio in government securities on the quantitative side, and (1) ceilings upon non-agricultural and non-industrial loans and (2) import pre-deposit requirements on the selective side.

Up to the end of the first quarter of 1964, as already observed, there were no obligatory minimum cash and liquidity ratios, the ratios being maintained by the banking system on a voluntary basis. In the circumstances the ratios could fluctuate and fall to very low points in total disregard of normal banking practice. In October, 1963 the cash ratio fell to 6.8 per cent and the liquidity ratio fell to 26.5 per cent in December of the same year. Between the end of 1962 and the end of 1963 the liquidity ratio fell from 46.3 per cent to this low level. The Bank of Ghana appreciated that the fixation of these ratios was one of the means by which the banks could be disciplined to promote sound banking and to regulate the level of bank credit so as not to cause an undesirable expansion in the money supply. At the same time however the Bank realised that the function of monetary policy in a developing economy was not only a stabilising one but was also, and perhaps even more importantly, one of promoting growth in the desired sectors of the economy. Even though commercial bank credit to the public had been expanding so rapidly that it was one of the causes of great monetary expansion, the greater part of it was still used to finance trade. It was considered desirable that the commercial banks should be made use of in the developing economy of the country by asking them to provide some of the needs for medium term loans for the directly productive branches of the economy. Quantitative and selective controls came to be applied on 1st April, 1964 so as to discipline the banks and make them practise discrimination in their lending activities by moving away from the traditional short-term credits to traders into sustained medium and long-term finance for development. At the end of 1962, loans and advances to commerce represented 57.1 per cent of the total; while loans to the agricultural sector accounted for only 4.2 per cent, to manufacturing 2.3 per cent, to mining and quarrying 0.9 per cent, and to building and construction 7.5 per cent. Since then there has been a shift in the distribution of the loans and advances of the banking system. In June 1964 agriculture accounted for 22.2 per cent, building and construction 22.5 per cent and manufacturing 4.6 per cent. But commerce was still the largest recipient of bank credit which comprised 24.8 per cent of the total.[1]

While there were previously no obligatory minimum liquidity and cash ratios, the central bank in exercise of the powers vested in it under Secs. 29 and 33 of the Bank of Ghana Act, 1963, now required the banking institutions to keep the following reserve ratios:

(1) Sight balances due to banks abroad to be covered by foreign currency deposited with the Bank of Ghana—100 per cent

This was to discourage commercial banks from holding idle balances with banks abroad.

(2) (*i*) A liquidity reserve ratio against the total deposit liabilities (all types—demand, savings and time)
Between 1st March and 31 August—48 per cent
Between 1st September and 28 February—54 per cent

The reason for directing the maintenance of different seasonal ratios was to restrict bank lending to the public (commercial sector) during the cocoa season (September to February) when bank credit was usually high. Liquid reserve was defined to include cash reserve and other liquid reserves including Government of Ghana treasury bills, approved agricultural and industrial loans and balances in special deposit account. Agricultural and industrial loans have been included in the definition of liquid reserve to direct more bank credit into productive fields rather than into the commercial sector.

(*ii*) Cash reserve ratio in the form of cash in tills, net balances with banks in Ghana and current account deposits with the Bank of Ghana—8 per cent
Other liquid reserve ratio—40 per cent/46 per cent
In addition to (*i*) and (*ii*) above,

(*iii*) In special deposits account with the Bank of Ghana (interest being paid at ¾ per cent below bank rate)—total deposit liabilities to be covered by 5 per cent.

[1] See Table LV *Report of the Bank of Ghana for 1964*, p. 70. pp. 89-90.

(3) A secondary reserve in Government of Ghana Stock in addition to (*i*), (*ii*) and (*iii*)—18 per cent.

(4) Individual loans above £G 5000 for purposes other than for agriculture and industry were to be granted by a banking institution only with the prior approval of the Bank of Ghana.

(5) Import pre-deposit requirements—A minimum down payment was required before opening a letter of credit in respect of imports of consumer goods including consumer durables to be kept with the Bank of Ghana so as not to expand the credit creating base of the bank concerned —15 per cent.

The following table brings out the various types of required reserve ratios to be maintained by the banking system under Credit Control Regulation and how far the banks were able to fulfil the requirements:

TABLE[1] No. 28

	1964		
	April	*May*	*June*
1. Cash Ratio (minimum 8%) ..	10.6	10.5	8.9
2. Other liquid reserve (minimum 40/46%)	56.3	56.2	57.9
3. Liquidity Ratio (minimum 48/56%) ..	66.9	69.5	66.8
4. Special Deposit (minimum 5%) ..	2.5	2.9	2.9
5. Govt. Stock ratio (minimum 18%) ..	15.6	15.6	15.6
6. Total Reserve Ratio (minimum 71/77%)	84.9	85.2	85.3

It is clear from the above table that the banks could not fulfil all the reserve ratio requirements e.g. special deposit and Government Stock ratios. But some of the banks are on the way to meet their requirements. It is hoped that as time goes on and initial difficulties are removed and the banks become more familiar with the regulations, they will fulfil all the requirements. In the earlier stages of the development of the Bank wide fluctuations in the cash and liquidity ratios of the commercial banks could be observed. Cash ratios are found to have fluctuated between a range

[1] *Bank of Ghana, Report for the financial year ending June 1964.* Table LVIII, p. 77. pp. 89-90.

of 45.9 per cent in September 1959 and 7.6 per cent in June 1960, while liquid assets ratios varied between 66.2 per cent in March 1959 and 42.9 per cent in March 1961. The movements in the liquidity ratio have a seasonality—being low in the main cocoa season because of expansion of bank credit to the public and high in the off season when advances for cocoa finance are paid back. But such wide fluctuations would have clearly impeded the operation of the variable reserve ratio as a sensitive weapon of credit control.

CONTROL POLICY OF THE LIBYAN CENTRAL BANK

Under the 100 per cent reserve system the Central Bank could have no control over the size of the currency component of the money supply. The size of this component was by and large a function of the availability of foreign assets and of public choice between sterling and Libyan currency. As a result of the substantial increase in foreign assets money supply had been increasing. Thus while the domestic money supply was kept in line with the foreign exchange reserves under the hundred per cent reserve system, the central bank was prevented from adjusting the money supply to the requirements of the national economy. Manipulation of the money supply to suit the needs of the economy is an essential function of central banking. It is clear without this indispensable power the Libyan central bank could not discharge its primary responsibilities in economic and financial matters.

Sixty per cent of the increase in money supply in 1960 is found to have been made up of demand deposits. It is obvious that even if the National Bank had the authority to control the amount of bank notes in circulation, it could not regulate the total money supply without a corresponding authority to control the amount of demand deposits. In the absence of any reserve requirements against bank deposits it was theoretically possible for the banking system as a whole to create an almost infinite amount of secondary deposits out of a given amount of primary deposits so long as there were willing borrowers. The only limiting factor was the 20 per cent liquidity ratio to be maintained against their liabilities. But in the computation of the liquidity ratio both inter-bank deposits and short-term foreign balances were included. In the circumstances the actual cash percentage of the required liquidity was quite low. Thus so long as there was the demand for bank credit, the commercial banks were in a position to generate considerable amounts of secondary deposits and increase the money supply out of any given cash in hand. The demand for credit was rising rapidly owing to the continued expansion of the tertiary sector of the economy. The credit-deposit ratio had reached almost 80 per cent and for some individual banks even 90 per cent. It was indeed quite a high ratio out of proportion to the domestic liquid resources of the banking system.

Thus the National Bank of Libya was powerless to regulate the quantity or rate of note issue owing to the 100 per cent reserve system. It was also prevented from controlling the rate of credit expansion by the commercial banks not only because of the absence of a system of legal reserve requirements, but also of an effective rediscount rate and of open market operations. It is rather curious that while commercial banks could create almost unchecked a substantial amount of purchasing power in the form of secondary deposits through credit extension, the central bank had no fiduciary powers.[1]

The above analysis points clearly to the imperative need of a major reform of the monetary system without which the National Bank could not be expected to assume the responsibilities of a full fledged central bank in a developing economy. The central bank had to be equipped with the necessary tools of quantitative, qualitative and selective control. An important initial step lay in persuading the commercial banks to eliminate their system of borrowing from their head offices. This step was taken in 1960. A second line of reform urgently necessary was the imposition of legal reserve requirements for the commercial banks. The regulation of the structure of assets and liabilities of commercial banks was a third desideratum as a necessary concomitant of any purposive monetary policy.

Economic growth by and large is usually, though not necessarily, associated with the generation of inflationary pressures in the economy as the result of a high level of investment, output and income. But even before the Libyan economy had been undergoing an extensive programme of development, it was clearly heading towards that stage. It is interesting to observe

[1] *Fourth Report of the National Bank of Libya 1960*, p. 51.

among the monetary authorities a heightened awareness of the complex and serious problems that might have to be faced when the inflationary forces stimulated by a development plan would be superimposed upon the existing situation. The National Bank of Libya, as it then was, directed its newly formed Research Department in June 1961 to undertake a study which would provide a systematic understanding of the inflationary forces that had been plaguing the country's economy since 1955. At the stage when the country was standing on the threshold of a gigantic programme of public investment for development purposes, it was confronted with the problem of a continuous inflationary trend which could impede the rate of economic growth or even stall it. It would be difficult to measure the extent of this inflation owing to lack of data about the price situation for the country as a whole in the absence of an official statistical organisation at the time. But some data about retail prices in Tripoli available from a foreign institution show that during the two years 1958-1960 cost of food, household equipment, restaurant meals, hotel accommodation and services increased by about 30 per cent. A survey of non-food items also revealed that prices of clothing rose by 32.86 per cent and fuel and light by 45.50 per cent during the period 1955-1960.[1] The figures reflect more or less the position in other regions of the country.

The main factors which may be said to have initiated the inflationary situation were foreign spending, local expenditures of oil companies and a large amount of deficit spending by the government.[2] In an underdeveloped economy, like Libya's and the consequent inelasticity of production the upsurge in the demand for goods and services caused by the heavy expenditure of the oil companies engaged in exploration brought about the inevitable upward movement in prices. Apart from the expenditures of the oil companies, there were the military expenditures of the foreign troops, and expenditures made by the U.N. and USOM. All these taken together showed a persistently increasing total and must have contributed to the inflationary spiral. The following table brings out the total expenditures on these accounts over the years 1955-1959:

[1] *Price Trends of Selected Commodities in Tripoli 1955-60*. Development Council of Libya, Tripoli.

[2] *Seventh Annual Report*, National Bank of Libya, March 1963, p. 32.

	In £L
1955	6.8 million
1956	12.2 ,,
1957	15.9 ,,
1958	19.3 ,,
1959	19.4 ,,

A great deal of these expenditures was for non-economic unproductive purposes such as the military and diplomatic ones which could not obviously create direct significant increases in output and thereby alleviate to some extent the prevailing inflationary pressure. They also constituted quite a large proportion of the gross domestic product. The percentage of foreign expenditure to gross domestic product was as high as 36.9 per cent and 32.4 per cent in 1958 and 1959 respectively.

The second important initiating factor was the rising level of public expenditure financed by deficit budgets in succession. The following table reveals a gap between total domestic expenditures and domestic revenue over the years since 1954. The continuous increase in deficit financing tended to create an excess demand for goods and services and accentuated the inflationary pressures in the economy.

TABLE[1] No. 29

1954-55 to 1958-59

	Surplus+ or Deficit—	In £L 000 Index 1954-55=100
1954-55	—3248	100
1955-56	—5917	182.17
1956-57	—7286	224.32
1957-58	—7436	228.94
1958-59	—10516	323.77

It is also interesting to observe that by far the greater proportion of the public expenditures was devoted over the years to administrative and other purposes while expenditures on economic and productive purposes were relatively small. Thus while expenditure on general administration and defence constituted on an average 39.41 per cent of total expenditure per year during

[1] SOURCE : *Economic Development of Libya*, (IBRD Mission), p. 247.

the four years, economic services constituted 33.90 per cent only. Expenditure incurred on economic services again was not wholly for direct production of goods and services. Expenditure on irrigation, agriculture, industry and minerals, which could be said by and large to be for purposes of direct production of goods and services, averaged only 11.19 per cent per year. From this aspect the expenditure pattern of the budget may be said to have been highly inflationary.

The tax structure of the country in which indirect taxes formed 68.81 per cent and direct taxes only 14.72 per cent of domestic revenue on the average during the period contributed to accentuation of the pressure on prices rather than alleviating it. So far as the indirect taxes like customs duties and sales taxes could be shifted on to consumers, they tended to raise the prices.

The inflationary effect of all these factors would have been still more serious but for the fact that it was partly offset by the flow of imports.

Without a knowledge of the magnitude of the consumption function, it would not be possible to attempt a quantitative analysis of the multiplier effect of this foreign spending and domestic government expenditure. But it will be reasonable to assume that the initial increases in expenditure were creating via the multiplier successive increases in the disposable income of a larger magnitude which exerted further pressure on the price situation. In view of the underdeveloped nature of the economy, handicapped as it was by a formidable array of social and economic problems and the consequent inflexibility of physical output, no relief could be expected from an increase of production in response to the price stimulus.

In the absence of any comprehensive and effective price regulation the inflationary effect could not be repressed and found ample scope for being reflected in spiralling prices which in many cases took the form of jerky, discontinuous spurts.[1]

This mounting inflation came to be financed by a tremendous increase in total money supply which rose from £L 13,835,000 to £L 23,746,000 during the period December 1956—December 1960, the index of change being from 100 to 171.64. The currency component of the money supply rose from £L 5,000,000 to

[1] *Inflation in Libya.* Prepared by the Research Department of the National Bank of Libya, March 1961, pp. 30-32.

£L 10,335,000, the index of change being from 100 to 206.70.[1] At the end of March 1962 total money supply reached the figure of £L 27.7 million which represented an increase of 18.2 per cent over the previous year. Under the existing monetary system the currency was not autonomously regulated by the monetary authorities but was subject to the pull and push of market forces. The National Bank of Libya was under obligation to issue new notes and coin for the amount of the approved foreign exchange tendered by the public for conversion.

The other component of the money supply, demand deposits held by the private sector, rose at the same time from £L 8,835,000 to £L 13,411,000, the index having increased from 100 to 151.80. The ability of the commercial banks to extend credit was not restricted except by the legal requirement to maintain a 20 per cent liquidity ratio. The liquid assets were interpreted very broadly and afforded ample opportunity to the commercial banks to augment their liquid assets by book borrowing from their head offices at any time for the purpose of credit expansion. The ratio of liquid assets to deposits amounted to about 38 per cent at the end of 1959 and was undoubtedly pretty high. But if deposits with foreign banks were excluded it was as low as 13 per cent.[2] Unless the practice of borrowing from head offices abroad could be controlled, there would be no check on their power to expand their liquidity base and their loans and advances.

While recognising the limitation of monetary policy and its complementarity with fiscal policies, it may be observed that the Libyan inflation being mainly of the nature of a demand inflation, there was some scope for monetary policy for controlling the existing pressures. Monetary measures that could be adopted to curb the inflationary forces should obviously provide a two-pronged attack, first, controlling the aggregate volume of money supply and secondly, controlling the direction of credit via selective controls. As regards the first, so far as the currency side of the money supply was concerned, the existing 100 per cent automatic monetary system had to be replaced by a regulated fractional reserve system. Such replacement would enable the monetary authority to adjust the quantity of currency in circulation to the requirements of the economy for quickening the pace

[1] IBRD Mission. p. 365.
[2] *Sixth Annual Report*, National Bank of Libya, 1962, p. 31.

of economic growth or maintaining price stability or both. Such a change in the monetary system received support from Mr. E. C. Hald, U.N. Economic Adviser to the Government of Libya in a memorandum submitted to the Minister of Finance on November 29, 1960. Control of the volume of credit created by the banking system was of greater importance. From this point of view it was necessary to arm the central bank of Libya with all the weapons needed to control the credit activities of the banking system. The first step to be taken in this direction was to prohibit the banks to borrow from their head offices abroad and induce them to approach the Central Bank for assistance in their hour of need. This was essential to enable the central bank function as a lender of last resort. The National Bank of Libya asked the commercial banks to abstain from borrowing from the head offices abroad without obtaining its prior approval. The minimum liquidity ratio of 20 per cent had to be interpreted much more rigidly and narrowly in this connection so that bank liquidity could be related to actual liquid funds available.

The next important step was to empower the central bank to control the direction of credit so as to channelise the flow of bank credit to preferred categories of productive investment and divert it away from the financing of activities like wholesale and retail trade, purchase of automobiles, construction of expensive residential buildings and purely private consumption. It has already been noted how the existing distribution of credit among various uses had been pulling in the opposite direction and accentuating the inflationary pressures. As the bulk of credit was being extended to activities which did not automatically provide a base for sound economic growth, any restriction of credit could not obviously hamper the rate of economic progress.

Let us now consider how far the traditional quantitative methods of control like the bank rate and open market operations could be effectively employed by the National Bank of Libya.

As regards the bank rate weapon, it is well known that it is by and large ineffective when the banking system enjoys a very high degree of liquidity. The commercial banks in Libya had been enjoying a plethora of liquid resources and had no need to make recourse to the central bank for assistance. In such circumstances the manipulation of the rediscount rate by the National Bank could hardly exercise a restrictive effect upon their credit policies. The rediscount rate was rendered further ineffective because of the practice of holding bills to maturity and because of the predominance of advances and overdrafts in the structure of bank credit. At the end of December 1961 advances and overdrafts constituted 76.9 per cent of total bank credit while bills maturing within 3-6 months formed only 21.4 per cent.[1] Thus the raising of the official rediscount rate from 4 per cent to 5 per cent in October, 1957 proved to be ineffective. When the rate was subsequently pushed up to 6 per cent in August 1960, the result was the same. There seems to be hardly any relationship between the bank rate and the volume of credit or the market rates of interest. In spite of the raising of the rediscount rate to 6 per cent it is observed that the total volume of credit rose from £L 8.4 million in December, 1958 when the bank rate was 5 per cent to £L 13.7 million by the end of 1960. In February 1961 the rate was reduced to 5 per cent but both the volume of credit and lending rates of the commercial banks remained at high levels. At the end of March 1962 when the rediscount rate still remained at 5 per cent, the volume of bank credit amounted to nearly £L 14 million and the commercial banks were charging 10 per cent on advances and overdrafts.[2]

Owing to the absence of the necessary institutional framework, the use of open market operations was not possible. So far there had not been any issue of government securities. The establishment of a capital market, however rudimentary, was urgently called for so that the central bank could have for use a second tool for controlling the prevailing inflation. It has been observed that the issue of treasury bills by the government in the required amount and maturities provided the original stimulus to the development of a capital market in many underdeveloped countries in Africa and elsewhere. It would be highly desirable for the government to take the initiative to build up a capital market in the prevailing circumstances in the country. That would not only add another instrument of control in the shape of open market operations to the armoury of the central bank but would help in the mobilisation of the excess purchasing power of the people to canalise it into productive investment—

[1] *Sixth Annual Report of the National Bank of Libya*, 1962. p. 35.
[2] *Sixth Annual Report of the Board of Directors*, National Bank of Libya. 31 March, 1962, p. 39.

excess purchasing power which would otherwise be spent upon consumption and thereby further aggravate the inflationary forces. From time to time the central bank had made a number of proposals to enable it to cope with the rising tempo of inflation but these could not be implemented owing to lack of planning and organisation in the sphere of monetary-fiscal policies.

It is clear that institutional, legal and administrative changes were called for to enable the central bank to play the vital role of monetary management in a developing but predominantly oil exporting country.

An important addition to the central bank's instruments of quantitative credit control would be to require the commercial banks maintain minimum statutory balances with the central bank amounting to a certain specified percentage of their deposits/liabilities and also to empower the central bank to vary the reserve ratios so that it could exercise the necessary control over their credit policies.

Apart from quantitative controls, selective controls had to be introduced so that commercial bank credit might be directed to flow into desired lines which would serve to curb inflation and quicken development. In this connection regulation of the hire-purchase activities may also be called for through what is known as the "terms of trade" control. Last but not least, with the growing status and prestige of the central bank it would have to rely a great deal upon the technique of moral suasion which has been found to be a relatively more effective weapon of control in many of the newly independent and developing countries.

Legal and institutional developments of far-reaching significance took place in the monetary-banking sphere of the country during the financial year ending in March 1964. The most important development in this respect was the coming into effect of the new Banking Law on April 15, 1963. The Law conferred on the Bank of Libya full powers of a central bank. The broad objective of the new law was to enable the Bank to discharge smoothly and effectively the basic functions of controlling the monetary and the banking system and maintaining monetary and fiscal stability in a manner which would serve the needs and requirements of balanced economic growth and development.

Chapter 4 of the new Law gave to the Bank of Libya substantial powers of control and supervision of the commercial banking system. The Board of the Central Bank was empowered:

1. to regulate methods used in assessing the various assets of banks;
2. to fix the proportion and kind of liquid funds which must be maintained by the banks;
3. to determine the channels in which banks are to be prevented from investing their funds;
4. to fix the proportions of advances and the value of the security and determining the kind of such security;
5. to determine maximum interest rates on all creditor and debtor accounts;
6. to determine the permitted difference to be maintained between the interest rate or the rediscount rate as fixed by the Bank of Libya and the discount rate charged by the banks to their customers;
7. to fix the percentage of each type of credit in relation to the total of these operations and determine the maximum amounts and durations of credit operations;
8. to determine the maximum limits of cost margins for opening documentary credits in general.[1]

It was further provided that commercial banks should maintain reserves with the Bank of Libya without interest against their deposit liabilities. The Board of Directors of the Bank should specify the percentage of reserves to each component of these deposits, the percentage being 5 to 20 per cent on time and savings deposits and 10 to 40 per cent on demand deposits. The Bank was authorised to vary the percentage within the above limits but in as gradual a manner as possible. Except in emergencies at least 15 days' notice was to be given prior to effecting any change.[2]

Immediately after coming into force of the new Banking Law, two important measures were taken by the Bank of Libya. First, the legal minimum reserve required under the above provisions was made effective from July 20, 1963 at 5 per cent of time and savings, and 10 per cent of demand deposits. Secondly, maximum rates to be paid on deposits as well as those to be charged to

[1] Art. 35 *Banking Law*, February 5, 1963.
[2] Art. 36. *Banking Law*, February 5, 1963.

bank customers on various types of advances were fixed with effect from October 5, 1963. A kind of correlationship was established between the interest rates on secured and unsecured loans on the one hand and the rediscount rate on the other, being 2 and 2½ per cent respectively over the latter. Time and fixed deposit rates were fixed between 1½ per cent to 4 per cent according to the period for which the deposits were made. On savings deposits the maximum was fixed at 3½ per cent while no interest was to be paid on current accounts.[1]

The reserve ratios were not altered by the Bank but the Board of Directors decided that liquid assets should also be maintained at all times at a level not below 20 per cent of each bank's deposits and other liabilities including borrowings from other banks. The maintenance of statutory liquidity ratios was imperative in the context of the prevailing credit conditions in Libya where, as observed before, the liquid assets-deposits ratio had been declining over the years. It may be recalled that this ratio had been steadily falling from the high of 71 per cent in 1952 to 39 per cent in 1961 and further to 28 per cent and 23 per cent at the end of 1963 and 1964 respectively. A declining trend in the liquid assets-deposit ratio is not by itself alarming. It may be a natural development as a result of further opening out of outlets for the employment of the reserves of the banking system. It is certainly not economic for banks to maintain liquidity ratios at inordinately high levels. There has indeed been a parallel growth of bank credit owing to the developing nature of Libyan economy, as is evidenced by the rise in the credit-deposits ratio from 34 per cent in 1952 to 78 per cent in 1963 and 89 per cent in 1964.[2] But these declining trends make it all the more necessary for the central bank to exercise constant vigilance over the maintenance of minimum liquidity ratios so that over-extension of credit may be inhibited. There is not only the need for ensuring optimum levels of credit expansion but also the appropriate end-uses of bank credit.

There were obvious limitations to the monetary policy of a central bank in the context of the Libyan economy. In recent years external factors have been responsible for the largest magnitude of increase in the money supply. The causal factors,

[1] *Eighth Annual Report*, Bank of Libya, 31 March, 1964, p. 21.
[2] *Ninth Report of the Bank of Libya* 1964-65, pp. 26-27.

for instance, which affected the changes in money supply during the financial year ending 31 March, 1965 were an increase of £L 16.7 million in net foreign assets, a decrease of £L 2.6 million in government deposits, an increase of £L 1.8 million in the net liabilities of the public to the banks, and a decrease of £L 1.4 million in other non-classified net liabilities. It was difficult to offset wholly the monetary influence arising out of external factors like the net balance of payment position. The Bank of Libya has always been aware of the vital need to keep a watchful eye on the monetary front but the persistent inflationary pressure could not be combatted by exclusive reliance on monetary policy. What was called for was a package of policy measures embracing monetary, fiscal and direct controls co-ordinated with the development policy.[1]

GENERAL APPRAISAL OF CENTRAL BANK POLICIES IN THE CONTEXT OF INFLATIONARY PRESSURES IN DEVELOPING ECONOMIES

The general picture presented above is one of chronic inflationary pressures in most of the developing economies under review. Just as the development process itself has generated the inflationary pressures, it has also led to the emergence of the central banking system which provides facilities for monetary management aimed at economic growth with stability. In all the countries there has been a phenomenal increase in money supply in the sense of currency and demand deposits. Without a continued excessive monetary expansion, such chronic inflation could not have occurred. The question naturally arises why the central banks did not play their part in regulating the rate of monetary expansion. To make an appraisal of the monetary policy of the central banks as an anti-inflationary measure, it is necessary at the outset, first, to appreciate the main factors responsible for monetary expansion in the developing economies, and secondly, to define the lines along which the rate of monetary expansion should be regulated. In an expanding economy the rise in the volume of money is conditioned by three factors: First, an increase in the gross national product which calls for a corresponding increase in money supply for transaction purposes; secondly, the widening of the exchange sector with the development of the economy, which requires additional money for the

[1] *Tenth Annual Report of the Bank of Libya, 1965-66*, p. 25.

monetization of the hitherto non-commercialised sector; thirdly, the increasing proportion of money balances, as a result of rising incomes, in the total assets of individuals and firms. What are the economic criteria on the basis of which the rate of expansion may be judged to be excessive, inadequate or safe? The concept of a "safe rate" of increase in money supply is being recently employed in this connection.

The growth of money supply should conform to the growth of the economy in real terms. Broadly speaking a "safe" rate of monetary expansion may be considered to be related to the average rate of increase in real output. That supply of money which is just enough to finance the increased real output at the same prices may be regarded as "safe". It is determined quantitatively at any point of time by dividing the total national income at current prices by total money supply at that point of time. In other words the "safe" increase in the supply of money is equal to the increase in real output divided by income velocity. When the economy of a country is developing rapidly and national income is increasing, the rise in national income should be financed with a "safe" increase in money supply. If the actual supply of money exceeds this safe quantity, an inflationary gap is created and other things being equal, a price spiral would be generated, as was to be witnessed in Ghana in recent years.

As a recent commentator has shown, the effect of any given primary expansion on the money supply will be determined by the credit multiplier,* whose ex-post order of magnitude is indicated by the ratio of the increase in the money supply to the increase in the total monetary liabilities of the central bank.[1] The credit multiplier and consequently the scope of secondary credit expansion with given changes in monetary liability of the central bank may increase or decrease with changes in the ratio of currency in circulation to money or changes in the banking system's legal or customary reserve ratio. Monetary authorities are not likely to directly influence any changes in the former but they can influence the multiplier by altering the latter. If the multiplier is larger in one country than in another, the scope

* The credit multiplier is defined to be equal to the reciprocal of $c+r\ (1-c)$ where $c=$ratio of currency in circulation to money and $r=$legal or customary reserve ratio maintained by banks against their deposits.

[1] Art. by Joachim Ahrensdroff entitled "Central Bank Policies and Inflation" in the *IMF Staff Papers*, Oct. 1959.

of secondary expansion would be more significant in the first than in the second. Although currency counts for a relatively higher proportion in the total money supply in most of the underdeveloped countries as compared to mature economies, yet it is not true that the currency component of the money supply is always larger than deposits in the developing economies. In some countries as in Libya demand deposits comprise a high percentage of the total money supply. In Tunisia the relative percentage of fiduciary money compared with bank money in the total money supply is almost similar to that of certain developed countries. Fiduciary money and bank money represented 33.6 per cent and 66.4 per cent in December 1964 and has been practically stable since December 1963.[1] Further with the increasing development of the economy, the currency component of the money supply is also found to fall. To control the secondary expansion of credit, the central bank has to steer the banking system in such a manner that it releases precisely the amount which in the judgment of the central bank is "safe" as defined above. The central bank does this by working on the demand deposits segment rather than on the currency issue. In the circumstances in the countries where demand deposits constitute quite a sizeable proportion of money supply relatively to currency, central banking regulation of the supply of money through the control of the credit activities of the commercial banks is facilitated.

It must be observed, however, that the supply of money may have to be augmented beyond the "safe" limit under certain special conditions. For instance, where there are idle resources and excess capacity, it may be necessary to increase money supply for the purpose of stimulating output. But this argument assumes the condition of a highly elastic output in the short run which is not to be generally witnessed in underdeveloped countries. Supplies in such economies are inelastic and monetary expansion may raise prices rather than output even though unemployed resources exist. The rate of growth of money supply, however, must not fall short of that in real output; otherwise deflationary trends may set in. All this is well illustrated in the price trends in Indian economy during the Plan period. During the First Plan monetary imbalance was responsible for price declines, the rate of growth of money supply being outpaced by the rate of

[1] *Report of the Societe de Tunisiene Banque for the fiscal year 1964*, p. 20.

growth in real output. In the Second Plan, however, the rate of growth of real income fell so short of the expansion in monetary resources as to generate severe pressures on prices. In the first four years of the Third Plan the imbalance between the two rates was even greater with the result that the pressure on prices was still more serious.[1]

The importance of currency and the relative insignificance of bank money in the conventional computation of total money supply (currency plus demand deposits) may suggest that any restrictive action on bank credit may have an impact only on a limited portion of money supply and therefore monetary policy may not appear to be meaningful in an underdeveloped economy. It is quite true that this relationship between currency and bank deposits would impart an element of rigidity to monetary control. But the argument should not be pushed so far as to establish the case for complete negation of monetary policy in such economies. In most of these economies the institutional framework is rapidly changing and with the growing spread of bank deposits as a component of total monetary resources in the wider sense of currency plus aggregate deposits, central bank action on bank credit becomes quite relevant. Indeed in some developing economies the pace of aggregate deposit expansion has actually been observed to be greater than that of currency expansion. In India, for instance, during the four years ending in March 1965 the rate of aggregate deposit expansion at 63 per cent was much greater than that of currency expansion at 32 per cent. The area of transactions amenable to monetary control becomes wider and wider, and bank credit gradually tends to assume a dominant influence on overall economic activity almost in the same manner as is to be observed in relatively more mature economies. Central Bank control of bank credit then becomes meaningful.

It must be observed however that extravagant claims cannot be sustained in favour of a restraining effect on the level of prices through the policy of regulating the cost and availability of bank credit. The correlation between price trends and control of bank credit, as observed in these developing economies, is not strong

[1] "Recent Evolution of Monetary Policy in India" Art. in the *Reserve Bank of India Bulletin, April 1966.* (Prepared by Dr. V. G. Pendharkar and Mr. Narasimhan of the Economics Division, p. 4.)

enough to warrant an implicit faith in the ability of overall credit control to correct a rising price situation. The factors affecting the price situation in these economies are often very complex and emanate from the side of supply. They are structural in character and uncertain in the timing and incidence of their impact. A policy of credit restraint is aimed at reducing the pressures arising from the demand side rather than from that of supply. It can narrow the gap between aggregate demand and supplies to some extent but clearly it cannot be expected to restore price equilibrium when the underlying factors have their roots in the supply side or in fiscal deficits operating on demand.

Experiences of the underdeveloped countries suggest that of the two primary sources of inflation, central bank credit to the public sector and that to the private sector, the former has been more important. But whether the source of inflation lay in the one or the other sector, the history of monetary policy of the central banks in these underdeveloped economies amply demonstrates that central banks have been either impotent or unwilling to exercise monetary restraint of the required degree of rigorousness. The impotency of central banks has arisen either because the kit of tools with which they have been equipped has not given them the necessary technical capacity or because the structural and psychological factors characteristic of these economies have blunted the edge of these tools. In the circumstances the task for the central bank to enforce an effective monetary policy has been to invent new weapons or refashion old ones so that they could be adapted to the particular environment or to take steps to alter the institutional and psychological setting. But even though they may have the technical capacity to neutralise excessive credit expansion, they tend to be reluctant to exercise the appropriate degree of restraint. This reluctance is to be mainly ascribed to their particular views about the aims and objectives of central banking policy or to their fears that they will offend the government or the banks and the private entrepreneurs or both. The central banks in these countries have come to regard themselves as engines of growth rather than as stabilising agencies. As such they are inclined to believe that they need not be significantly concerned with controlling the overall volume of credit; on the contrary they should be concerned with encouraging supposedly non-inflationary production credits. They are afraid that a severe restraint of credit may lead to a curtailment of output and in the process inhibit growth. Such apprehensions regarding the output effects of a reduction of credit expansion explain the unwillingness of the monetary authorities to use the restrictive weapons more vigorously. Further, the reluctance to pursue a vigorous policy of monetary restraint may not have been politically feasible. In the perspective of their standing, power and maturity they are naturally unwilling to antagonise the banks and the private sector by a sharp restriction of bank credit. As the commentator quoted above has shown, in Paraguay and Nicaragua during 1949-57 the primary source of inflation was central bank credit to the banks and the private sector. The technical conditions in both the countries were favourable for the central banks to raise rediscount rates to a level required to curb the rate of secondary credit expansion. But neither of the banks permitted a rise of the official interest rate to anything near this level. In Indonesia and Mexico during the same period government borrowing was the primary source of inflation. What was needed was to neutralise the inflationary effect of government borrowing by a corresponding freezing of credit to the banks and the private sector. Central bank action could have reduced the rate of inflation in these countries, if the authorities had restricted more severely the extension of central bank credit to the banks and the private sector through the exercise of a stiff bank rate. Because of the agricultural sector's heavy dependence on credit, the monetary authorities were apprehensive that the adoption of a much too restrictive policy would adversely affect output and the utilisation of productive capacity.[1] In the same way the Central Bank of the Philippines has not been quite successful in countering internal or external instability because the government itself was the primary source of inflationary finance. Various measures were adopted by the Philippines Bank to counter recent inflationary pressures in the economy including raising reserve requirements, issuing its own securities, prescribing margin requirements, transferring government time deposits of the commercial banks to the central bank but monetary expansion was not arrested. The nature of the

[1] "Central Bank Policies and Inflation : A Case Study of Four Less Developed Economies (1949-57)". Art. by Joachim Ahrensdroff in the *IMF Staff Papers* October, 1959.

economic problem in growing economies is such that it can be attacked only by the simultaneous employment of a package of monetary, fiscal and physical controls. There is no mathematical formula which can draw the line between the areas of the respective operations of each of them. Indeed there may be considerable overlapping and even conflict of the areas of their operations. It would be misleading to suggest that in this policy-mix, the role of monetary control is insignificant.

In developing economies monetary policy has some crucial roles to perform. The monetary authorities in such economies can aid the growth process through money creation not only in the matter of monetising the economy but also in meeting an increased asset demand for money, as with the rise in per capita income a larger proportion of additional income comes to be held in money form. An adequate money supply, it may be observed, is a *necessary,* though not a sufficient condition for economic growth. Secondly, monetary policy assists in the institutionalisation of saving and investment. The accumulation and wide-spread dispersion of financial assets among the different strata of the economic society condition the rate of economic development. Central banks in the underdeveloped countries of Africa, as in Latin America and Asian countries, have played an important part in initiating and developing various categories of financial institutions.[1]

[1] See Lecture by Dr. C. D. Deshmukh on the "Balance between Monetary Policy and other Instruments of Economic Policy in a Developing Economy" under the sponsorship of the Per Jacobsson Foundation, Oct. 1st 1965. Washington D.C.

A NOTE ON CHAPTER EIGHT

Table No. 30 given below brings out the relative growth of the national income and money supply and rise of the price level in the four countries under study.

TABLE No. 30

Countries	*P.C. rate of growth of N.I.*	*P.C. rate of increase in money supply*	*P.C· rate of rise of price level*
Ghana	7.4	75	36
Nigeria	8.7	21	4
Libya	14.0	185	21
Sudan	3·5	43	13

All the countries except Nigeria record a remarkably high percentage of price rise relatively to the rise of National Income.

From the relevant data presented in Table No. 31 it will be observed that the increase in total Central Bank Credit has exceeded the estimated 'safe' limit. This expansion of Central Bank Credit has been in favour of both the public and the private sector. To neutralise the inflationary pressure generated by the excess increase in central bank credit, the expansion of such credit should have been contained within the 'safe' limit either by maintaining its flow to the public sector and freezing a corresponding amount for the private sector or alternatively restricting the amount partly to the public and partly to the private sector.

TABLE No. 31

FACTORS DETERMINING SIGNIFICANCE OF CENTRAL BANK CREDIT AS SOURCE OF INFLATION OF THE FOUR COUNTRIES NIGERIA, GHANA, LIBYA AND SUDAN DURING 1960-'65

Annual Averages

Countries	*Increase in real income (In millions of national currency)*	*Income velocity (a)*	*Credit multiplier (b)*	*Increase in money supply*	*Increase in Central Bank monetary liabilities*	*Increase in Central Bank Credit*	*Safe increase in money supply (c)*	*Safe increase in Central Bank monetary liabilities (d)*	*Safe increase in Central Bank Credit (e)*	*Excess increase in Central Bank Credit (f)*
				In thousands of national currency						
	(1)	(2)	(3)	(4)	(5)	(6)	(7)	(8)	(9)	(10)
Nigeria 1960-65	493	19.1	0.36	25715	7645.36	15200	25000	6944	5687.64	9512.36
Ghana 1961-64	485	5·4	2·80	88000	42131	20418	89800	22071	10358	10060
Libya 1960-65	65	1·1	1·09	61598	58329	14311	59000	54127	10109	4202
Sudan 1960-65	31.75	0·49	4·09	66660	16633	14596	64900	15843	13806	790

(*a*) Average national income at current prices divided by average money supply.
(*b*) Total increase in money supply during the period concerned divided by total increase in Central Bank monetary liabilities minus increase in Government deposits during the same period Col. (4) ÷ Col. (5).
(*c*) Col. (1) ÷ Col. (2). (*d*) Col. (7) ÷ Col. (3). (*e*) Col. (6) minus Col. (5) minus Col. (8). (*f*) Col. (6) minus Col. (9).

SOURCES: Annual Reports and Statements of Accounts, Central Bank of Nigeria 1960-1965, Economic and Financial Review (Published by the Central Bank of Nigeria).
Annual Reports of the Bank of Ghana 1961-1964.
Annual Reports of the Bank of Libya- 1957-64, Monthly Economic Bulletins (Published by the Research Department of the Bank of Libya.)
Annual Reports of the Bank of Sudan, 1960-65 Economic and Financial Bulletins (Published by the Bank of Sudan).
Statistical Year Book 1965, Published by the United Nations.

Chapter Nine

Promotional Role of the Central Banks

The promotional role of these central banks may be reviewed in relation to the part they have played and may further play in the development of money and capital markets, in the creation of banks and other financial intermediaries so as to provide an institutional framework favourable to rapid economic growth, in acting as the governments' financial and foreign exchange advisers and generally in implementing their overall economic policy. The statutes of most of these Banks have equipped them for all these tasks. In Ghana and Nigeria central banks have striven from the start to create money and capital markets. In Tunisia the creation of the inter-bank monetary market in July 1962 on the initiative of the central bank of Tunisia has been an important contribution. The monetary market is allowed to act as a regulator of the banking system's liquid assets through centralisation of supply and demand while all operations are accomplished with optimum security and rapidity.[1] In Morocco and Rhodesia they have endeavoured to support markets already in existence. In Sudan the Bank has since its inception been planning to extend the scope and possibilities of the country's money and capital markets. As far back as 1961 the Bank of Sudan had submitted a scheme to the government aimed at the creation of a market for long and medium-term government bonds as the first step towards the creation of a capital market ultimately capable of canalising private savings for meeting a part of the government's growing financial needs.[2] The establishment of the first commercial bank under Sudanese ownership and control, it may be recalled, was due to the direct initiative of the Bank of Sudan in 1960. It has since continued its assistance to the Sudan Commercial Bank by providing technical advice and in various other ways. But its policy was never to provide special treatment too far so as to undermine its private character. The principle that guided the central bank was that assistance should be extended only when it was necessary to promote speedy and sound development.[3]

[1] Annual Report of the STB for the year 1963, p. 18.
[2] *Bank of Sudan*. Annual Report for the year 1961, p. 4.
[3] *Ibid.*, for the year 1960, p. 30.

It has been much too commonplace an observation that underdeveloped countries are in the grip of a vicious circle of low income and low productivity because of an inadequate volume of capital per head; the low stock of capital and capital formation again are due to the smallness of the incomes. In such countries capital is not only in short supply but the scarce capital resources are further employed in a manner which does not facilitate an optimal rate of economic expansion. The absence of well organised and reputed financial intermediaries which could provide both liquidity and income has caused a diversion of the savings of the people into the traditional forms of investment in real estate, gold and ornaments, away from productive investment in industry and agriculture. A more rational allocation of the scarce savings of these countries calls for the creation and encouragement of money and capital markets. The creation of a variety of financial intermediaries in such territories is not indulging in an expensive luxury. It is the essential preliminary condition for economic development. On the one hand it is a means of providing appropriate liquid assets to investors in the country; on the other it is a channel through which the internal flow of savings can be stimulated and directed to the desired categories of investment. In the initial stages of economic growth it is the government of the country working through its most important agency, the central bank, which has the primary responsibility for developing and broadening the money and capital markets.

The foundations of the capital markets must have to be laid on domestic sources of funds. Reliance on the flow of foreign funds may subject the market to serious crises when the inflow is interrupted owing to political or other factors. The volume of business in the market must be relatively large, otherwise there will be wild price movements. There must also be a short-term credit market with an adequate volume of lending and borrowing. The existence of borrowers and lenders for short-term funds will ensure the movement of liquid assets from the short-term to the medium and long-term and conversely with the decline or the rise in the prices of the respective securities.

A common characteristic of the economy of these countries is that a substantial proportion of their productive activities is of a seasonal nature with the consequence of a considerable amount of short-term funds seeking temporary outlets for suitable and profitable employment. What is needed, therefore, to build up a market is in the first instance to provide a supply of short-term assets comparable to those which led to the development of active short-term markets in the financially mature countries of the world. It will be idle to think of creating overnight the sophisticated instruments which are to be witnessed there; only those instruments which are suited to the requirements of the particular economy should be encouraged to grow. The central and the commercial banks of the country can stimulate, through the liberal offer of rediscount and discount facilities, the use of these indigenous instruments by lenders as well as borrowers. Such instruments again may not immediately grow in quantities adequate enough for the establishment of a broad, active and resilient market. In most cases the treasury bills may have to play a predominant part in the earlier stages. The central banks in the underdeveloped countries have therefore proceeded to issue treasury bills on behalf of their governments and extended at the same time liberal rediscount facilities to the purchasers of such papers. The greater the number and the more diversified the maturity patterns of these bills and more regular the intervals at which they are issued, the stronger will be the encouragement to the growth of the market. The governments may indeed meet their requirements more cheaply than by increasing their short-term debt in the form of treasury bills. But in the larger interests of the economy the creation of a market in short-term debt may be necessary. In the circumstances the governments may have to borrow through the treasury bill method even more than their requirements. Such a market will provide an appropriate avenue through which suitable assets may be furnished to private investors and at the same time enable trade and industry to get an access to funds which would not otherwise have been invested within the country. Indeed as a commentator has well observed, public debt has a special role to perform in an underdeveloped economy, not limited to the financing of public expenditures.[1] It provides the machinery through which funds can be obtained from local investors and canalised into government accounts and then transmitted to the private as well as the public sector for real capital formation.

[1] E. Nevin, *Capital Funds for Underdeveloped Countries*, p. 91, p. 95.

Not only a short-term credit market but also a long-term capital market has to be created in the interests of the country's economic development. It may be necessary for the governments to issue from time to time bonds, in addition to the treasury bills, with a diversified maturity pattern, and much beyond their immediate financial requirements. A regular and adequate flow of medium and long dated securities will prove to be an attractive outlet for the investment of the reserves of banks and other financial intermediaries. This points to the necessity of establishing a market in long-dated government securities even as much as in short-term where buyers and sellers can trade at prices which do not fluctuate over a wide range but are fairly and reasonably stable. Such a market however cannot thrive without the operation of a healthy stock exchange. The provision of a stock exchange has been regarded by many underdeveloped countries as having the same status symbol as a national central bank. It would be entirely impractical to attempt to build up stock exchanges in these underdeveloped countries on the lines of their more sophisticated counterparts in London or New York. Such complex and refined machineries would be entirely uncalled for in the context of the economic and financial structures of the countries. The creation of a rudimentary stock exchange may be the first step in this direction. In countries where stock exchanges already exist in an elementary form, steps may be taken to regulate and develop them further. In the beginning operations in private securities cannot be expected. In these underdeveloped countries there would hardly exist a requisite number of industrial companies with fair prospects of profitability which could issue securities and find ready investors. The main trading will in the circumstances be in government securities. As the economy of the countries develops and stock exchanges grow more mature, the marketing of private securities will take place. By that time experience with government securities would have inspired the confidence of the investors in private stocks. This is what has exactly happened in Rhodesia where there was considerable expansion of activity in 1964 and both the value and the number of transactions rose in relation to previous years. There was also an active market in other types of securities. The number of locally registered shares is still small. Domestic investors have thus limited opportunities to participate in the equity of many locally established companies.[1] The transactions at the Lagos Stock Exchange (Nigeria) during the years 1962-66 in this connection are highly interesting. While the volume of transactions in industrial securities was only £6.3 thousand, that in government securities was £34.3 thousand in April 1962, the respective figures for December 1964 were £264.1 thousand and £516.8 thousand. The total volume shot up from £1737.4 thousand in 1962 to £7927.7 in 1965.[2]

In the Federation of Rhodesia and Nyasaland as elsewhere the weekly issue of treasury bills by the Bank on behalf of the Federal government had been an important factor contributing to the growth of the money markets. Before the Federation had a central bank, a local money market could not be developed. Again without the development of a money market, government operations in short term finance had to be inevitably small. Indeed treasury bills had been issued prior to the creation of the Bank of Rhodesia and Nyasaland. But it was with the commencement of the regular weekly issue of treasury bills offered for tender, on behalf of the Federal government in September 1957 that the growth of the market may be said to have been stimulated.[3] For the first time the advantages of a system of open trading whereby the supply of and demand for short-term money could find equilibrium and therefore reflect market conditions were introduced into the country. Before the year was out the value of treasury bills on issue amounted to £12.4 million.[4] The establishment of the money market has provided an avenue for the productive employment of funds within the country which would otherwise have found their way to the London money market. As the volume of fine trade bills continued to rise and the supply of treasury bills regularly increased, the avenue for the employment of short-term funds has been assured. The government has also been able to benefit from the resources available in the form of short-term finance. The amount offered throughout the months has varied from week to week during the three years 1962, 1963 and 1964. The value of bills on issue reached a record figure of £39.5 million in June, 1964, declining steadily thereafter till the more normal level of £33 million was

[1] *Bank of Rhodesia and Nyasaland*, Annual Report for the year 1964, p. 8.
[2] *Economic and Financial Review*. Central Bank of Nigeria, June 1966, p. 53.
[3] *Commonwealth Banking Systems*. Ed. by W. F. Crick. p. 349.
[4] *Bank of Rhodesia and Nyasaland*, Annual Report for the year 1961, pp. 2-3.

reached.[1] From time to time the Bank has absorbed a large volume of bills so that stable conditions can be maintained. The figures quoted above are no doubt very small compared with developed financial centres; but the rate of progress reflected is remarkable in view of the short period taken to develop the market. On the dissolution of the Federation and the constitution of three territorial governments, it was decided that the Bank of Rhodesia should issue its own bills in replacement of the treasury bills previously issued by the Federal government so that a common money market could be maintained. The first 91-day bills issued by the Bank were offered through the weekly tender at the end of September, 1963. It was not practicable for the Bank of the Federation to issue its own bills after February 1964 in view of the termination of the monetary area in June, 1965. The Central Banks in the two territories of Rhodesia and Zambia assumed responsibility for issuing treasury bills on behalf of their own governments thereafter. The Malawi government was also expected to issue its own treasury bills through the agency of the Reserve Bank of Malawi.

It is interesting to observe that discount houses and merchant banks were operating in the territory of the old Federation. The two discount houses which were formed in 1959 dealt not only in commercial bills but also in short-dated government and municipal bonds. They employed money at call from commercial banks and did not compete with them for deposits. The Central Bank has further encouraged the development of the short bond market and helped it to grow. With its growth dealings in short-dated government bonds tended to increase. Prior to the dissolution, building societies were found to operate under territorial legislation in all the three territories, Rhodesia, Zambia and Malawi. Between March 1954 and March 1962 loans of building societies other than those against shares and deposits rose from £7.66 million to £52.4 million. Land banks and hire purchase finance houses could also be witnessed. The outstanding debt due to the hire purchase finance companies has tended to remain steady round about £8 million. Since December, 1964 when the outstanding debt fell to £7.2 million the finance houses have been experiencing increasing competition from commercial firms offering instalment credit facilities. But the hire purchase com-

[1] *Bank of Rhodesia and Nyasaland*, Annual Report for the year 1964, pp. 6-7.

panies also compete with them in the matter of attracting deposits which varied between £2.5 million and £3.4 million during 1962.64.[1] There has been a concentration of these finance houses in Salisbury but subsidiaries of these finance houses are being registered at Zambia after the dissolution.

It had already been observed that the Central Bank of Nigeria had appreciated at a very early stage the limited scope for monetary policy in the absence of a relatively developed financial mechanism. Ever since its inception it had directed its efforts towards the creation of a suitable institutional framework for the operation of modern central banking. Not only new institutions were created but those which had already existed were also sought to be reorganised. Within a few years of its operation, it was able to alter the monetary banking environment. The development of a short-term money market, the establishment of a clearing system, and the fostering of a stock exchange and a development bank may be listed among its important contributions.[2]

Let us now turn to review the policy adopted by the Central Bank in Nigeria to broaden the money and capital markets in the country. As early as 1960 the central bank introduced on behalf of the government treasury bills with the objective of developing the local money market. These bills were in units of £1,000 and had a maturity of 91 days. As steps taken by the central bank to foster the expansion of the money market, introduction of weekly issues and diversification of their maturities in 1963 may be particularly mentioned. The treasury bills provided for the first time an outlet for investment of short-term surplus funds of the banking system which traditionally flowed out to London. The offer of rediscount facilities or repurchase guarantees by the central bank, it is well-known, helps to encourage the growth of the market. An active and expanding money market has been observed to have grown in many countries with the issue of treasury bills by tender and the creation of rediscount facilities. In India, for instance, when rediscounting facilities were offered from 1937, considerable encouragement was given to the growth of the market. In

[1] *Bank of Rhodesia and Nyasaland*, Annual Reports for the years 1962, p. 43. Table 13 and 1964, p. 66 Table 15.

[2] The *Bankers' Magazine* March 1966, p. 182. Art. by O. Olakanpo entitled "Banking Problems in Nigeria".

Nigeria the central bank has since the beginning contributed to the growth of the market by its systematic policy of encouraging the local investment of funds and standing ready at all times to rediscount treasury bills. The maintenance of a small differential between the issue rate and the rediscount rate in this connection has constituted an important feature of its policy. Thus when the treasury bill issue rate was reduced in January 1963 by ½ per cent to 3½ per cent, the discount rate was simultaneously lowered by ½ per cent to 4 per cent. The central bank has also purchased treasury bills from commercial banks, when pressed for cash they had to sell out their investments in such bills to finance the marketing of agricultural produce and to meet other seasonal demands. It has also purchased such bills in order to enable holders to make investments in the country's Development Stock.[1] In 1964 the monthly average of treasury bill issues rose from £8.1 million in 1963 to £10.9 million. The average amount outstanding also increased from £23.5 million to £31.4 million.[2]

TABLE No. 32

TREASURY BILLS TRANSACTION
TOTAL ISSUE

(*In £ thousands*)

	1 *Total Issue during the period*	2 *Taken up by Central Bank*	3 *By Public* (including *commercial banks*)	4 *Bills Outstanding*
1963. Dec.	8,000	5,331	2,669	30,000
1964. Dec.	14,000	6,527	7,473	34,000
1965. Dec.	11,000	6,231	4,769	40,000

The central bank has lent its support to the produce bill finance scheme by providing rediscount or refinance facilities upto a defined limit. The scheme was introduced in 1962 for the marketing of agricultural produce handled by the regional marketing boards. Initially limited to the marketing of ground nuts and cotton for the Northern Nigeria Marketing Board, it was extended to cover produce handled by the Western Nigerian

[1] Annual Report and Statement of Accounts, *Bank of Nigeria*. for the year 1963, p. 29.

[2] Annual Report and Statement of Accounts, *Bank of Nigeria* for years 1964 and 1965, p. 45 and p. 46 respectively.

Marketing Board in 1963. For the marketing season of 1963-64 the central bank stood ready to refinance a total of £27 million commercial bills under the scheme. Money market assets are now available in Nigeria at all times of the year. A market for call money appears to have also developed. The Call Money Fund managed by the central bank has proved to be a valuable outlet for temporarily surplus funds of commercial banks and other eligible financial institutions. The Fund not only provides an interest-earning avenue for these funds but also ensures their recall on demand. Thus the Fund is acting as a cushion which absorbs the immediate shock of liquidity pressure in the money market and the volume and direction of Fund movements is a barometer of money market conditions. A welcome development has been the growth of call money facilities outside the central bank.[1]

With regard to the capital market the central bank has continued to stimulate its growth particularly in the gilt-edged sector by issuing on behalf of the Federal Government Development Loans and stocks and underwriting the issues of stocks not initially subscribed by the public. The Bank gradually disposes of the holdings of these stocks as the market conditions improve. A problem however has been posed for the central bank by the difficulty in disposing of the stocks so underwritten before the new issues were floated. The central bank's own subscriptions amounted to 34.8 per cent and 61.8 per cent of Third and Fourth Development stocks respectively.[2]

With the reorganisation of the Investment Company of Nigeria Ltd., (ICON) into the Nigerian Industrial Development Bank Ltd., (NIDB) in July, 1964 an important milestone was reached in the structure of the country's capital market.[3]

THE BANK OF GHANA AND MONEY AND CAPITAL MARKETS

The fiduciary provisions in the original Bank of Ghana Ordinance offered the possibility of creating the real beginnings of a money and securities market in the country. One of the ways in which the Bank could advantageously employ its fiduciary

[1] Annual Report for the year 1963. *Bank of Nigeria*, pp. 29-30.
[2] *Ibid*, p. 32 (Table).
[3] Annual Report for the year 1964. *Bank of Nigeria*, p. 45.

issue in the interests of further development of the national economy was to stand ready at all times to purchase domestic government securities from any holder and conversely to sell from its own portfolio when there was an opportunity to do so. The Bank of the Gold Coast had initiated the process long before. With the coming into existence of the Issue Department of the Bank of Ghana, the fiduciary clauses gave the central bank considerable scope for developing the market.[1]

The adoption of a system of bill finance for the marketing of cocoa crop is an interesting feature of the expanding functions of the Bank of Ghana. Upto 1959-60 the marketing of the cocoa crop had been financed by the Cocoa Marketing Board of Ghana by cash, a portion of which had to be raised by borrowing. This method of financing involved holding idle for about 6-9 months by the Board of a substantial part of its resources in cash and liquid assets. The resources were maintained in the form of demand and time deposits in London. The Board could be allowed to hold large idle balances when the government had ample liquid funds. But with the increasing tempo of government's development expenditure, its liquid assets suffered considerable strain and recourse had to be made to borrowing from the Board in 1959. The old system of financing by cash also meant that the Board's financial affairs were conducted mainly in London and not in Accra.

The new system of bill financing adopted in 1960 had the two-fold objective of making it unnecessary for the Board to hold large idle balances and enabling the government to siphon off the surplus liquid assets of the Board in exchange for its own holding of longer-dated sterling giltedged securities or as a straight loan to the government. Secondly, the Board's financial transactions would be transferred from London to Accra when they would be within the purview of the monetary authorities at home. The cocoa crop requires finance at two stages, first as between the licensed buying agent and the farmer and second, between the Board and its licensed buying agent. It is at this stage that the Board requires finance to accommodate the buying agent upto 90 per cent of the purchase declared from time to time.[2] Under the bill finance scheme the Board met its

[1] *Bank of Ghana*, Annual Report of the Board. 30 June, 1958.
[2] *Bank of Ghana*, Annual Report of the Board. 30 June, 1961, pp. 5-6.

requirements of cash by drawing a 90-day bill of exchange on its subsidiary, the Ghana Cocoa Marketing Company of London. The Bank of Ghana backed the scheme by giving rediscounting facilities. The rediscounted bills were taken into the Issue Department as part of the currency cover assets under Sec. 28(d) of the Bank of Ghana Ordinance 1957. For the 1961-62 crop, however, a different method of financing the purchase from the farmers and the cost of marketing the cocoa was adopted owing partly to the transfer of the marketing from London to Accra.[1]

AFRICAN CENTRAL BANKS AND COMMERCIAL BANKING BUSINESS: RELATIONS BETWEEN THE CENTRAL BANKS AND THE COMMERCIAL BANKS

The classic observation of Prof. Sayers that in an underdeveloped country wherever there are gaps in the financial system, the central bank should be prepared to step in and close them has been invoked by some of these underdeveloped countries to support the entry of their central banks into the field of commercial banking in the transition period. Indeed some of these banks have been expressly empowered by their statutes to undertake commercial banking business. Thus the Bank of Sudan has been authorised to enter into credit operations and open accounts for and accept deposits from persons other than banks and the government with the previous approval of the Minister of Finance.[1] The credit operations with private persons may be of the same form as stipulated for the banks and the government. In Nigeria the Central Bank may also open accounts for and accept deposits from ordinary persons in the country with the prior agreement of the Minister [Art. 29(1) and (*c*)] but it is prohibited from paying interest on any deposits. In both Sudan and Nigeria as well as in Ghana central banks have been enjoined, by their statutes using identical language, to seek the cooperation of and cooperate with other banks in their respective territories to promote and maintain adequate and reasonable banking services for the public, to ensure high standards of conduct and management throughout the banking system and to further such policies not inconsistent with the national interest [Nigeria Art. 39(*a*), (*b*) & (*c*), Sudan Art. 49, Ghana Ordinance Art. 40].

[1] *Bank of Ghana,* Annual Report. 30 June, 1962, p. 6.
[2] Arts. 62 (a) and 63 (1). *The Bank of Sudan Act,* 1959.

The new Rhodesian Bank's statutes are entirely flexible in this respect. The general provisions empowering it to grant loans and advances and to accept money on current account and collect money for its customers have not stipulated anywhere that such operations should be limited to commercial banks only [Rhodesia Art. 9(*b*) & (*c*) '64]. But there is an interesting feature borrowed from the Bank of England Act, 1946 under which the Rhodesian Bank may, if it thinks in the public interest, request information from and make recommendations to bankers and may if so authorised by the Minister, issue directions to any banker for the purpose of ensuring that effect is given to any such request or recommendation, provided that no such request or recommendation shall be made in respect of the affairs of any particular customer of a bank and provided further that an opportunity is given to the banker concerned to make representations.[1] This provision was missing in the original Bank of Rhodesia and Nyasaland Act 1956.

In Morocco as well as in Tunisia there is a commercial banking department in the central bank. Article 36, Section IV of the chapter has expressly authorised the Bank of Morocco to open and hold current accounts, and deposit accounts, receive in deposit securities and let out safe deposit vaults and effect all operations for the collection of securities. Such central-cum-commercial banking business appears to be traditional in Morocco and has been functioning smoothly. Through its commercial banking department the central bank is able to deploy credit into new and preferred categories of trade, industry, agriculture and where there is considerable need of such credit. Thus the central bank may be said to be filling a void in the financial system. Until special credit institutions for financing agriculture and industry are built up, the central bank must be performing a useful role in this way. Instances of central banks usefully supplementing the activities of commercial banks are to be witnessed in several under-developed countries of Latin America and elsewhere. For instance, the model of a mixed central bank was embodied in the statutes of the central banks of Indonesia, Chile, Paraguay and Nicaragua. The most interesting case of an intermixture of central and commercial banking business in an African country is to be witnessed

[1] *The Reserve Bank of Rhodesia Act, 1964.* Art. 23(1) (*a*) & (*b*).

in Libya. It has been noted earlier that the National Bank of Libya from the inception has been a mixed type of central bank. This feature has not impaired the good relations of the central bank with the ordinary banks nor has it stood in the way of central banking control over the latter. The National Bank of Libya has reported the continued existence of extremely good relations with the commercial banks and absence of misunderstanding.[1]

The Banking Department of the National Bank of Libya which was responsible for the conduct of normal banking business on behalf of the government had a commercial section. Through this section it catered for the financial requirements of private firms and individuals who wished to do business with what was at that time the only pure indigenous institution providing full banking facilities. Besides functioning as the banker to the government, the Banking Department under the original law of 1955 accepted money on deposits or current account, granted overdrafts, made advances for fixed periods against prescribed securities, accepted from customers the custody of securities and other articles of value and undertook on behalf of its customers the purchase, sale, collection and payment of securities, currencies, gold or silver. The duration for which advances could be made and the types of securities that could be accepted as cover for overdrafts and loans were specifically limited. Unsecured advances and overdrafts were strictly prohibited. There was however no bar against the conduct of high class banking business.

As originally structured the commercial banking business was non-differentiated in organisation from the central banking business with a common board of directors. Under the new Banking Law of April 15, 1963, the Banking Department came to be split up into a central banking and a commercial banking department. Under the provisions of the new law the Minister of Finance should specify by agreement with the Board of the Bank the ordinary commercial banking operations which might be undertaken by it; the accounts of such operations were to be kept "separate and distinct" from all other accounts, and the deposits and reserves of commercial banks should not be used for the purpose of making commercial loans.[2] The Law did not go as

[1] Annual Report for the year 1960. *National Bank of Libya*, p. 57.
[2] Art. 22. *Banking Law, February 5, 1963.*

far as the Australian Law of 1959 which transformed the Commonwealth Bank of Australia into a pure central banking institution—the Reserve Bank of Australia,—and the Commonwealth Banking Corporation. The commercial banking functions of the Commonwealth Bank were separated from those of pure central banking where they had been previously combined together and entrusted to the Commonwealth Trading Bank, one of the three constituents of the Commonwealth Banking Corporation.[1] The Trading Banking Department of the Commonwealth Bank had been earlier competing with the private banks in the field of ordinary banking business and in the process had aroused their hostility. During most of the interwar period, the Commonwealth Bank under conservative governments had been advised not to compete with the private banks. But when the Labour Government came to power, not only the war-time framework of controls was re-imposed on the private banks but the Commonwealth Bank was also actually advised to enter into direct competition with them. The climax was reached when the Labour Government true to its own ideology wanted in its impatience to nationalise the whole banking system. The Labour Government was subsequently defeated at the polls on this issue. The Conservative Government which stepped in established the Reserve Bank and the Commonwealth Trading Bank as separate institutions. The combination of central and commercial banking was ill-advised in the case of Australia where a highly developed commercial banking system had already been functioning.[2] It was quite proper for the central bank there to shed its non-central banking functions with the growing maturity of the economy. But it was a different story with Libya. The country had hardly any indigenous banking system. The few expatriate banks with their head offices in the metropolitan cities abroad which were functioning in Libya could not be expected to cater for the needs of indigenous trade, commerce and industry in the same way as national banks would do. There was no question of the open hostility of the Libyan banks because they did not exist. After the segregation of the commercial banking department from the

[1] *The Reserve Bank of Australia Act, 1959*. Sec. 26 (a) and (c). Also Hans Aufricht, *Central Banking Legislation*, p. 47.

[2] *Indian Economic Review*, January-March 1965, p. 241. Art. by H. W. Arndt entitled "Central Banking in Developing Countries".

central banking department the former department has been treated on the same basis as other commercial banks.[1]

The activities of the commercial banking department of the Bank of Libya which has shown systematic progress expanded remarkably during 1964-65 in response to the increasing demand for banking services from a developing economy. The department played a significant part in the implementation of the country's Five Year Development Plan by providing credit to new contractors engaged in construction projects under the Plan.[2] How the business of the department has expanded may be seen from some 'key' figures relating to its assets and liabilities. On the assets side during the year ending 31 March, 1964 total bills discounted rose by 203.9 per cent as against the year ending 31 March, 1963; loans and advances by 50.1 per cent; and customers' liability for credits opened and letters of credit issued by 81.2 per cent. On the liabilities side the value of current accounts rose by 68.1 per cent, of time deposits by 64.2 per cent and of savings accounts by 76.5 per cent.[3]

The combination of central and commercial banking to be witnessed in Libya is a peculiar but not a singular characteristic of underdeveloped countries. A mixed type of central banking is no doubt foreign to the traditions of the Bank of England, but is quite familiar in the continental type of central banking which is characterised by the conduct of a substantial amount of private business in direct competition with the commercial banks. In France particularly, the Bank of France has operated as a central-cum-commercial bank through a network of its branches spread over the whole country, accepting deposits from the public and bringing loan and discount facilities so to speak to the very door of the small trader and industrialist.[4] In the statutes there was virtually no distinction in terms between business with the ordinary public and that with the banks. The central banks of Morocco and Tunisia had a French heritage and following French tradition had imbibed this feature of mixed central banking which in their case has worked satisfactorily.

[1] Eighth Annual Report, *Bank of Libya*, 1964, p. 2.

[2] Ninth Annual Report, *Bank of Libya*, 1965.

[3] Seventh and Eighth Annual Reports, *Bank of Libya* for 1964, pp. 62-65 for 1965, pp. 52-55.

[4] Parker Wills, *Theory and Practice of Central Banking with particular reference to the Federal Reserve System*, pp. 22-23. Also *Midland Bank Review*, March-April, 1927.

It is interesting to find that the charters of a number of newly established central banks, all of which may not be influenced by French tradition, have given them broad powers to discount for, make advances to, and accept deposits from the non-banking public. The cases in point are Mali, Somalia, Burundi and Jamaica. Of the three only Mali is a member of the French franc zone, while Somalia and Burundi are members neither of the sterling area nor of the French franc zone. Although the Bank of Jamaica (established 1960) has been endowed with the necessary powers, it has declared its intention to refrain from commercial banking business, possibly because of its British heritage and membership of the sterling area. But the central banks of Somalia and Mali have been doing a great deal of commercial banking business. Indeed in the case of Somalia, the central bank's rediscounts for commercial banks are insignificant, while its claims on the private sector are larger than similar business of commercial banks by two-thirds. In line with its commercial credit policy the Somali National Bank opened 9 branches during 1960-1965. The central bank of Mali's business with the private non-financial sector is as heavy as its business with the banking sector for while it discounts heavily for commercial banks, its claims on private borrowers are nearly four times as large as those of ordinary banks.[1]

The theoretical case for a central bank undertaking commercial banking business has been examined by us elsewhere and need not be repeated.[2] As already noted, no less an authority than Prof. Sayers has given his blessings to the undertaking of commercial banking business by central banks in underdeveloped countries where there are gaps in the financial machinery to be filled. But it should be made quite clear that his argument is applicable only to the transition period when the financial system is still immature. In the case of a country where the banking system is adequately developed, it is obvious that his argument cannot be invoked. Whatever might be the advantages in a marriage of central and commercial banking functions in the earlier stages of a developing economy, a divorcement of the two

[1] *Federal Reserve Bank of New York, Monthly Review*, July 1964, p. 135. Art. entitled "New Central Banks". Also *The Bankers' Magazine*, May 1965. Art. by M. Buonomo, p. 350.

[2] *A Survey of Contemporary Banking Trends* (3rd Ed.) by the present writer, pp. 12-19.

functions is called for as the economy grows more and more mature. The central banks, to use an expression of Prof. Sayers, should then "retire gracefully" and operate as distinct institutions.[1] Not only in Australia but also in another group of countries which include Iran, Ireland, Ethiopia, Nicaragua and the U.A.R. where institutions which had previously conducted both central and commercial banking business at the same time have now been converted into central banks proper, and their commercial banking operations entrusted to existing or newly formed commercial banks.[2] Neither the theoretical argument of Prof. Sayers nor the practical logic of the Australian precedent seems to have any lesson for the Reserve Bank of India. The Indian institution has been continually "diluting" the essence of central banking by extending more and more the scope of its functions beyond the frontiers of central banking proper.

[1] R. S. Sayers, *Central Banking After Bagehot*, p. 118.
[2] *Federal Reserve Bank of New York Monthly Review*, July 1964, p. 133.

Chapter Ten

Central Banks and Development Banks

In the advanced economies of highly industrialised countries specialist institutions for meeting the various kinds of financial requirements have gradually evolved in the normal process and have attained maturity only after passing through various stages of growth and experiment. The building up of such institutions cannot be left to the processes of evolution in underdeveloped countries. The evolutionary process will inevitably be slow, too slow indeed, and may involve many years and even an indefinite period. Agriculture and industry in these underdeveloped economies are badly in need of capital, both loan and equity, as well as proper technical advice and guidance without which their development cannot be accelerated. The promotion of such specialist institutions by the government and the central bank is, therefore, an important desideratum for quick economic growth. The wide range of specialised banking and other financial services to be witnessed in the industrially advanced countries to-day does not exist in the underdeveloped countries or is only in a rudimentary stage. An agency will be required to create and foster them. The most appropriate agency for the task is the central bank. In the advanced countries the central bank had the basis for its operations in the variety of financial intermediaries already in existence. In the emerging countries the usual pattern is reversed; and it is the central bank itself which will have to sponsor and develop the institutions which will provide it with the necessary basis for its operations. Central banks in the underdeveloped countries have to perform a very significant role in assisting the institutionalisation of saving and investment. As observed before, the rate of economic growth is conditioned by the accumulation, disposition and diversification of financial assets. Such accumulation of financial assets with a diversified pattern of risk and reward attaching to them ensures a wider and more rational choice for savers. It also provides a more efficient mechanism for allocation of investible resources through the operation of financial intermediaries in their various forms which tend to grow with the increasing tempo of economic development. Most of the central banks operating in the newly independent African colonies have been fulfilling important roles in creating and developing a variety of financial intermediaries, extending short, medium as well as long-term credit. As a well known central banker of an underdeveloped country has observed, such a central banking policy would clearly be unorthodox and unconventional in the "lexicon of classical central banking"; but is now regarded to be in the very nature of central banking in developing economies.[1]

It is in this context that reference must be made to the institutional device of development banks in the sphere of industry and agriculture which has come to be adopted by many underdeveloped countries to attain a rapid rate of economic development and has attracted a great deal of attention in recent years. Designed to provide some of the most fundamental ingredients of economic development such as capital, enterprise, technical know-how etc., they have come to be established in the various underdeveloped countries not only of Latin America but also those of Asia and Africa. Specialist institutions for providing development finance are to be witnessed in advanced countries also to cope with specific problems posed by the after effects of wars and the great depression and wide-spread unemployment. In some cases they have been totally government owned; in others partly government and partly central bank owned and in yet others privately owned or even mixed. There are one or two remarkable instances of development banks being completely owned by central banks.[2] Whatever may be the structure of ownership of the banks, they have almost invariably been sponsored by the governments and/or the central banks of the countries concerned. In almost all countries whether developed or underdeveloped, wherever development financing institutions have been set up, it is the central banks which have assisted in their formation by participating wholly or partly in their share capital, by subscribing to their bonds, by refinancing their loans, and by guaranteeing their obligations in the internal as well as in the international capital market. Thus central banks in the developed countries of Great Britain and Canada in the West and underdeveloped countries of India, Pakistan, Ceylon, Nepal etc. in

[1] "Balance between Monetary Policy and Other Instruments of Economic Policy" by C. D. Deshmukh, op cit., p. 22.

[2] The Industrial Development Banks of Canada and India.

Asia have assisted in the establishment of development finance institutions through one or more of the methods mentioned above.

I have examined elsewhere the question whether central banks should wholly own a development bank and through it directly provide and administer industrial loans.[1] Central banks do not possess the expertise for running a development bank and directly financing or administering industrial and agricultural enterprises. The institutional arrangement under which the Reserve Bank of India is owning and administering the Industrial Development Bank is ill-conceived and unsound. It is in direct opposition to the established traditions under which central banks divest themselves of commercial and other non-central banking activities with the increasing tempo of economic growth. If there is true "dilution" of central banking anywhere, it is to be found here.

In the African countries under review development banks (or corporations) are found to be already operating in Nigeria, Ghana, Sudan, Morocco, Tunisia, Libya and Rhodesia. The anxiety of the countries to participate in the promotion of various kinds of financial institutions for facilitating their economic development is reflected in the statutes of the Banks. Thus the Sudanese Bank has been authorised to buy, hold and sell shares of any enterprise, the participation in and the initiative of which promote the Bank's aims or are generally in the interests of the national economy.[2] Limitations placed on the power of the Bank to participate in the capital of other financial institutions have been removed by an amendment in 1962. In Nigeria the statutory provision in this respect is more explicit. The central bank may subscribe to, hold and sell shares of any corporation set up with the approval of or under the authority of the Federal Government for the purpose of promoting the development of a money market or securities market in Nigeria or of improving the financial machinery for financing the economic development of the country.[3] The Bank of Morocco similarly has been authorised to subscribe to the capital of as well as the obligations issued by financial institutions incorporated under a particular law. It may even be charged by the Finance Minister to create certain

[1] See *Theory and Practice of Development Banking* (1965), Ch. 9, by the present writer.

[2] Art. 64. *Bank of Sudan Act. 1959 (As amended up to 1962).*

[3] *Central Bank of Nigeria Act. 1958 (As amended up to 1962).* Art. 29 (1)(i).

financial institutions.[1] The Central Bank of Tunisia has also been authorised to invest its funds, after authorisation by the Secretary of State for Finance, in papers issued by financial institutions or economic enterprises registered under particular law or placed under the control of the state up to 25 per cent of its own funds.[2] It is clear that they were intended from the start to assist in the formation of development finance institutions.

THE INDUSTRIAL BANK OF SUDAN

The establishment of the Industrial Bank of Sudan by an Act of October 26, 1961 marks an important landmark in the series of efforts made by the government and the central bank for the social and economic development of the country. Its objects were to assist in and promote the establishment of privately owned and operated new industrial enterprises and the expansion and modernisation of existing enterprises belonging to this category in the Sudan and to encourage and promote the participation of private capital in such enterprises. The fact that the government may have assisted an enterprise by providing a loan or equity capital without having acquired a controlling interest therein will not render the concern ineligible for the assistance of the Bank, provided it is managed or operated by private interests. The usual functions of a development bank have been assigned to it. Thus it has been empowered to provide finance by making loans ranging from 2 to 15 years, or by taking up debenture bonds and by participation in common or preference stock, to sponsor and underwrite shares and securities, to guarantee and counter-guarantee loans, etc. and finally to furnish managerial, technical and administrative advice. The loans have to be secured for an amount equal to 120 per cent of the amount of the loans by a first mortgage on the borrower's fixed assets and on his movable assets, if he has no fixed assets. The authorised capital of the Bank was fixed at LS 3 million divided into 3 million shares of LS 1 each. The shares could be subscribed to by the government, government boards and by the public.[3] In view of the lack of private capital in the Sudan, the Bank has been initially financed

[1] Art. 30 and Art. 39 *Statute of the Bank of Morocco,* 1959 (as amended 1962).
[2] Art. 53. *Statute of the Bank of Tunisia,* 1958 (as amended 1963.)
[3] *The Industrial Bank of Sudan Act.* 1961. Art 6(1) and (2).

by the government and the central bank. But the Act provided that to ensure future participation of private capital, domestic or foreign, part or all of the authorised but unissued balance of the Bank's share capital (LS 1.9 million) might be offered to the public. Of the Bank's authorised capital of LS 3 million, the government of Sudan took up LS 500,000 and further agreed to provide to the Bank a loan of equal amount repayable in 30 equal semi-annual instalments commencing 15½ years after disbursement. The Central Bank's Annual Report for the year ending December 1964 shows that it subscribed and paid up LS 400,000 of the share capital. It was also agreed that the balance of LS 600,000 would be subscribed and paid up in amounts and at times to be settled in the light of the loan commitments and the liquid position of the Industrial Bank.[1] The Bank of Sudan increased its shareholdings to LS 600,000 in 1965.[2] Of the eight members of the Board of Directors of the Industrial Bank it was statutorily provided that there should be a representative of the Bank of Sudan.[3]

Since the commencement of its operation on August 15, 1962, the Industrial Bank received generous co-operation from the Bank of Sudan and was able to draw upon the national foreign exchange resources whenever necessary for its loans. Out of the total cost of 21 projects about LS 700,000 (65/70 per cent) was to be paid out in foreign currencies over a period of two years. The lacuna in its original structure under which it was not provided with an initial fund of foreign currency was thus made up. On July 14, 1963 a tripartite agreement was signed by the Government of the Sudan, the U.S. Agency for International Development and the Industrial Bank under which the Bank received a loan of 2 million dollars from the AID. Under the terms and conditions of the loan, it was to be repaid by the Bank to the government over 12½ years plus a grace of 3 years, the latter repaying the AID in dollars over 31 years plus a grace of 10 years. The loan was very significant in that it was the Bank's first foreign loan and was intended to be utilised to the fullest extent for industrial development in the Sudan.[4]

[1] Annual Report of the Industrial Bank of Sudan 1964, p. 5.
[2] Annual Report, *Bank of Sudan*, 1965, p. 61.
[3] *The Industrial Bank of Sudan Act*. 1961 Art. 8(2) (c).
[4] Report of the Board of Directors of the Industrial Bank of Sudan No. 2 for the year ending 31-12-1963, p. 2.

The resources of the Industrial Bank of Sudan available for lending were seriously depleted by the second half of 1963 so much so that action for additional capital had to be taken. Disbursement of the loans made by the Bank which showed an upward trend in the second half of 1965 prompted the Bank to apply to the Bank of Sudan under its agreement with the latter for a further subscription of LS 200,000 to its share capital. This was paid by the Bank of Sudan in December 1965 bringing the amount paid by it to LS 600,000 out of its total agreed commitment of LS 1 million. The Industrial Bank's total subscribed and paid up capital together with the government's original subscription of LS 500,000 stood at LS 1,100,000 on 31st December 1965. Together with the interest-free loan of LS 500,000 from the government the total resources in paid up share capital and quasi-equity capital amounted to LS 1,600,000 on that date. The proceeds of the 2 million dollar-loan granted to the Bank by the American AID could not be utilised owing to a state of administrative and procedural difficulties.[1]

In the performance of its functions the Industrial Bank is guided by sound economic, financial and business principles. It is authorised to assist only those projects which are technically and financially sound and are calculated to contribute to the economic development of Sudan. In examining and appraising projects the Bank gives priority to those which belong to the category of "approved enterprises", a list of which is available at the Bank to serve as a guide line. The aggregate indebtedness of the Bank shall not exceed one and a half times the sum of paid up capital, reserves and loans from government. It is precluded from investing in any project more than two-thirds of the total cost of that project. The maximum investment by the Bank is limited to 15 per cent, 10 per cent and 7 per cent of its paid up share capital, reserves and loan capital, if the private enterprise is owned and operated by a co-operative society or limited company, by a partnership; and in other cases respectively.[2]

Since the Industrial Bank commenced operations in August 1962, it has provided both loan and equity capital, the propor-

[1] Annual Report of the Industrial Bank of Sudan 1965, p. 2.

[2] *See* The Industrial Bank of the Sudan Bye Laws 1962. Secs (3) (4) and (7).

tion of loans being higher than investments as is generally the case with industrial development banks in other underdeveloped countries. Thus the proportion of loans to total investments during the four years ending 1965 is found to be as follows:

Table[1] No. 33

	1962 (*four months*)	*1963*	*1964*	*1965*
Proportion of loans to total investments	63.1%	60.0%	62.8%	59.4%

The Bank's policy is to contribute to the decentralisation of industrial development through private enterprise by providing its technical assistance and its financial co-operation, by establishing new industrial enterprises in the provinces and by modernising and expanding existing ones. There are several limiting factors in the implementation of its policy such as inadequate transportation, power and water facilities and skilled manpower shortage. That the Bank has been able to achieve its objective of decentralisation is evidenced by the trend towards the emergence of smaller projects in its scheme of financing. Between 1963 and 1965 the share of projects with a total individual investment below LS 25,000 rose from 47.6 per cent to 66.0 per cent in number, from 9.3 per cent to 16.4 per cent in the amount of total investment and from 10.4 per cent to 17.0 per cent in the amount of loans by the Bank.[2] Moreover, the very novelty of industrial activity in many parts of the country calls for intensive guidance in the understanding of the requirements of such activity. During the first four years of its operation (1962) it assisted by loans and investments 46 projects spread over various categories of industries, such as building and carpentry materials, paper, textile, iron and steel, electrical appliances, food, ice manufacture, chemicals etc. and some services like dry cleaning and laundry. These industries represent only the initial stages in the industrial development of Sudan through private enterprise and their direct contribution to the national income may not be very great. But the authorities of the Bank would not minimise their "radiating"

[1] Annual Report of the Board of Directors (No. 3) Industrial Bank of Sudan for 1964, p. 5 and for 1965, p. 1.

[2] Annual Report of the Board of Directors, The Industrial Bank of Sudan for the year 1965, p. 4.

future impact. It is estimated that the 46 projects sanctioned should ultimately create about 1,450 new employment possibilities, save valuable foreign exchange by import substitution and produce increased tax revenues for the government.[1] The Bank lays great stress on the need for practical research to reveal the industrial potential of the country and hopes to contribute to the creation of a climate in Sudan to attract the interest of domestic and foreign capital for investment in private industry in the country. As they have observed in the prospectus of the Bank, it is for the first time that financial and technical assistance, consultant services and research will be simultaneously available to Sudanese industry and these facilities should effectively serve to encourage private enterprise.[2]

It is no doubt true that the pace at which the operations of the Bank should develop, as estimated at the time of the formulation of the Ten Year Economic and Social Development Plan, has not been attained. But at the same time they reflect the rate at which industrial development through private entrepreneurship can reasonably be expected, if it is to be based upon the application of available resources, human and material.

As it is, the progress of the Bank of Sudan since its inception though not spectacular indicates that it has fulfilled an important role. The number of loans approved increased from 5 involving LS 67,000 to 46 involving LS 979,000 during the period 1962-1965. The total amount of investment in projects rose from LS 124,000 to LS, 1,648,000 during the same period. It is of interest to find that most of these 46 projects were operating satisfactorily in 1965. Only one concern is reported to have encountered difficulties in respect of working capital shortage. There is only one instance where the borrower had not at the time of reporting reacted to the invitation to sign the loan agreement. In the case of two or three projects where the operations have not yet begun, building construction has been completed and machinery and plant are being installed.

It cannot be denied however that the time taken for completion of the projects assisted by the Bank can be improved. Apart from the inhibiting effect of the continuing lacunae in infra-

[1] Annual Reports of the Board of Directors, The Industrial Bank of Sudan for the year 1964, p. 10 and for 1965, p. 6.

[2] Prospectus of the Industrial Bank of Sudan (2nd Edition) p. 3 (Furnished by the courtesy of the Bank).

structure and administration, the main delaying factors can be summarised as follows.[1]

1. Non-availability of land for industrial sites in several provincial towns and villages;
2. Inadequate experience of the private entrepreneurs;
3. Insufficiency of recognition and appreciation by the Bank's customers of the benefit of a closer co-operation with their creditor Bank, based upon a misunderstanding of the Bank's role and functions and upon unfounded apprehensions of officious interference.

The regular and recurring end-use supervision by the Bank of all approved projects may clear away some of these misunderstandings and allay the fears and suspicions of the clients, and thus pave the way for fostering closer relations between them.

THE INDUSTRIAL DEVELOPMENT BANK OF NIGERIA

The National Industrial Development Bank of Nigeria Ltd. (NIBD) is another interesting case of a development bank of an emerging African country where the Central Bank has been an important participant in its capital structure. It was established on January 22, 1964 through the reconstruction of the Investment Company of Nigeria Ltd. (ICON). The ICON had been set up in 1959 as an industrial development financing institution owned almost wholly by British banks and industrial companies. The Federal Government of Nigeria played an active role in the formation of the NIBD through negotiations with the representatives of the ICON and a Nigerian steering committee and gave its support to the Bank by providing it with a long term interest-free loan of £N 2 million. On 22nd January 1964 the Bank had an authorised capital of £N 5 million made up of ordinary stock (£N 2 million) and non-voting preference stock (£N 250,000). 51 per cent of the Bank's voting capital designated as "A" ordinary stock was reserved for Nigerian subscribers and international organisations like the IFC (W). The remainder of the voting capital designated as "B" ordinary stock could be taken up by any investor whether Nigerian or foreign. The paid up share capital and the government loan increased the NIDB's

[1] Annual Report of the Industrial Bank of Sudan for the year 1965, pp. 5-6.

original resources of £N 1 million by £N 3.25 to a total of £N 4.25 million. Of this amount £N 1.25 million came in the shape of additional equity capital contributed by the Central Bank of Nigeria, the IFC (W) and leading financial institutions in Europe, Japan and the U.S.A.[1] The NIDB has been further empowered under Art. 64 to borrow up to three times the issued share capital, reserves and subordinated borrowings so that the total potential resources of the Bank amount to £N 17 million. IFC's total investments (equity) amounted to $1,399,516.* The holdings of 'A' ordinary shares by foreigners are severely restricted under the Articles of Association as follows: "No 'A' ordinary share shall be issued or transferred to or held by or in trust for, or in any way under the control of a foreigner". Wherever not less than 50 per cent of the Directors have reasons to believe that any 'A' ordinary share is held in violation of the previous article, the foreign holder shall be required to transfer the same to some Nigerian national.[2] The number of shares held by or under the control of an individual whether alone or jointly with others has been restricted to 20 per cent of the voting share capital of the Bank. The limit has been fixed at 30 per cent in the case of the Central Bank of the country or an international institution of which Nigeria is a member.[3]

The NIDB was established to assist industrial, commercial and agricultural enterprises and the exploitation of natural resources in Nigeria. The various ways in which the Bank has been authorised to provide its assistance are by (1) creating, expanding and modernising such enterprises, (2) encouraging, sponsoring and facilitating participation of capital, domestic and foreign, in such enterprises, (3) creating and stimulating security markets and in particular by providing long and medium term loans and participating in their share capital, underwriting issues of shares and bonds and giving its guarantee and finally by furnishing managerial, administrative and technical advice as well as assisting in obtaining such services for Nigerian industry, agriculture, and commerce.[4]

[1] Report and Accounts of the Nigerian Industrial Development Bank for the year 1964, p. 11.
* *Report of the International Finance Corporation* 1964-65, p. 29.
[2] Memorandum and Articles of Association. Art. (*B*) & (*C*).
[3] *Ibid.*, Art. 7(*A*).
[4] Articles of Association Art. III (1) (A) (i-v) and (B) (i-v).

The scope of its activities normally includes privately owned and managed Nigerian enterprises. As in the case of the Sudanese Industrial Bank, the mere existence of a government or other public interest in an undertaking does not necessarily exclude it from the purview of the NIDB, especially when the government's interest is not predominant or is only temporary, pending its selling out to private investors. Although under the Articles of Association it has been authorised to cover agriculture and commerce, it normally restricts its operations to the industrial and mining spheres. It does not engage in commercial banking business and does not accept deposits, whether demand or time. Investments in social infra-structure projects, such as hospitals, roads and schools are outside its sphere of activity. The financing of cottage and small scale industries is also outside its purview. It is primarily interested in enterprises which by reason of their size are expected to contribute significantly to the country's economic growth. As such its interest does not lie in proprietary and partnership concerns.[1] In this respect it bears close analogy to the Indian Industrial Finance Corporation.

Apart from providing finance in various forms, the NIDB is prepared to assist its customers to obtain the necessary technical advice and services of technical know-how. It has considerably enlarged its role and has been undertaking more and more promotional work by assisting promoters in sound project preparation and analysis, by advising on appropriate financial structures, and helping clients in carrying out the feasibility studies and financial planning which have to precede actual investment. It also makes arrangements for a close watch over the projects during the construction and early gestation periods. The progress of the concerns during the crucial stages is carefully watched through periodic visits and reports. By this close follow-up the NIDB is enabled to remedy any unhealthy trends that may develop in their management and financial control and adversely affect their profitability.

The NIDB has adopted certain guiding principles for its financial participation in an enterprise and has laid down criteria regarding the economic desirability, technical feasibility and commercial viability which the projects must satisfy in order to be eligible for its participation. The NIDB will be prepared to

[1] Nigerian Industrial Development Bank Ltd., Explanatory Memorandum, p. 3 (kindly furnished by the Management of the Bank to the present writer).

extend its financial participation in a project only when it will satisfy all the conditions and present all the information required by it. Detailed information regarding the industrial and commercial experience of the promoter, the nature of the project, total cost involved with its breakdown, sources of finance, equity, preference, and loan, requirements and availability of technical and managerial personnel, and of water, electricity, fuel and transport, expected average annual prices and sales, extent of government support, if any, and in the case of existing enterprises balance sheets for the last three years have to be furnished. All this material will be carefully examined by the staff of the NIDB and a technical appraisal of some aspects of the material may be made by specialist consultants at the expense of the applicant firm. If the detailed scrutiny is found to be satisfactory at the staff level, it will be forwarded to the Board of the NIDB for approval or rejection according to its wisdom. The NIDB keeps in touch with the project and is always ready to provide its advice and assistance whenever necessary.[1]

The present policy of the NIDB is to restrict its overall financial assistance to any one enterprise between a minimum of £10,000 and a maximum of £200,000. The minimum limit may be relaxed in exceptional cases. Its investments or underwritings are not to exceed 25 per cent of the capital of the company concerned. Its overall participation in a project, i.e. share capital and loans taken together, should not exceed 50 per cent of the value of the total fixed assets after allowing for similar coverage by other secured lenders nor should it be more than £200,000. Financial assistance is flexible and may be made available in the form of direct subscriptions or underwriting of equity, preference stock or debentures, medium and long-term loan and long-term debt instruments with convertibility features or any mixture of these types of assistance.

The minimum duration of its loans is 5 years, while the maximum is normally a period of 15 years but in exceptional cases a longer amortization schedule may be arranged. Loans are not disbursed in a lump sum but are provided against evidence of expenditure actually incurred or plant and equipment installed. All loans have to be secured, the acceptable types of

[1] Explanatory Memorandum and Guide to Applicants. Issued by the NIDB. (Kindly provided to the present author by the Authorities of the Institution).

security being legal mortgages of fixed assets, floating charges in other assets, guarantees given by banks and pledges of government securities. Besides security certain other safeguards may also be asked for, such as ceilings on the rates of dividends to be declared or on the creation of additional debt. The NIDB, it may be observed, is not an ordinary provider of finance, it is a financial partner as well. In suitable cases it undertakes to arrange for additional finance from other sources. A study of the operations of the NIDB during the last two financial years, 1964-1965 shows the wide coverage of its activities. The enterprises to which it has extended its assistance in various forms comprise diverse lines of industry such as textiles, food, sugar, chemical and metal products, wood, rubber, shoes, engineering, plywood, paints and varnishes etc. It has also kept itself closely associated with the Lagos Stock Exchange which is housed in its own premises, and has taken a significant part in the development of the capital market.

On December 31, 1964 the NIDB held equity investments in 9 companies of a total value of £367,500. Holdings of convertible debentures amounted to £84,600. Other debentures and loans to 7 companies totalled £322,026.[1] During 1965 the NIDB sanctioned a total of £1,172,000 in loans and debentures and £155,050 in equity investments to 19 companies. The total fixed capital involved in these projects amounted to £6.6 million. It is clear NIDB has been responsible for bringing this much of new investment in private industry started in Nigeria during the period. There has been a remarkable increase in the volume of applications for the financial assistance of the NIDB. The business of the Bank has been growing at such a rate that the funds available at present are likely to be fully used up very soon. Steps have already been taken to increase its resources. The World Bank has been approached for a loan in foreign currencies equivalent to U.S. $6 million. The Federal Military Government has also granted a loan in Nigerian currency amounting to £2 million at a concessional rate of interest.

The following table shows total sanctions since the incorporation of the NIDB.[2]

[1] Annual Report of the NIDB for 1964, p. 12.
[2] Annual Report of the NIDB for 1965. Schedule 3, p. 17.

TABLE No. 34

			£	
Total sanction of the NIDB.	Loans and Debentures	=	2,301,214	
	Equity	=	439,050	
				2,740,264
Total sanction of the ICON.	Loans and Debentures	=	504000	
	Equity	=	217550	
				721,550
				3,461,814

LA SOCIETE TUNISIENNE DE BANQUE (STB OF TUNISIA)

The objectives of the STB, as outlined in its statutes, are as follows: [1]

(1) To receive deposits of current or term types from all persons (physical or legal), public, semi-public or private.

(2) To enter into the business of discounting and collecting commercial bills, the negotiation and the rediscount of all assets, making advances on bonds, on goods and all other (acceptable) guarantees; extending credits with or without hypothecation of securities, financing of the money and the stock market and more generally, all the operations of bank-credit capable of facilitating the normal exercise of the activities of its customers.

The advances shall not be made for periods longer than one year and discounting shall not be undertaken of assets with maturities longer than 9 months.

The total amount of credit extended to a single client, be it credit extended on discountable assets or direct credit, is fixed by the decision of the Committee for Discounts and by the initiative of the Director-General.

(3) The Bank can also extend credit for medium or long term but only against obtainable funds equally middle or long term, such as, deposits, ordinary loans or obligatory (first-call) loans or all other special resources.

(4) As an exceptional case, always in conformity with its resources and with the express agreement of the Secretary of State for Finance, the Bank may participate in commercial, industrial or financial enterprises whose objective presents the characteristics of the general interest, and more particularly in investment societies or development

[1] Art. 3 *Object. Statuts. Societe Tunisienne de Banque 1957-1964.*

societies created for promoting the objectives of the plans for the development and industrialisation of the country.

As already observed, the Tunisian STB is a commercial-cum-development bank. As a commercial bank, taking deposits and making short-term loans, it has moved into all fields of commercial and industrial activity. Aid on a short-term basis is the fundamental objective of the Bank in this connection. As a development bank, it operates as a medium and long-term lending institution and participates in business concerns of unquestionable national interest through purchase of shares and stocks. As such, it takes a more dynamic view of its mission and directs its activities towards the creation of new "riches" through industrialization of Tunisia. With its own resources supplemented by Government and U.S. ICA grants, it has been able to promote the financing of 52 enterprises within a very short time engaged in a wide variety of industries such as leather, sugar, transportation, textiles, fishing, hotels and public works. In this respect the Bank's policy is to expand the development of small and medium size business which according to its authorities should form a basis of industrialization of the country.[1]

By 1961 the STB had confirmed its role as the leading bank of Tunisia. Within a year in December 1959 the amount of its deposits was double of what it was in December 1958 and 25 per cent of all bank deposits. On December 31, 1961 sight deposits at the STB had come to total 38.2 per cent of such deposits in all banks as against 34.8 per cent on December 31, 1960. This increase in deposits coupled with enlarged rediscountable credits enabled the Bank to increase its commitments by 32 per cent corresponding to 40 per cent of the total funds allocated to the economy in the same year. These credits were employed in the various sectors of the economy including financing of the olive oil campaign and building of a storage unit for olive oil of a very modern design. Of these medium-term credits for financing capital goods and construction goods rose by 45 per cent. Industrial and commercial construction loans were facilitated by the extension of a Government guarantee. The activity of the Bank in foreign trade was quite important, amounting to 26.8 per cent of total foreign exchange transactions in the form of remittances,

[1] Report of the Board of Directors, *Societe Tunisienne De Banque* for the fiscal year 1959, pp. 6-9. Also *Report* for the year 1960, pp. 5-7.

documentary credits and transfers.[1] The recently created Security Department also registered expansion. The Department administers the insurance companies portfolio and securities of a number of companies, such as the debentures of the National Loan of the Republic of Niger, the Réseaux Electricité et Transports etc. The Bank has contributed to the economic development of the country, conducting various feasibility studies and investing in new ventures. A chemical complex, a ceramics complex and a project for manufacturing 25 items of industrial and domestic hardware were the result of these studies. Among the new investments of the Bank, the following may be particularly mentioned —Societe Tunisienne D' Industrie Automobile (a truck assembly plant), Societe Commerciale Tunisienne et Societe D' Acconage et de Manutention (for handling operations in Tunisian harbours), Societe Tunisienne Immobiliere (for construction of an international type hotel in the centre of Tunisia), Societé Nationale D'Investissements (participating in industrial ventures, conducting studies of industrial projects and engaged in Tunisification of important existing concerns). A remarkable assistance provided by the STB was its participation to the extent of 10 per cent in the capital of the Development Bank of the Republic of Niger. This was in response to the government of Niger's request to help in the creation of a National Bank similar to the STB.[2]

Since its creation in 1958 down to 1964 the STB has been playing a more and more dynamic part in the economic development of Tunisia. The object of the first 3-year Plan and particularly of the next 4-year Plan is to quicken the pace of the country's industrial expansion. The STB has been acting as a development bank in this context effectively. There has hardly been any project which has not been established without its efficient and untiring assistance. The STB can, therefore, be considered as the most efficient tool of the Government's planning policy.[3] According to the estimate of the Central Bank, the STB is ahead of all banks in Tunisia with regard to the volume of its own funds, the total of its deposits and the credits granted.[4]

Between 31 December 1962 and 31 December 1964 sight

[1] Report of the Board of Directors, STB for the fiscal year 1961 pp. 10-12.
[2] Report of the Board of Directors, *Societe Tunisienne De Banque* for the fiscal year 1961. pp. 14-15.
[3] Report of the Board of Directors of the STB for the fiscal year 1963, p. 29.
[4] *Quarterly Review No. 20, Central Bank of Tunisia.*

deposits which had been declining registered an increase and represented 33.2 per cent of the banking sector's deposits as compared with 28.7 per cent at the end of 1963. The total amount of its commitments rose at the end of December 1964 so as to constitute 46.5 per cent as against 42.7 per cent of the credits granted to the economy by the banking system in 1963. Since its creation its medium and long-term loans have been growing in importance. At the end of December 1964 they increased by 40.8 per cent over December 31, 1963, representing all economic sectors of which the Bank's assistance to the tourist industry has been remarkable. Besides construction loans and bank guarantees in the framework of its activity as a development bank, it has participated with the approval of the Secretary of State for Planning and Finance in the capital of a number of new companies in all economic sectors, which totalled 36 on December 31, 1964. Aggregate investments rose from D 683,983.833 on December 31, 1962 and D 861,130.468 on December 31, 1963 to D 1,043,469.264 at the end of December 1964. The following may be particularly mentioned: the Tunisian Sugar Company, the Tunisian Automobile Industry, the Tunisian Cellulose Company, a real estate management company, a cork company, a printing concern and a phosphoric acid manufacturing company, and three integrated plants viz. the Skanes Furniture Plant, the Djemmal Brick Plant and the Sahel Mechanical Plant. Its other banking activities have included as before provision of documentary credits, currency exchange for facilitating tourist operations, purchase and sale of securities through the Security Department etc.[1] Medium and long-term loans of the STB have experienced a remarkable growth and increased from D 4,310,464 on December 31, 1961 to D 9,986,251 on December 31, 1964. The growth

Year	*Amount*
1961	4,310,464
1962	7,916,939
1963	8,714,685
1964	9,986,251

[1] See Reports of the STB for the fiscal years 1963, pp. 9-15, pp. 24-28 and for the fiscal year 1964, p. 1, pp. 26-31.

of such credits (cumulative) during the period 1961-1964 is brought out in the table on the previous page.[1]

THE NATIONAL INVESTMENT BANK OF GHANA

As far back as November 1947 an Industrial Development Corporation had been established in the Gold Coast by an ordinance with the object of financing new industries and industrial undertakings, laboratories for investigating commercial possibilities of products and schemes for the modernisation, expansion and better organisation of existing industrial undertakings. The entire capital of £350,000 was provided by the Government. The working of the corporation was severely criticised by traders and industrialists in their memorandum to Sir Cecil Trevor. Sir Trevor, however, found that most of the criticisms were unwarranted. Most of the complaints came from intending borrowers who had no idea of the basic functions of these corporations or had no experience of the industry they were desirous of starting or were reluctant to supply all the necessary information called for in the corporation's questionnaire. The centralisation of the corporation's activities too much at Accra, its headquarters, which was another charge against it, was according to Sir Trevor inevitable because of the acute shortage of staff which stood in the way of opening up branches at all principal centres. But Sir Trevor found that there was no special provision to meet the requirements of small artisans and craftsmen. The Industrial Development Corporation was providing finance for comparatively larger concerns. He recommended that a subsidiary Industrial Finance Corporation should be started to cater specially for the financial needs of this class of small entrepreneurs.[2]

A National Investment Bank was established by an Act of 1963 in Ghana after independence which has to be sharply distinguished from the Sudanese Bank with respect to its scope and coverage. Its activities are not restricted to the field of industry alone but are intended to extend to the sphere of agricultural, commercial and other enterprises. Nor is its interest confined to the private sector only: it may operate in all sectors of the national economy, including the public, the private and the co-

[1] Report of the STB for the fiscal year 1964 (June 25 1965), p. 28.
[2] See Report by Sir Cecil Trevor paras 112, 113 & 143.

operative sectors. The objects of the Bank are by and large the same as in other similar institutions: to assist in the establishment, expansion and modernisation of such enterprises; to stimulate and facilitate the participation of domestic and foreign capital in such enterprises; counsel and encourage small Ghanaian business concerns; and finally to bring together internal and external capital, investment opportunities and experienced management.[1] For the purpose of its operations in the public sector, the Bank may receive on special deposits money allocated by the National Assembly for development purposes and the proceeds of any loan, external or internal, specified for public sector enterprises. For purposes of operations in the private and the co-operative sector it may use its general funds, funds borrowed generally on the Bank's own account from internal and external sources, and any funds allocated by the Government for employment in such sectors.[2] As in the case of the Sudanese Industrial Development Bank, the Ghanaian Institution has to conduct its affairs in accordance with sound business, financial and investment standards. The funds at its disposal have to be employed with due regard being paid to the principle of diversification of risks. As such it is precluded from investing more than 10 per cent of its paid up share capital in the ordinary or preference shares of enterprises financed by it: It is further prohibited from investing a part of its borrowed funds in such shares; and from making loans or giving guarantees for more than £G 5,000 nor except in the case of public sector enterprises, for more than £G 100,000 in any one enterprise or group of enterprises controlled by a single interest. It is further provided that the Bank should not normally finance more than 75 per cent of the total cost of any project.[3]

An interesting feature of the Bank's business is the authority given to it to make long and medium-term loans without security. This allows ample discretion to the Bank in the matter of its lending policy and resembles very closely similar powers granted to the Industrial Development Bank of India set up later. All other powers usually provided to such institutions have been written down into its charter. Thus it may purchase or subscribe

[1] *The National Investment Bank of Ghana Act 1963* Sec. 3 (1) and (2).
[2] Sec. 3 (3) and (8). *The National Investment Bank of Ghana Act 1963.*
[3] Bye Laws of the National Investment Bank, Ghana 1963. Secs 3-5.

for shares and other securities; underwrite new issues of stocks, bonds and debentures; transact all kinds of guarantee business; draw, issue and endorse and rediscount bills of exchange and promissory notes for the purposes of its business; issue medium and long-term bonds, and finally furnish technical, managerial and administrative advice to industrial, agricultural and commercial enterprises.[1]

The share capital of the Ghanaian Investment Bank had been fixed at 10 million pounds divided into one pound shares of which 75 per cent was to be taken up by the government and the remaining 25 per cent was to be issued to the public at such times and in such amounts as might be determined by the Board of Directors. On the establishment of the Bank the Minister of Finance was to have paid up $33\frac{1}{3}$ per cent of the nominal value of the shares taken up by the government, the balance of $66\frac{2}{3}$ per cent remaining uncalled for one year. The Bank commenced its operations on 15th June 1963. According to the balance sheet of the Bank, December, 1965 out of ₵ 24,000,000 worth shares of ₵ 2.40 each (1 cedi = 8*s* 4*d* of the old Ghanaian Currency) shares worth ₵ 7,800,000 were issued. The present position is that the Investment Bank is jointly owned by the government and private investors including some reputable overseas financial institutions.

The policy of the Bank ever since it commenced its operations has been cautious and conservative. The Board has followed this guarded policy with a view not to subjecting the Bank to undue risks and in the belief that in that way a sound foundation could be built up to enable the Bank to embark upon its future operations in the various sectors of the economy. The loan commitments by the Bank during the period since its inception down to December 1965 have amounted to ₵ 4,796,042.29 (after deducting repayments) for 26 projects in the different sectors of the economy. Among various industrial and agricultural projects, the Bank has financed commercial printing, ceramic products manufacture, facility for curing heavy leaf tobacco, a fleet of commercial buses for long distance passenger transportation, tobacco cultivation, poultry farming and beef cattle production.

[1] See Sec. 4 *The National Investment Bank of Ghana Act 1963.*
The total amount of moneys borrowed and owing or outstanding shall not exceed at any time the total of paid up capital.

During 1965 loans granted to the public sector less repayments amounted to ₵ 4,418,088.85 (of which ₵ 1,274,759.62 remained to be disbursed) and those to the private sector including co-operatives less repayments to ₵ 377,953.44 (of which ₵ 50,085.66 remained unutilised). The total balance of guarantee liabilities at the end of 1965 was ₵ 12.6 million as against ₵ 13.9 million a year before.[1]

A distinguishing feature of the Ghanaian Development Bank is the Development Service Institute built into its organisation. It is the technical wing of the Bank and has continued to play a crucial role in the operations. All investments by the Bank are made only when the Service Institute has fully investigated and favourably reported upon the technical, economic and market feasibility of the projects as well as the managerial competency of the borrowers and entrepreneurs. Loan analysis, feasibility studies, planning of the distribution and marketing of the products of the assisted enterprises and rendering consulting services to the clients of the Bank constitute the main tasks of the Institute. It is a pity that what Ghana could do at the very commencement of the working of its development bank, the Industrial Finance Corporation of India, although set up as far back as 1948, has not been able to organise even the semblance of such a technical department all these years in spite of the present writer's persistent efforts to draw the attention of the Board and the Government to this lacuna.[2]

The Bank has drawn up a well-conceived programme of projects to be implemented during 1966 which are so designed as to produce a significant impact on the national economy. These include a wide range of agricultural, commercial and industrial projects as well as a number of services, such as caustic soda and chlorine production, dry cell batteries, ceramics, building hardware, electrical equipment and household appliances; distribution and marketing of foodstuffs; sugar-cane, oil, palm and pineapple production; low cost housing for industrial workers and vegetable cultivation under irrigation. Feasibility studies of a number of projects will also be undertaken such as production of fish nets, hurricane lanterns, asbestos cement, shoe laces, candy, surgical

[1] Report of the Director, National Investment Bank for the year ending 31 December 1965, pp. 12-13. Also Balance Sheet of the Bank for 1965.

[2] See *Industrial Finance in India,* (Fourth Ed.) by the present writer.

cotton, garments, plastic goods, mirrors and buttons. The new economic policy of the National Liberation Council which took over on 14th February 1966 would, according to the authorities of the Bank, be sure to create a favourable climate for foreign investment in the private sectors. With the determined efforts that are being made to revitalise the entire economy, the Bank is expected to play the catalystic role of a true development financing institution. It is interesting to note that Lt. Gen. J. A. Ankrah, the Chairman of the National Liberation Council, was a director of the Bank before his elevation to the high office of State.[1]

The National Investment Bank of Ghana received up to the present year (1966) 740 applications involving an amount of ₵ 71,785,294.00 or £29,910,539. Of these 590 applications or 53.4 per cent for the amount of ₵ 37,307,386.00 or £15,691,410 had to be rejected, the reasons for rejection being as follows:

For 44 or 7.46 per cent of the rejectees amounting to £3,302,753 or 10.19 per cent because the projects did not fall within the purview of the Bank's activities; for 49 or 8.31 per cent amounting to £7,836,633 or 20.46 per cent because the projects were not considered to be of high priority; for 33 or 5.59 per cent amounting to £1,930,520 or 5.04 per cent because the applicants did not have adequate securities for the loans; and for the largest number 464 or 78.64 per cent amounting to £2,291,504 or 14.35 per cent because the maximum financial requirement in each case was very much below the minimum loan limit. Twenty-five loans amounting to a total of £1,606,641 have been approved.

So far the loanee firms are doing quite well. The Bank has still under active consideration as many as 85 applications amounting to £12,342,486; the remaining 40 loans being suspended because the applicants have failed to provide any estimate of the total financial requirements of their various projects.[2]

THE NATIONAL BANK FOR ECONOMIC DEVELOPMENT OF MOROCCO (BNDE)

Morocco's development bank under the above name (Banque Nationale Pour Le Developpement Economique) was established

[1] Report of the Board of Directors, National Investment Bank 31 December 1965. pp. 12-14.

[2] Source: Letter to the writer dated 28 November 1966 from the Secretary of the National Investment Bank of Ghana.

in 1959 with the objective of assisting Morocco's economic development.* For that purpose it can among other things:

(1) consent to provide long-term loans of at least two years' duration;
(2) discount or hold all representative bills of medium-term credit;
(3) give all kinds of guarantees particularly by means of endorsement and development of all types of companies or enterprises;
(4) manage all funds, public or private;
(5) assist in whatever form it may be, the state and all other institutions under the authority of the state which are engaged in the study and implementation of plans and programmes for economic development.

To realise these objectives the BNDE, as it is known, can adopt any method that appears appropriate. In particular, it can issue all types of bonds, conclude loans, accept all types of advances and subventions from the state. But it has been prohibited from receiving deposits from the public. In a general way it has been empowered to participate in all operations in securities or in real assets necessary to facilitate directly or indirectly the realisation of the activities mentioned above.[1]

The capital of the BNDE has been fixed at 30 million dirhams, divided into 600,000 shares of 50 dirhams each of which 400,000 shares represent the original capital and 200,000 shares represent the increase in capital as decided by Extraordinary General Assembly on 15th December 1962.[2] The Administration Council has been authorised to issue, without going to the General Assembly of shareholders, bonds and debentures, the total value of which must not exceed ten times the paid up capital of the company. The issue of bonds beyond this limit requires the previous sanction of the General Assembly.[3]

The BNDE is administered by a Council consisting of 8 to 20 members from among the shareholders and nominated by the

* *La Societe a pour objet de concourir au developpement eonomique du Maroc.*

[1] Statuts, Banque Nationale pour le Developpement Economique (Edition tenant compt des resolutions de l'Assemblee Generale Extraordinaire du 15 Decembre, 1962.)

[2] Art. 7 Statuts.

[3] Art. 20 Statuts.

General Assembly. The Administrators who have a tenure of 6 years must hold a minimum of 20 shares. The Council nominates from among its members a President and several Vice-Presidents as it thinks fit.[1]

On the establishment of the Bank, 50 per cent of the share capital (then fixed at 20 million dirhams of which 15 million dirhams was paid up) was taken up by the Government and public corporations, and the balance was subscribed by Moroccan banks and foreign banks in equal proportions. From the statutes quoted above other sources of finance are found to be long-term loans floated in the market, rediscounting of medium-term credits granted at the Central Bank of Morocco, and credits from the Government. In 1962 the World Bank and the IFC (Washington) provided financial assistance, the former in the shape of a U.S. dollar loan of $15 million in foreign exchange, and the latter in the form of an investment of 7.5 million dirhams (US $1.5 million) in the share capital of the BNDE amounting to three-quarters of a new issue.

Although it has statutory power to assist broadly in the economic development of the country, in practice it has confined its activity mainly to industrial and commercial enterprises in the private sector. Its loans may not be for a shorter period of two years but there is no reference to the maximum duration of the loans. In actual practice it has provided long-term loans to private enterprises for a term of 15 years and medium-term loans for a duration of 5 years. Its loans are generally intended to finance fixed capital expenditure rather than working capital requirements. Its loans to a single project are not generally below the amount of 50,000 dirhams.

As in the case of other development banks it has special departments to undertake feasibility projects and to keep a close watch over the end-uses of its loans.

Since its inception up to 1965 the BNDE has provided assistance to 317 operations for an amount of 443.6 million dirhams. Operations agreed upon in 1965 has increased substantially in number and amount, and accounted for 22 per cent of the total at the end of 1964. The table below indicates the progress of its operations classified under different types of credit and participations.

[1] Arts 21-25. Statuts.

TABLE[1] No. 35

(In millions of Dirhams)

	As on 31st Dec. 1964		New operations engaged in 1965	
Operations in force on 31.12.65	*Amount*	*No.*	*Amount*	*No.*
Long-term direct Credit	84.179	51	36.89	16
Medium-term direct Credit	9.340	17	2.95	9
Medium-term re-discountable	83.123	149	18.38	11
Industrial participation	4.183	10	5.01	1
Non-Industrial participation	2.164	5	0.36	2
Operations for the State	1.35	2	—	—
Total	185.819	243	63.610	45

The progress of long-term credit is particularly remarkable. An increase in underwriting participation both industrial and non-industrial is also to be observed. The former rose from 1.450 thousand DH in 1962 to 9.198 thousand DH in 1965, and the latter increased from 1.572 thousand DH in 1962 to 2.522 thousand DH in 1965. As regards the latter, at the end of 1965 the Bank participated in 3 principal institutions and 2 tourist Companies The medium-term rediscountable credit has however continued to decline. The portfolio of such credit which had executed 145 millions DH in 1961 stood at 54.4 million DH in 1965. The table below illustrates the progressive decline of this category of credit.[2]

(In millions of DH)

1960	1961	1962	1963	1964	1965
78	145	142	119	83	54

As a result of two important medium-term rediscount credits (furnished to O.N.E. and S.U.T.A.) amounting to 35 million DH, the share of direct credit was slightly reduced in 1965 as compared with the previous years. If these two credits are excluded, the tendency remains the same as in the past. Thus the number and amount of direct loans and participations constituted respectively 61 per cent and 73 per cent of the total of

[1] Rapport Annuel Excercice 1965 *Banque Nationale pour le Developpement Economique*—p. 84.
[2] *Ibid* p. 85.

operations. Excluding again the two loans to O.N.E. and S.U.T.A. the average size of the Bank's operations in 1965 did not exceed 0.62 million DH. The B N D E appears to have been mainly interested in assisting enterprises of medium-size which are particularly suited to the economy of Morocco. 75 per cent of the loans granted in 1965 were for less than 1 million DH; their total amount, however, accounted for only 18 per cent of the grand total.

As regards the duration of the credits provided, periods of less than 5 years accounted for 63 per cent and of more than 5 years accounted for 35 per cent of the total in 1965. Capital participation at the end of the year amounted to 2.14 per cent of the operations. If one considers the fact that medium-term rediscounting operations accounted for 54 per cent of the medium-term loans, it may be observed that most of the direct loans of the Bank have been granted for a period exceeding 5 years. Since its origin 255 operations involving an amount of 318 million DH have been agreed upon for a period of 5 to 8 years. These represented 71.6 per cent of the total amount. Only 29 operations amounting to 25 million DH were for shorter periods and were engaged in the earlier stages of the Bank's working. Operations for a longer period numbered 28 amounting to 92 million DH representing 20.8 per cent of the total. Participations numbering 15 amounted to 9.5 million DH.[1]

As regards the nature of the borrower, whether public or private sector, the ratio of $\frac{1}{4} : \frac{3}{4}$ between the two sectors that could be observed in the earlier years is found to be completely changed and even reversed in 1965. The operations in the public sector became more important in the year. Although there were only 7 undertakings, their receipts amounted to 58.3 million DH out of a total of 80.7 million DH. The table given below brings out the recent trends in this respect:

TABLE[2] No. 36

Percentage of assistance	*1959-60*	*1961*	*1962*	*1963*	*1964*	*1965*	*Cumulative Average*
Public	26.5	17.6	26.9	23.9	24.5	71.5	29.3
Private	73.5	82.4	73.1	76.1	75.5	28.5	70.8

[1] *Rapport Annuel* BNDE 1965 p. 91.
[2] *Rapport Annuel* BNDE 1965 p. 92.

The situation in 1965 is a complete break with the past trends and is probably an exception.

Classifying the operations according to the source of capital of the borrowing concerns, it is found that in 1965 domestic investors benefited to the extent of 67.1 million DH for 26 agreements, while enterprises with major part of capital from foreign sources accounted for 13.6 million DH for 18 agreements. Since the origin of the Bank the former category of enterprises received 264.5 million DH or 60 per cent of the total and the latter 179.1 million or 40 per cent. From the following table showing sector-wise distribution of the Bank's credit, it will be observed that it has covered a wide variety of industrial undertakings including mines, petroleum, textiles, mechanical, chemical, food, agriculture and transport. By far the greater proportion of the credits has gone in favour of mining with 22.95 per cent of the total, followed by food products and petroleum with 14.40 per cent and 14 per cent respectively.

TABLE[1] No. 37

(*In millions of DH.*)

	1965		*Total*		*per cent*
	No.	*Amount*	*No.*	*Amount*	
Energy:—					
Mines	1	15.000	15	100.694	22.95
Petroleum and its derivatives			7	61.450	14
Textiles	13	6.175	83	49.160	11
Food products	7	43.850	55	65.263	14·40
Mechanical	6	2.545	34	45.690	10.25
Chemical	3	3.250	30	32.067	8
Agriculture	2	1.850	15	4.425	1
Transport	2	1.740	16	36.790	8.25
Others	10	6.175	62	42.042	10.15
	47	80.685	317	443.584	100

The record of the B N D E has been quite impressive. It has sustained both public and private sector enterprises. It has brought together within the purview of its assistance concerns with domestic as well as foreign sources of capital. It has assiduously pursued its industrial objectives and has shown consider-

[1] *Rapport Annuel* 1965 p. 94.

able initiative in fostering tourism. It has doubled the level of its participations which bears testimony to its dynamism and creative faculty in fields where risks must be undertaken in the interest of the economy as a whole.

IDO AND IREB OF LIBYA

A public institution known as the Industrial Development Organisation was established in Libya by Law No. 2 of 1963 with the objective of developing Libyan industries in both private and public sectors by (1) creating or assisting in new industries, (2) expanding development of existing industries, (3) providing technical and financial assistance to industrial establishments, (4) keeping by various means the marketing of industrial products and finally (5) encouraging and facilitating the investment of private capital in the country's industries in conformity with the industrial and development policy of the State. For the achievement of these objectives the methods made available to the organisation consisted of granting short, medium and long-term loans to industrial establishments, guaranteeing of loans contracted by or of bonds issued by them, participating with others in the creation of joint stock companies for the exploitation of industrial projects up to 25 per cent of the capital and constructing, hiring and managing immovable properties. In the case of small industries, that is, industries whose fixed capital did not exceed more than £35,000, and the number of workers was not over 50 where the power was over 15 h.p. and 100 if power was 15 h.p. or less, the proportion of loans granted should not be less than 60 per cent of the whole amount provided for the purpose of loans; the rate of interest on such loans was not to exceed 4 per cent while the rate of interest on other loans should not be less than the rediscount rate plus 1½ per cent. The organisation was authorised to have its own representatives on the board of directors of industrial companies whose shares were taken up by it. It was not intended that the organisation should permanently retain the ownership of industrial units which it helped to set up or hold shares in private undertakings. These were to be transferred subsequently to the private sector.

The resources of I D O were to consist of funds allocated by the Government and subsidies, profits and interests accrued out of investments made by the organisation, loans contracted by it with the Government, banks and institutions whether local, foreign or international and bonds issued by it in Libya and abroad. In 1963 £L 700,000 was allocated to it under the budget. The Five Year Plan provided £L 5 million for this institution. The main recipients of credit from the I D O were the following industries, viz. tiles and building blocks, metal rods for building, textiles and garments, batteries, fisheries and handicrafts.

It is clear from the above analysis of the statutory functions of the I D O that it was formed on the same lines as and with the same objectives as those of most of the development banks in the underdeveloped countries. An important departure from the usual functions of development institutions, however, is to be observed in the authorisation of the Libyan I D O to provide short-term finance in addition to medium and long-term.

During the financial year 1965-66 the Law No. 2 of 1963 establishing the I D O was repealed and a new institution called the Libyan Industrial and Real Estate Bank was established in its place by a Royal Decree of October 1965 with a capital of £L. 10 million to be paid in full by the Government. To obtain further resources it was empowered to contract loans with the Government, ordinary banks and the Bank of Libya which under the decree has been permitted to grant loans to the Bank and to issue bonds and debentures. The total amount of such loans and bonds, however, should not exceed thrice the value of the Bank's capital. The object of the new Bank was to finance not only the development of national industry but also to encourage building construction and carry out banking transactions connected thereto. The scope of its activities has been defined as that of (1) granting industrial and non-farm real estate loans against guarantees, (2) guaranteeing loans contracted and bonds issued by industrial and real estate concerns, (3) issuing shares and bonds in favour of industrial and real estate concerns, (4) participating in their creation, (5) subscribing directly to the shares and bonds issued by small undertakings, (6) financing the marketing of national industrial products and (7) discounting or rediscounting financial and commercial stocks having connection with industries. It is interesting to observe that the Bank's coverage of activities includes not only private projects but also Government projects relating to industry and building.

The Bank is prohibited from accepting deposits either on

current account or on term except from clients who are dealing in industrial projects or building activities. Nor can the bank grant credit facilities to other than the above. (Art. 7)

The administration of the Bank has been vested in a Board of Directors under the Chairmanship of the Director General. The members of the Directorate are the Directors of (1) the Industrial and (2) Real Estate Departments and one representative each of the Ministries of Industry, Finance, Planning, Ministry of National Economy and of the Bank of Libya. The members, however should hold high technical qualifications or be particularly conversant in the fields of economy, industry, building and banking. The decisions of the Board of Directors shall not be operative before being sanctioned by the Council of Ministers. When these decisions relate to financing of governmental projects and involve an amount exceeding £L. 20,000, they will be operative only after sanction by the Minister of Industry. The Director General will be nominated by the Minister and will be appointed by a Royal Decree. The Minister may also convene a meeting of the Board and preside over such a meeting.

In the prevailing circumstances in Libya the combination of industrial and mortgage banking in the new Institution may have been justified. But it will be desirable to segregate the industrial and mortgage functions of the Bank at a later date by establishing a true industrial development bank as in other underdeveloped countries.

DEVELOPMENT INSTITUTIONS IN RHODESIA AND NYASALAND

The Federation of Rhodesia and Nyasaland, as noted earlier, possesses a variety of financial intermediaries and a diversified structure of financial instruments, as are to be witnessed in more mature industrial economies. Apart from the Post Office Savings Bank with its savings certificates we find acceptance houses and merchant bankers on British lines, hire purchase companies and building societies. During the period 1954-64 the total balance outstanding on hire purchase agreements and other instalment sales registered a continuous rise till 1960 when the peak figure of £10.1 million was reached. In 1958 specific measures to restrict hire purchase finance had to be adopted. The reduced demand for consumer durables owing to various factors and the increase in the rate of payments served thereafter to check the growth and even to bring about a decline. It is interesting to note that the instalment finance facilities available under hire purchase were not only used by individuals for purchasing consumer durables, a larger proportion of which were imported, but also by industry and the agricultural sector for the purchase of capital equipment. Development institutions have significantly assisted in the economic development of the Federation. Besides the Industrial Promotion Corporation of the Federation, development corporations were found to be working in Northern and Southern Rhodesia.

On the dissolution of the Federation legislations relating to the financial institutions were revised so that they could operate in all the three territories of Rhodesia, Zambia and Malawi. In all these territories again, the problems of financing industrial development have received considerable attention. In Malawi and Rhodesia industrial development corporations were formed in 1964. In Zambia the capital of the Industrial Development Corporation was reconstructed and was again altered in 1964, when the Government took up the private shareholdings. All these development corporations provide long-term capital and managerial and technical device. Supplementing the work of these territorial Government-sponsored corporations there is the Industrial Promotion Corporation of Rhodesia and Nyasaland. It is a private company which had formerly confined its attention to industrial projects only but has now expanded the scope of its activities. It has recently undertaken to finance the promotion of a Coffee Planting Scheme in Rhodesia and an industrial estate in Zambia.[1]

ILLUSION OF A CAPITAL SHORTAGE IN UNDERDEVELOPED COUNTRIES

The raison d'etre for the establishment of development finance institutions in the underdeveloped countries lies principally in their capital shortage. Inadequacy of investment capital has been almost universally regarded as one of the most pressing needs of underdeveloped countries and to constitute one of the most

[1] *Annual Report of the Bank of Rhodesia and Nyasaland 1964*, pp. 8-10.

fundamental obstacles in the way of their economic growth. Development banks have been sponsored by the state and the central bank in these countries to provide this scarce capital along with technical advice and enterprise. A recent commentator, however, has challenged the prevailing view that capital shortage offers the most effective impediment to indigenous private investment. He has advanced in its place his own thesis that what really exists is not a current shortage of capital at all, but a shortage of "viable" projects. The chief source of evidence to support his thesis is the loan experience of Nigeria's Federal Loans Board during the period 1956-62. From a scrutiny of the applications for financial assistance to the FLB up to August 1961, he finds that 79 per cent were rejected on the basis of viability and only 2 per cent were approved. Again, among those which stood the viability test, security could be accepted in 89 per cent cases only. The percentage of figures of viability and security rejectees clearly indicates, according to him, that there was only a false demand or desire for capital and no effective demand for it. Taking both the types of rejectees it is found that only 11 per cent of the capital demand was genuine and 89 per cent was false. There may thus be ample reason to believe, he argues, that there exists actually a shortage of viable projects in Nigeria. The conclusion is supported, first, by the fact that the amount loaned by the FLB was quite small in spite of its assiduous search for viable projects, and secondly, by the poor record of the loanee concerns, 39 per cent of which proved unsuccessful and 25 per cent of which were "shaky". Most of them had to be taken to court as loan defaulters. The disappointing "scorecard of success and failure" of a selected group of indigenous enterprises, which had been well established, had been carefully appraised and had, moreover, been recipients of special Government aid prompts Mr. S. P. Schatz to conclude that capital shortage is a myth. "It is not viable projects vainly running after capital but it is capital which is vainly seeking viable projects".[1]

It is difficult to agree with the naive contention of the commentator, particularly with his suggestion that it is true not only of Nigeria but "of many other of the more economically underdeveloped countries as well". The hard core of the functions of

[1] Art. by S. P. Schatz entitled "Capital Shortage Illusion: Government Lending in Nigeria" in the *Oxford Economic Papers*, July 1965, pp. 369-316.

development banks all over the underdeveloped world is provision of finance in various forms. Along with financial assistance, they usually provide technical guidance and managerial advice. Development banks in all the countries in which they are operating have fulfilled a valuable role in coping with the problem of inadequacy of industrial capital. In the earlier stages of their operations, their objectives and scope are not clearly known to the potential customers nor are the methods of financing well understood nor again are they well adapted to the needs of the industrial community. A large number of applications at such stages is apt to flow into them which have not been properly processed; or the technical and economic feasibilities of the projects under them have not been carefully assessed; or which may be outside the scope of the Banks' activities; or again very low in the national priority list. In such circumstances the percentage of "rejectees" on the ground of economic and technical viability as well as on other grounds may be quite large. It is only when the institutions have been able to make their objectives fully known and financing methods well developed, that the right type of projects will be presented before them. The business community themselves gradually realise that new projects must be planned with care and responsibility and maximum human effort must be applied to their execution and operations. It should also be borne in mind that shortage of imported raw material and equipment for which there may be strict import licensing may be responsible for the slow progress of some of the loanee concerns. Rising capital costs in an inflation-oriented developing economy and frequent increases in import duties on capital goods have posed additional problems for industries in the emerging economies, involving recalculation of estimates, delay in installing of equipment and creation of factories. It is quite natural that in such economies industrial concerns would be likely to be exposed to serious hazards. The Ghanaian Investment Bank reports that several enterprises in the private sector had to be temporarily shut down owing to shortage of imported raw materials and spare parts as a result of foreign exchange scarcity, but at the same time some assisted firms are doing well.[1]

[1] Annual Report of the National Investment Bank of Ghana, p. 14.

In many cases it is the policy and the financial methods adopted by the institutions themselves which are responsible for the rejection of the applications. For instance, what is wanted by the applicant enterprises may not be loan finance but equity capital. The particular institution may not have been authorised to provide this kind of capital. Again, it is well known that industrial enterprises in underdeveloped countries, particularly small scale industries, can hardly offer any tangible security movable or immovable or even if such security is offered, its appraised value is inadequate for the required statutory margin. In such cases the rejections on the ground of unacceptable security may be numerous. Development banks in many countries have, therefore, been authorised to make loans and advances "with" or "without" security. The IDB of Burma, the Indian ICIC and the Pakistani ICIC furnish interesting instances of authorisation to "lend money with or without security". In the case of the recently established IDB of India the nature and type of security that may be accepted by the Bank against its loans has not been prescribed in the statute. The Bank has been allowed fullest discretion in the matter. Indeed, too much importance should not be placed by a development bank upon the security to be accepted or upon the appraised value of the security. What is of greater significance is the prospect of profitability of the applicant concern and reasonable ability to meet payments for instalments of principal and interest out of the income earned. The charge that most of the projects that are financed by development banks are "shaky" and show a very poor record of working, and are defaulters is much too sweeping. It may have been the experience of one particular institution in a particular country and during a particular period. From this it would be a hasty and misleading generalization that such is also the case with development banks in most underdeveloped countries. In India the record of the IFC shows that the percentages of rejectees and defaulters have been extremely low in recent years when the institution has grown into maturity and its policies have become well known. Thus during 1964-65 out of 186 applications for all kinds of financial assistance received by it, as many as 134 or 72 per cent were sanctioned for a total assistance of Rs. 33.44 crores. Of these only four applications could not be actually sanctioned, the rest having either lapsed or been withdrawn. An amount of Rs. 31.92 crores has already been disbursed. As regards the percentage of defaults, the following table relating to defaults under interest and principal during the last 5 years is revealing.[1]

TABLE No. 38

INDUSTRIAL FINANCE CORPORATION OF INDIA

Percentage of Defaults in Interest and Principal to total amount due (cumulative)

		Interest	*Principal*
1961	..	0.25	2.34
1962	..	0.18	1.24
1963	..	0.26	0.87
1964	..	0.66	0.88
1965	..	1.40	0.86

It is clear that Mr. Schatz's contention that the percentage of "rejectees" and "defaulters" is high enough to suggest that the problem in underdeveloped countries is not that of capital shortage but of viable projects cannot be substantiated. The Indian IFC during its working of 17 years has sanctioned a total net financial assistance of Rs. 226.96 crores to 390 industrial units in various forms, such as loans, underwritings, direct subscription to debentures and guarantees. In none of these cases has the Corporation relaxed the requirements of technical, economic and financial viability demanded of the projects. Thus the demand for capital was genuine and effective, and not false.

In Nigeria itself the NIDB which is an outgrowth of the old ICON is working satisfactorily as an instrument of economic development. In the case of the Industrial Bank of Sudan, it is observed that by December 1964 since it began operations in August 1962, it received a total of 178 applications for loans of which 37 or 20.79 per cent were approved. Of the remaining 141 applications only 35 or 24.82 per cent were declined by the Bank or withdrawn by the applicants for failing to comply with the requirements of technical, economic and financial feasibility. This is the percentage of what Mr. Schatz has chosen to

[1] Seventeenth Annual Report of the Industrial Finance Corporation of India 1965. pp. 11-12 and p. 28.

characterise as "viability rejectees". Of the rest of 106 applications again 45 or 42.45 per cent were under active consideration and 61 or 57.55 per cent were kept in abeyance for various reasons. Immediately after the Bank commenced operations in August 1962, there was a sharp increase in the volume of its business though there was a decrease in the subsequent year as is brought out in the Table No. 39.

Table No. 39

	1962 (*4 months*)	*1963*	*1964*
Total amount of loans approved	LS 67,000	LS 561,000	LS 299,000
Total amount of investments	LS 122,000	LS 935,000	LS 411,000

As a result, the Bank's funds available for lending came to be sharply reduced and additional capital had to be called for in the shape of increased equity capital and loan from the US AID.[1] The Bank reports that 13 of the 37 approved projects or 35.14 per cent were already operating satisfactorily and 15 projects or 40.54 per cent were under completion with building construction and machinery installation being completed. It is in the case of 8 or 24.62 per cent of the approved projects that loan agreements could not be signed.[2]

It has been already observed that the Industrial Bank of Sudan has filled an important need and that most of the projects assisted by it have been operating successfully. There has no doubt been delay in the completion of some of the projects but there have been specific delaying factors, such as non-availability of suitable land for industrial sites and shortage of working capital.

It has been noted earlier in the case of the National Investment Bank of Ghana that by far the largest number of applications had to be declined because the maximum financial requirement in each case fell far below the institution's minimum loan limit. The rest of the rejections was due to the inadequacy of the securities offered or because the projects did not fall within the Bank's purview or because they had a low priority in the national plan. All this does not help to establish the thesis of

[1] Annual Report (No. 3) of the Board of Directors, the *Industrial Bank of Sudan* for the year ending December 31, 1964, p. 5

[2] *Ibid.*, Appendices 1A and 1B, pp. 17-19.

the "capital shortage illusion" as propounded by the recent commentator. The firms actually assisted by the Bank are not at all "shaky" but to quote the Secretary of the Institution, "are doing very well".[1]

[1] Letter to the present writer from the Secretary of the Bank dated 24 November, 1966.

Chapter Eleven

Central Banks as Financial Advisers, Exchange Control Administrators and Organisers of Research Departments

In a developing economy central banks make a valuable contribution in their capacity as financial advisers and advisers on foreign exchange policy to their Governments. Indeed, Prof. Sayers has placed a great deal of emphasis on this aspect of the role of the central banker in underdeveloped countries.[1] By virtue of their close and continuous contact with the markets and by virtue of their expertise they are undoubtedly best qualified to advise the Governments on all economic and financial issues. Their advice again is the uninhibited advice of an impartial observer whose judgment is not warped by considerations of sectional or vested interests. The responsibility for this function has been specifically written down into the statutes of the central banks. In one particular case, Tunisia, it is obligatory for the central bank to warn the Government of any condition which may pose a threat to the country's monetary stability. Such a provision is reminiscent of similar statutory obligations in the case of some earlier central banks in Latin American countries. The Nigerian Central Bank has been specifically enjoined by its statute to act as banker and financial adviser to the Government of Nigeria.[2] The Advisory Committee of the Bank of Nigeria holds meetings under the chairmanship of the Federal Minister of Finance and exchanges views on monetary and financial developments in the country.[3] The Bank of Morocco also under its charter is the financial adviser to the Government and is the agent of the Treasury for all banking and credit operations.[4] The Government consults the Bank in all matters. The role of the Bank of Rhodesia and Nyasaland as a general financial adviser has been remarkable. It acted as such not only for the Federal Government but also for the Governments of the three constituent territories. The smooth functioning of this aspect of the Bank's responsibility bears testimony to the Bank's skill and judgment. The Bank was

[1] R. S. Sayers, *Central Banking after Bagehot*, p. 113.
[2] *Bank of Nigeria Act, 1963* Art. 4(1).
[3] *Annual Reports and Statements of Accounts for 1963 and 1964. Bank of Nigeria* p. 36.
[4] Art. 6 *Statutes of the Bank of Morocco.*

careful not to dabble in matters which might have political implications. It confined its advice to financial and economic issues on which it was qualified to advise by virtue of its technical competence.[1]

All the central banks are holders of the entire foreign exchange reserve or a good part of it. In the absence of a central banking organisation foreign exchange reserves could not be concentrated in the hands of a particular institution. Their holding was scattered among Governments, market boards and private companies. Thus cotton boards in Ghana and Nigeria and the mining companies in Rhodesia were holding and administering substantial amounts of foreign assets on the eve of the attainment of independence by the countries. Expatriated banks in Ghana, Rhodesia and Morocco also held substantial amounts of foreign exchange reserves. In Sudan foreign exchange holdings were in the hands of the Bank of England. It was not an easy task for the central banks to collect all these reserves for mobilising them in their own hands. Gradually it came to be appreciated that in the interests of the countries' economy they should be transferred to the central bank and be concentrated there. With the initiation of the development plans in the newly independent countries, which called for considerable expenditure of foreign exchange, the careful husbanding of the scarce foreign exchange reserves in the hands of the central banks became all the more necessary. Thus systematic efforts had to be made in Nigeria to collect the foreign exchange reserves not only from marketing boards but also from regional Governments to be placed in the hands of the central bank. The Central Bank of Nigeria found its position considerably strengthened thereafter and became all the more equipped to discharge its responsibilities efficiently. The Banks of Morocco and Tunisia were also able to bring within their hold all the foreign exchange reserves of the countries. During the second-half of 1963 the Bank of Ghana took over almost all the foreign assets of the non-banking sector, local governments, public boards and educational institutions; and for the efficient management of foreign exchange reserves, it was decided to centralise the reserves. In the later part of 1963 the Government took over almost all the foreign securities of the public institutions and sold them to the Bank of Ghana. By June 1964 all the

[1] Art. in the *Commonwealth Banking Systems*, *op. cit.*, p. 341.

foreign securities of the cocoa marketing board, local authorities higher educational institutions and some private institutions were acquired by the Bank.[1]

The discussion of the mobilisation of foreign exchange reserves brings us to the interrelated problem of the administration of foreign exchange control. Exchange control is to be witnessed in all these countries. Legally the Minister of Finance is responsible for its administration. But usually the task is delegated to the central bank of the country. The officers of the central bank possess all the technical knowledge and experience for the administration of such control. Reliance again has inevitably to be placed on the central bank where exchange control is being employed as an instrument of monetary policy. Thus in all these countries central banks have had to be entrusted with the administration of exchange control. Thus the Bank of Rhodesia and Nyasaland was entrusted with the administration of exchange control at an early stage of its career in March 1957. When the scope of exchange control was extended in February 1961, the Bank's responsibilities correspondingly increased.

RESEARCH DEPARTMENTS OF THE CENTRAL BANKS

An important responsibility of the central banks in these developing economies has been the organisation of research departments. Statistical information of various sorts and current analysis of the economic situation provide useful bases for the formulation of monetary policy. In underdeveloped countries reliable data of any kind relating to economic, monetary or financial matters are hardly available. In the circumstances central banks from the very start have to apply their minds to the establishment of their own research departments. Indeed, the setting up of such departments has been considered to be so important that it has been made a part of the statutory obligation of central banks in some underdeveloped countries. Thus the Bank of Korea has been enjoined by its charter to establish a Research Department. The duties of the Department have been defined and it has been empowered to request from any natural or juridical person as

[1] *Bank of Ghana.* Annual Report for the year 1964, p. 51..

well as the government any data or information necessary for the proper execution of its duties.[1]

Central banks in most of the developed and underdeveloped countries have established research departments of their own. Their main tasks are preparation of statistical data, and conducting of economic research relating to money, banking, public finance, prices, wages, production, balance of payments etc. The objective of the research department is to furnish the Board of the Bank with the information necessary for the proper formulation and execution of its monetary, credit and foreign exchange policies. The Department also assists in the preparation of the Annual Report of the Bank and may also publish a monthly statistical bulletin. Its collaboration with other departments of the Bank and with official agencies is often envisaged. It is also expected to make efforts to improve the country's statistical service.

The central banks in these African countries had to take steps from their start to establish their research departments. Even the most rudimentary statistical material relating to the banking and financial system was not available. Data regarding the number of banks and their branches, their capital structure, their advances/deposits ratio, the distribution of their loans and advances, the structure of their assets and liabilities by size and class, money supply and its components etc. are necessary to provide a basis for the formulation of central bank policies. Surprisingly in a very short time the central banks have been able to organise efficient research departments of their own. They have been ever since enlarging their scope and introducing the most modern mechanical aids to eliminate the possibility of errors and inaccuracies. Thus the Central Banks in Nigeria, Rhodesia, Sudan, Ghana, Tunisia, Morocco and Libya are all publishing their annual reports, which are certainly not "dull reading" at all. These reports through graphs and tables provide all the necessary data relating to money supply, analysis of loans and advances of commercial banks, their total deposits and investments, bank charges, treasury bill issues, public debt and activity on the stock exchanges. Besides the Annual Reports their publications include economic and financial reviews (Nigeria), bulletins

[1] Arts. 36 & 38. *Bank of Korea Act*. April 21, 1960. See H. Aufricht *op. cit.*, p. 467.

(Sudan, Tunisia and Libya) and Etudes et Statistiques (Morocco). All these furnish a wealth of statistical material relating not only to the banking and financial system but also to prices, production, agriculture, industry, and balance of payments and also provide commentaries on the current economic and financial situation. Indeed, they are comparable in their usefulness to similar publications of older established central banks in the advanced countries. It would not have been possible for the present writer to prepare this study without the wealth of material provided therein and generously supplied to him.

In these emerging countries, the challenge of establishing traditions of economic research is very great. Qualified research personnel, economists and statisticians, have to be recruited and have to be properly trained, well-equipped libraries have to be built up, appropriate machineries for collection of systematic and reliable statistical material relating to various fields and for their scientific processing have to be organised. All these tremendous tasks pose a formidable array of problems. The central banks in all the countries studied here have been endeavouring to meet this challenge ever since their inception. In the case of one of these new central banks, the Bank of Libya, we have been told by the Governor of the Bank how it is meeting this challenge.[1] The Bank has been able to collect a large amount of useful data relating to the banking and allied monetary and financial spheres. It has not only undertaken a regular review and analysis of developments in the monetary-banking fields and those of public finance, foreign trade and balance of payments, but has also published a number of useful studies. One such study relates to the analysis of the problem of inflation in Libya which was published in 1961 within a few years of the establishment of the Bank and which we have drawn upon with profit. Another study on public finance was prepared and published in 1964. The basic objective of such studies is to present to the policy makers and businessmen some necessary factual information and forecasts for making rational decisions. Another aim has been to provide the students of economics and commerce as well as the general public with reliable and timely appraisal of some important aspects of the national economy. The coverage of the activities

[1] See Preface contributed by the Governor of the Bank of Libya to the Study on "Inflation in Libya" June 15, 1961.

of the Research Department is being systematically extended as is demonstrated by its endeavours to collect relevant data relating to the oil sector for the purpose of evaluating the impact of this sector upon the country's economy. The Department has maintained all these years a close and continuous co-operation with various Government departments, banks and oil companies, which has helped in the presentation of the relevant material on a truly scientific basis.

Chapter Twelve

Concluding Remarks

In conclusion it may be observed that by and large the establishment of the central banks in all these countries has been justified. Indeed, it is a development to be welcomed particularly in the context of their growing economy. The most important task of a central bank in such economies is the promotion of money and capital markets. All the banks admittedly have not been able to establish equally broad and equally well-organised markets in their territories. The degree of their sophistication has indeed varied from one territory to another and has depended on local conditions and conceptions. But it has been abundantly clear from the preceding analysis that their endeavours have been fruitful. Where the rudiments of a money and capital market and of a stock exchange existed, their efforts in broadening their scope and possibilities have been significant. Where these did not exist, they have assisted in their gradual development. The gaps in the financial structure were numerous. In all these cases the central banks helped to foster not only the growth of an indigenous banking system but took steps to promote the development of various types of financial intermediaries. These led to the creation of a diversified volume of financial assets which are comparable with some of the money market assets to be witnessed in the advanced countries of the world. The hopes and expectations of the founders of the central banks in the various territories under discussion have not been belied; and the fears of the opponents of central banking in underdeveloped countries have largely proved to be illusory. The Banks have taken over the functions of currency management from the previous currency boards. Regularisation, simplification and stabilisation of the national currencies have been their accomplished objects. They have mobilised the external assets of the countries in their hands and have improved the management and investment of these assets. They are acting as bankers and financial advisers to their respective Governments; they are steadily developing into lenders of last resort; they are looking after the administration of exchange control and providing the requisite technical advice in this respect; they have assisted in the promotion of the money and capital markets, and in the creation of an indigenous banking system and of specialist financial institutions to fill the gaps in the machinery of industrial, agricultural and export finance. Most of these African countries may be said to possess almost all the financial intermediaries they require. Closely related to these major promotional functions, they have to their credit, as we have observed, a number of other activities such as the collection and improvement of financial statistics, economic intelligence and research and last, but not least, the creation of a trained indigenous banking personnel. Their role in the sphere of monetary control has not been insignificant and in some cases has been quite effective. The staffing problem with which the authorities of the Banks had been faced in their earlier stages has been practically solved. The banks except in Rhodesia are on the way to complete "Africanisation" which had been their policy ever since their inception. In Africa as in all underdeveloped countries there was an almost complete lack of indigenous financial expertise or trained banking personnel. In Rhodesia the difficulty was solved by a complete Europeanisation of the staff. But other countries considered such an arrangement to be ill-suited to a national monetary system The policy of Africanisation dictated that eventually all the banks should be fully African with a national outlook in monetary policy. At the same time they realised that the staffing of the Banks with untrained, inefficient, indigenous personnel would lead to utter monetary chaos. Different methods were adopted by the different Banks to meet this dilemma. One group of Banks, such as those of Nigeria and Morocco, made recourse to appointing expatriates to senior technical positions. Foreign commercial banks operating in the country had a few trained African officers; and these were persuaded to make their indigenous staff available to the central banks. The senior expatriate officers proved to be of considerable value in training up indigenous personnel in the medium and junior ranks who could replace them subsequently. In Sudan a great deal of preparation was to be witnessed. In Ghana the probationary trainee appointment under which members of the staff including officers are sent abroad for training in a variety of courses at the International Monetary Fund and the London School of Economics has yielded good results. The increasing trend towards Africanisation is shown in the fact that in June 1961, only four years after the establishment of the Bank there were only five non-Africans in a staff of 142. The employment of some female clerks has been a recent interesting feature. Non-African personnel were appointed on short-term contract for a year or so on whose expiry they returned to their original posts. By 1962 the Bank reached the stage of being completely managed by Ghanaian staff, except for one expatriate officer in the exchange control department. The Bank of England had loaned one of its officers on a contract basis to advise on the implementation of the Exchange Control Act, 1961. Another expatriate officer had also been lent on a contract tour of 18 months by the Deutsche Bundesbank to assist in the administration of the Compulsory Savings Scheme introduced in 1962. A banking school has also been established under the auspices of the College of Administration for the members of the staff at home.[1] The President of the Sudan Currency Board which was formed as a transitional device was a Sudanese but he had British, Swedish and Egyptian advisers. The Sudanese Currency Board during this transition period showed considerable imagination in sending nationals to foreign central banks and foreign universities for suitable training with the objective of building up an indigenous staff for the future central bank at the time it was set up. The foreign central banks with which it came in contact after it was established were requested to 'loan' some of their senior technical officers who could explain and 'teach' their speciality.[2] This arrangement proved to be at once successful and popular. The foreign officers were on a contract basis retaining their lien with their own institutions. They would automatically return to their original post after the termination of the contract. Thus neither any vested interest could be created nor any national jealousy excited.

Admittedly the decision to create these Central Banks has been partly a matter of "fashion" and status symbol and partly the influence of "demonstration effect" upon the new-comers. But the previous analysis has given ample evidence to justify the decision on economic grounds. The Central Bankers in these developing economies cannot be said to be "sitting in splendid

[1] *Bank of Ghana,* Reports for the financial years ending June 30, 1961 and 1962, p. 10; pp. 5-8.

[2] E. E. Jucker Fleetwood, *Monetary and Financial Problems in Certain New Countries in Africa* (B.I.S), pp. 4-5.

isolation twiddling their thumbs". Instead of "thumb-twiddling", versatility and venturesomeness, as envisaged by Prof. Sayers, have been their characteristic virtues. The manner in which both conventional and unconventional weapons have been pressed into service, the exciting experiments they have made in the refashioning of old tools and adapting them to their own needs have served to increase dramatically their powers of monetary control. By reason of the wealth of experience they have garnered and the expertise they have built up during the period of their operation, they are already in a strong position to provide the necessary guidelines for the accelerated economic development of their respective countries. If currency boards had continued to operate, as many advisers had desired or "Monetary Institutes", as recommended by Mr. J. B. Loynes for Sierra Leone, had been established, it seems most unlikely that a money market would have been created or development financing institutions founded. Nor would there have been any machinery for coping with the problems posed by the over-extended position of the banking system in the countries' developing economy. Last, but not least, an important potential source of advice in the field of finance and foreign exchange would have been lost to the Government. Currency boards or 'monetary institutes', with hardly any credit creating powers beyond a limited fiduciary issue, and with few close relationships with the governments, would not have been able to command their attention as central bankers with their control over financial resources would. They could not provide the leadership which central banks having a status detached from and not subordinate to the Finance Department could inspire.

There are, indeed, observers who have expressed a definite preference for the continuance of currency board arrangements in the developing economies rather than their replacement by full-fledged central banks. But the controversy that has centred round the question whether the currency board or the central bank should be the most appropriate monetary arrangement for such countries appears to us to be basically irrelevant and sterile. Those who favour the continuance of currency boards do not certainly envisage them in their regular, traditional form. They are inclined to redesign them and arm them with some powers of the central bank. Currency board arrangements, modified in the direction of changes as observed in the working of the East

African Currency Board, rather than central banks proper, have made a profound appeal to some recent commentators in this connection.[1] They have welcomed the move of that Board into areas of central banking as a significant evolution fraught with great possibilities. But currency boards modelled on the lines of the reformed East African Currency Board or "monetary institutes" as envisaged by Mr. J. B. Loynes have to be equipped with increasing central banking functions to cope with the complex problems of rapidly growing economies. Even then it will be found that the functions have reached their limits quickly, inhibiting the full and effective performance of the tasks of a central bank even in restricted spheres. The coverage of powers would have to be steadily expanded and the design of the Boards continually altered until their original character is lost and they have almost imperceptibly shaded into full-grown central banks. There would hardly be any difference with the central banks except in designation.[2] In conclusion, it may be observed that if one bears in mind the time that the central bank in the most developed territory of Africa—South Africa—took to reach maturity, and the central bank in Australia took in developing a capital market in spite of its relatively well-developed banking system and its possession of all the ingredients required for the development of a sophisticated capital market, the achievements of the new central banks have not been insignificant.

[1] "The Framework of Inter-Relations" contributed by W. F. Crick to *Commonwealth Banking Systems*. Ed. by him, p. 13.

[2] See Report of Dr. Erwin Blumenthal (of the Deutsche Bundesbank) on the working of the East African Currency Board and the possibility of Establishing an East African Central Bank. (He was invited by the Government of Tanganyika).

Appendix I

Graph I

Ghana: (Gross domestic product at market prices)
Dec. 1960-Dec. 1964.

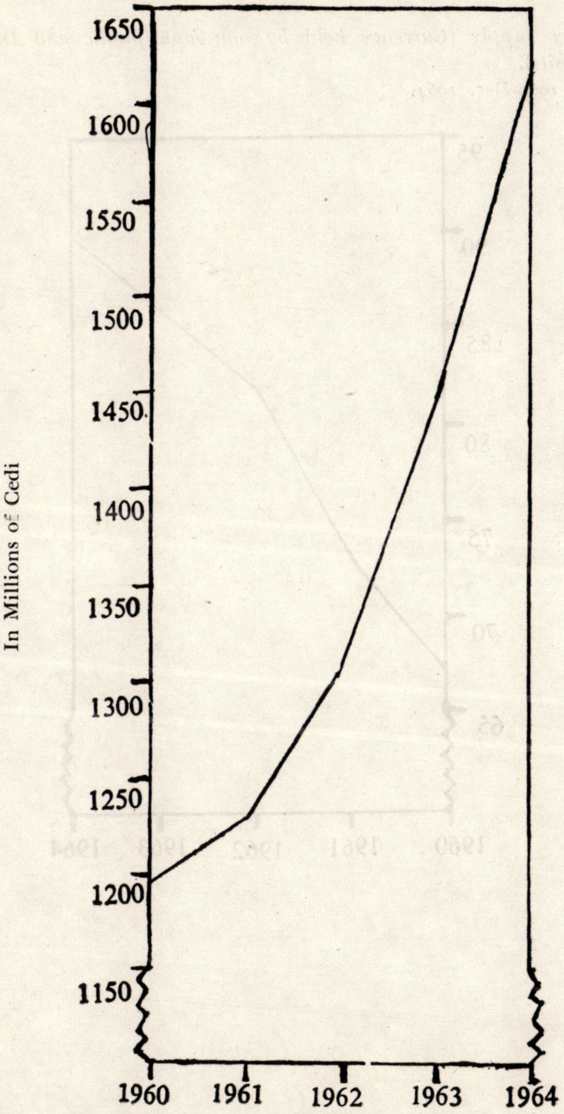

1 Cedi = 8s. 4d.
£1 = 2.40 cedis.

GRAPH II

Ghana: Money Supply (Currency held by non-bank public and Demand Deposits).
Dec. 1960-Dec. 1964.

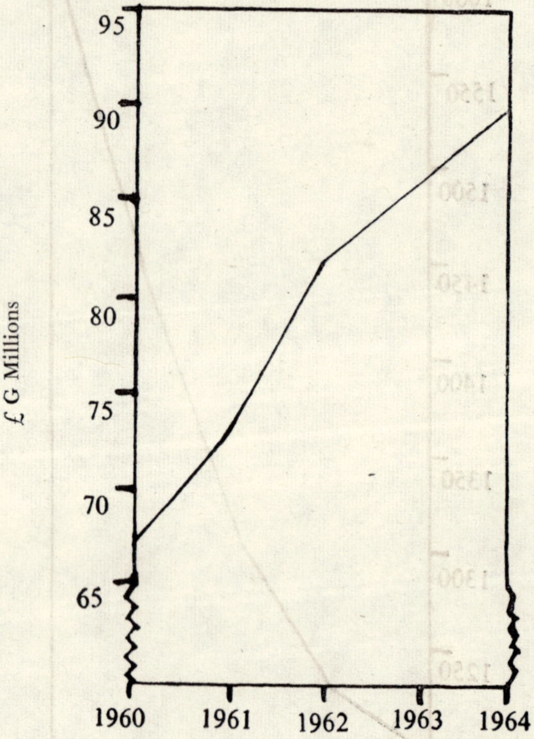

GRAPH III

Libya: National Income (Gross Domestic Product at factor cost) Dec. 1960-Dec. 1965.

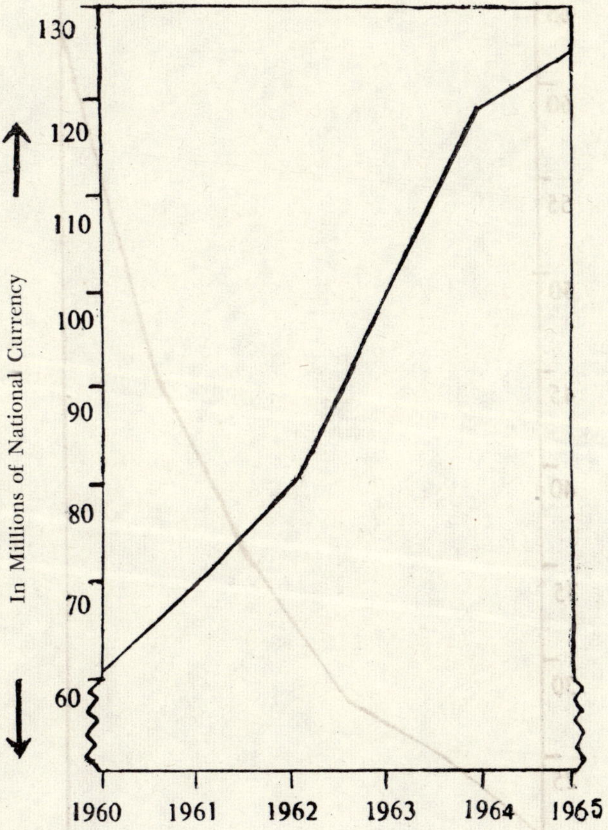

GRAPH IV

Libya: Money Supply (Currency with non-bank public and Demand Deposits) Dec. 1960-Dec. 1965.

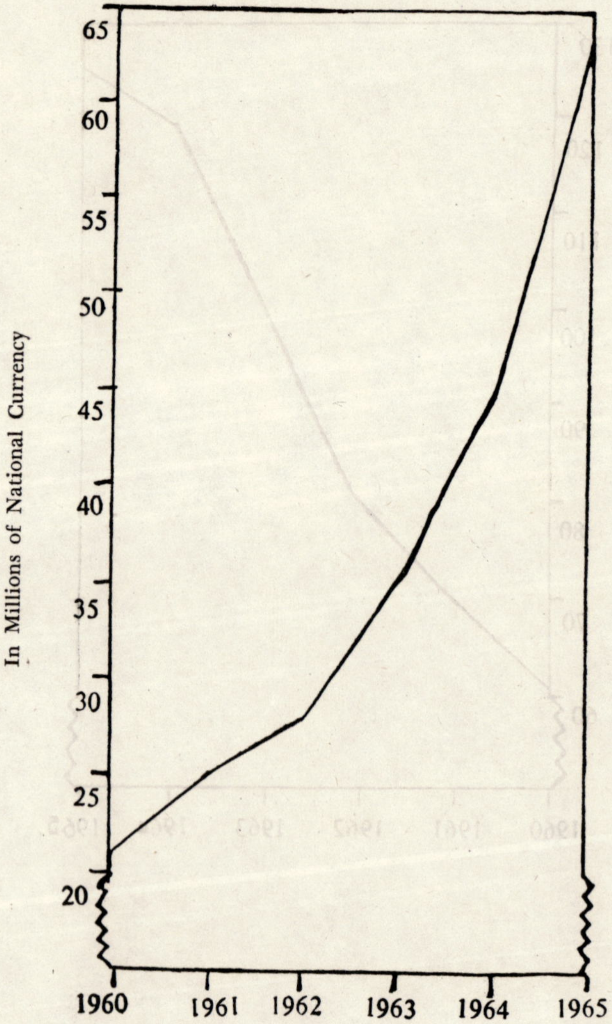

GRAPH V

Morocco: National Income (Gross Domestic Product at market prices) Dec. 1960-Dec. 1964.

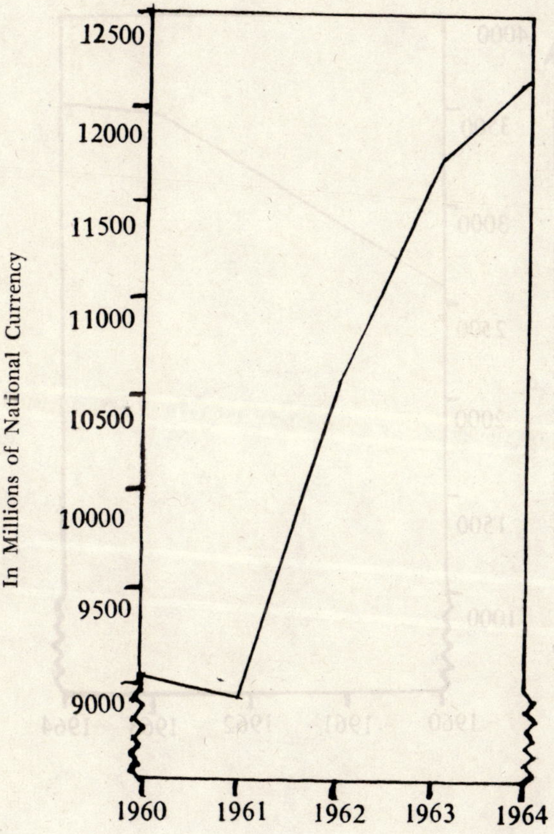

GRAPH VI

Morocco: Money Supply (Currency and Demand Deposits). Dec. 1960-Dec. 1964.

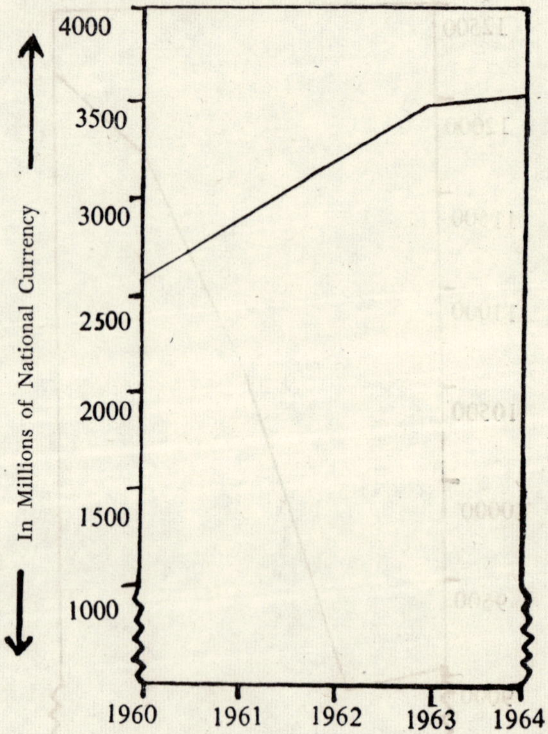

GRAPH VII

Nigeria: National Income (Gross Domestic product at factor cost) Dec. 1960-Dec. 1965.

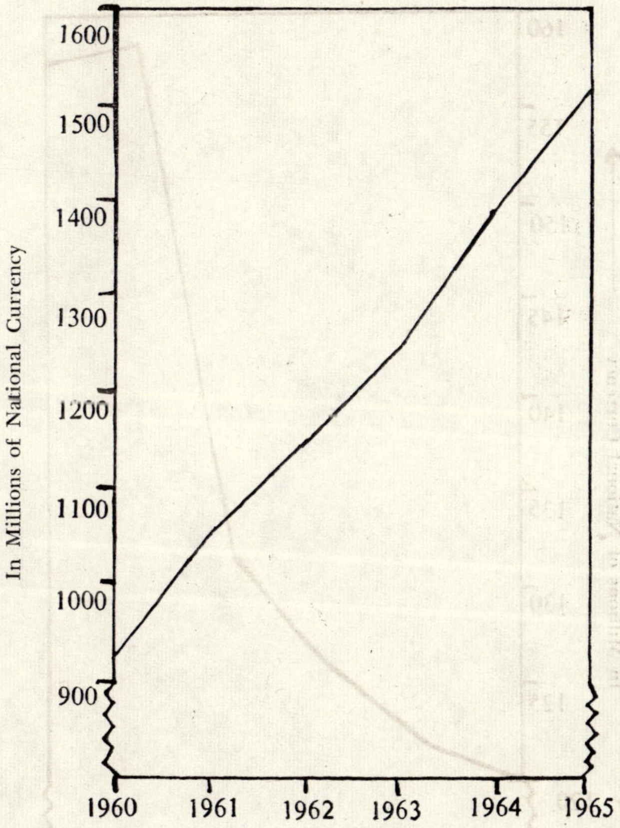

GRAPH VIII

Nigeria: Money Supply (Currency with Non-bank public and Demand Deposits).
Dec. 1960-Dec. 1965.

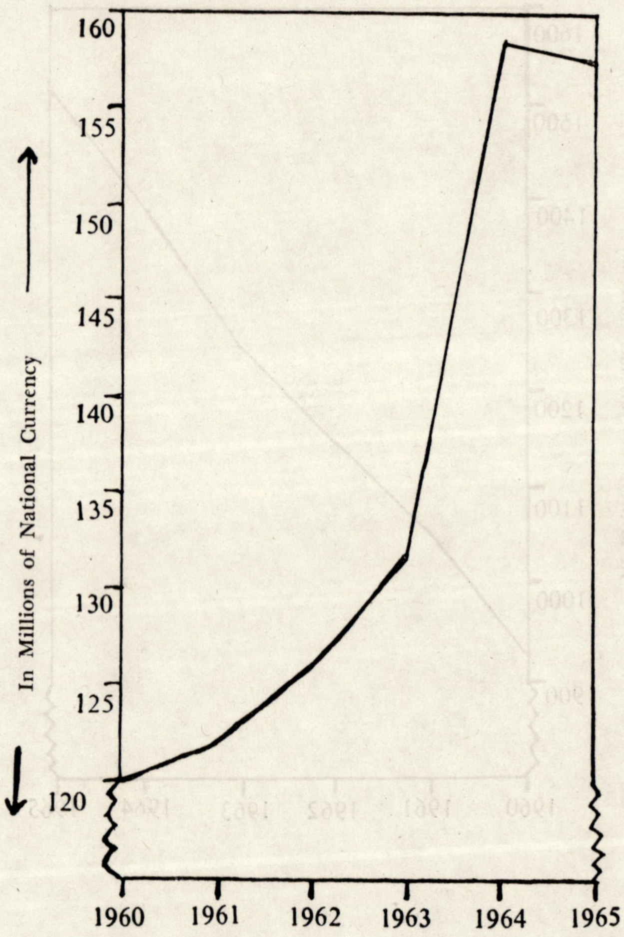

GRAPH IX

Sudan: National Income (Gross domestic product at market prices). Dec. 1960-Dec. 1963.

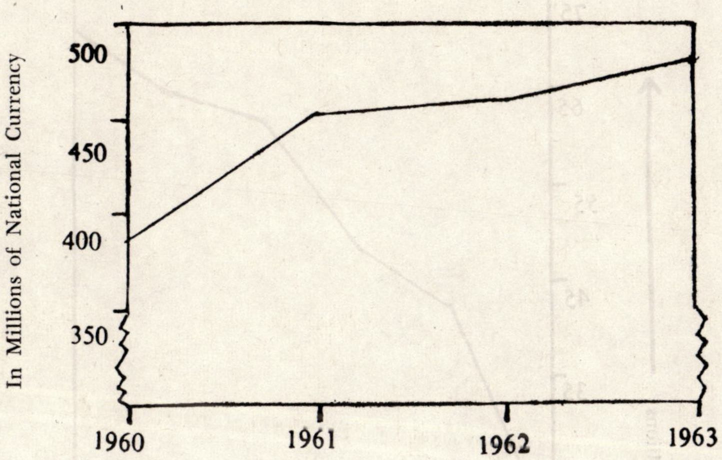

GRAPH X

Sudan: Money Supply
Dec. 1960-Dec. 1965.

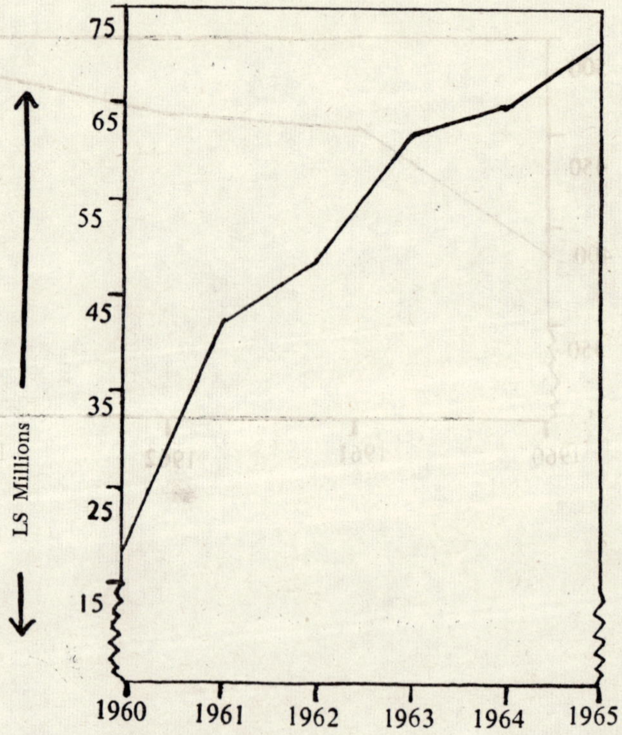

GRAPH XI

Tunisia: National Income (Gross domestic product at factor cost). Dec. 1960-Dec. 1964.

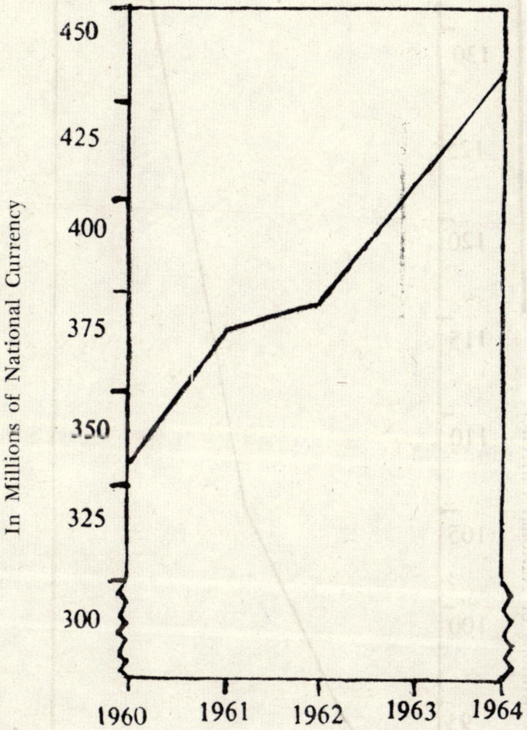

GRAPH XII

Tunisia: Money Supply (currency plus demand deposits).
Dec. 1960-Dec. 1964.

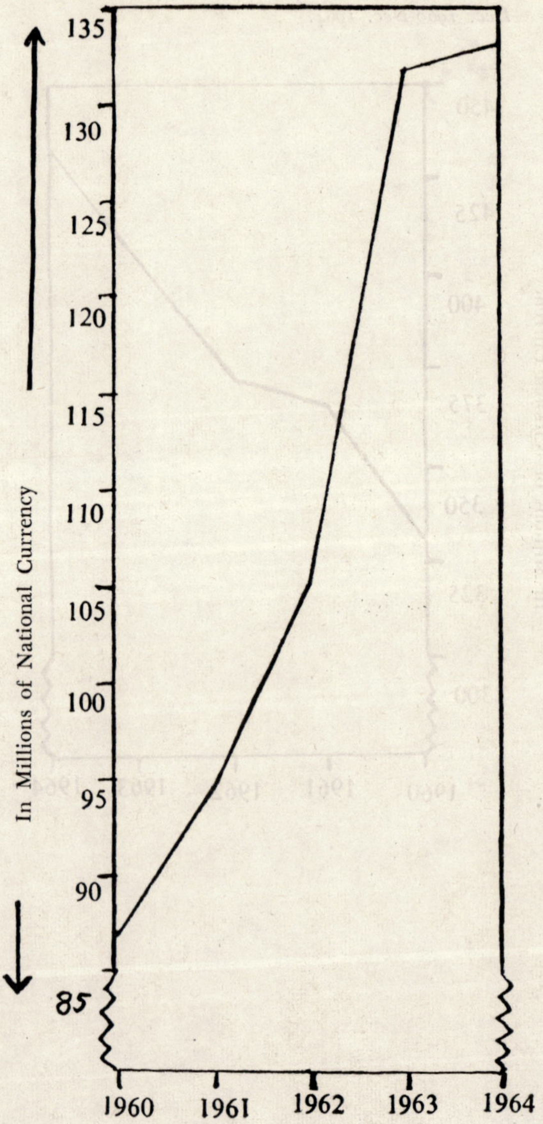

Appendix II

Specimen Statutes.

SAMPLE PROVISIONS ARE BASED ON THE FOLLOWING DOCUMENTS

1. The Bank of Ghana Act, 1963. Arts 1—58.
2. Central Bank of Nigeria Act, 1958 as amended 1962. Arts 1—52.
3. Statutes of the Bank of Morocco established by a Royal Decree of June 30, 1959 as amended December 30, 1962. Arts 1—70.
4. Act No. 58—90 of September 19, 1958 on the creation and organisation of Central Bank of Tunisia. Arts 1—74. *Textes Organiques, Banque Centrale de Tunisie.*
5. The Bank of Rhodesia and Nyasaland Act, 1956. Arts 1—29.
6. The Reserve Bank of Rhodesia Act, 1964. Arts. 1—28.
7. Bank of Sudan Act 1959 as amended by Bank of Sudan Amendment Act, 1962.
8. Law No. 4 of February 5, 1963. Promulgating the Banking Law, Libya. Arts. 1—84.

I. CAPITAL AND OWNERSHIP

THE BANK OF GHANA

4. The authorised capital of the Bank shall be ten million pounds which shall be taken up from time to time by the Government, and may be increased from time to time.

BANK OF RHODESIA AND NYASALAND

3. The capital of the Bank shall be one million pounds, which shall all be held by the Federal Government.
4. The capital of the Bank may be increased to such extent and in such manner as may be determined by the Governor-General.

RESERVE BANK OF RHODESIA

3. The capital of the Bank shall be one million pounds, all of which shall be held by the Government.

BANK OF SUDAN

7. The authorised capital of the Bank shall be one and a half million Sudanese Pounds and shall be provided wholly by the Government on the establishment of the Bank.

CENTRAL BANK OF TUNISIA

Art. 2. The Central Bank of Tunisia, called the 'C.B.' hereafter, is a public national establishment endowed with civil personality and financial autonomy.
Art. 6. (1) The capital of the Central Bank is constituted by donations entirely subscribed by the state and the amount of which is fixed by law.

(2) The capital of the Central Bank can always be increased by incorporating reserves on the consideration of the Council of Administration approved by a decree.

CENTRAL BANK OF NIGERIA

6. (1) The authorised cepital of the Bank shall be one million five hundred thousand pounds. There shall be paid up such amount as shall be resolved by the Bank and confirmed by the Minister and this amount shall be subscribed by and paid up at par by the Federal Government upon the establishment of the Bank.

(2) The paid-up portion of the authorised capital may be increased by such amount as the Board may, from time to time, resolve with the agreement of the Minister, and the Federal Government shall subscribe and pay up at par the amount of such increase.

(3) All the paid-up capital shall be subscribed and held only by the Federal Government.

BANK OF LIBYA

Art. 1. The authorized capital of the Bank shall be one million Libyan pounds and may be increased by decision of the Council of Ministers on the proposal of the Bank. Subscription to this capital shall be restricted to that of the Government.

BANK OF MOROCCO

6. (1) The authorised capital of the Bank shall be fixed at 20 million dirhams and shall be subscribed by and paid up at par by the state upon the establishment of the Bank.

(2) All the paid-up capital shall be subscribed and held by the Federal Government.

69. The subscription of the Capital of the Bank of Morocco will be paid by the State to the extent of 1660 million francs in conformity with the real assets and securities acquired by virtue of the convention passed between the State and the State Bank of Morocco on June 15, 1959.

II. OBJECTIVES

THE BANK OF GHANA

3. The principal objects of the Bank shall be,

(*a*) to issue and redeem bank notes and coin;

(*b*) to administer, regulate and direct the currency system;

(*c*) to regulate and direct the credit and banking system in accordance with the economic policy of the Government and the provisions of this Act;

(*d*) to promote by monetary measures the stabilization of the value of the currency within and outside Ghana;

(*e*) to propose to the Government measures which are likely to have a favourable effect on the balance of payments, movement of prices, the state of public finances and the general development of the national economy and monetary stability;

(*f*) to do all such things as are incidental or conducive to the efficient performance of its functions under this or any other enactment.

CENTRAL BANK OF NIGERIA

4. (1) The principal objects of the Bank shall be to issue legal tender currency in Nigeria to maintain external reserves in order to safeguard the international value of that currency, to promote monetary stability and a sound financial structure in Nigeria and to act as banker and financial adviser to the Federal Government.

(2) The objects of the bank shall include the issue of legal tender currency in the Northern and Southern Cameroons in accordance with any arrangements in that behalf between the Government of the Federation and the Governments of the Northern and Southern Cameroons.

BANK OF RHODESIA AND NYASALAND

To provide for the establishment of the Bank of Rhodesia and Nyasaland, to regulate the issue of bank notes and coins, to authorize the said Bank to take over the assets and liabilities of the Central Africa Currency Board, to confer and impose on the said Bank diverse other powers and duties, to provide for matters connected with banking, currency, and coinage, and for matters incidental to the foregoing.

BANK OF SUDAN

5. The principal objects of the Bank shall be to regulate the issue of notes and coins, to assist in the development and maintenance of a sound monetary, credit and banking system in the Sudan, with a view to the orderly and balanced economic development of the country and the external stability of the currency, and to serve as banker and financial adviser to the Government.

BANK OF MOROCCO

5. The Bank of Morocco exercises the privilege of issuing money. This Bank is bound to contribute within the limits of its powers and in accordance with the economic and financial policies laid down by the Government:

(1) to stabilize the money and to assure its convertibility;

(2) to develop and to regularize the money and capital markets in relation to the needs of the national economy;

(3) to expand the posibilities of employment and to raise the level of the national income.

CENTRAL BANK OF TUNISIA

33. The general objective of the Central Bank is to exercise control over monetary circulation and distribution of credit.

34. (1) The Central Bank lends its support to the political economy of the state.

(2) It can propose to the Government all measures which, in the opinion of the Government or of the Council, are of a nature to exercise a favourable action on the balance of payments, on the movement of prices, on public finances and generally on the development of the national economy.

(3) The Bank informs the President of the Republic about all facts which, in the opinion of the Governor or of the Council, can injure the monetary stability.

BANK OF LIBYA

Art. 13. The Bank shall:

(1) Regulate and issue the Libyan currency.

(2) Maintain the stability of the Libyan currency internally and externally.

(3) Regulate credit and banking policy and supervise its execution within the framework of the general policy of the state in such manner as would promote the national economy. To accomplish this objective, the Bank may:

(*a*) Influence the direction of credit with regard to quantity, quality and price in such manner as would ensure that the real requirements of commercial, industrial and agricultural activities are met.

(*b*) Take the appropriate measures to combat economic or financial disorders whether local or general.

(*c*) Supervise banking concerns with the aim of ensuring their sound financial position and safeguard the rights of customers.

(*d*) Manage the State's reserves of gold and foreign exchange.

III. DIRECTION, ADMINISTRATION AND SUPERVISION

THE BANK OF GHANA

6. (1) There shall be a board of directors which shall consist of a Governor, Deputy Governor and five other directors.

(2) The general administration of the affairs of the Bank shall be entrusted to the Board, to which the Governor shall be answerable for his acts and decisions.

7. (1) The Governor and the Deputy Governor shall be persons of recognised financial or banking experience and shall be appointed by the President on the recommendations of the Minister.

(2) The Governor and the Deputy Governor shall each be appointed for a term of five years and shall be eligible for re-appointment. Executive Directors shall be appointed by the Minister after prior consultation with the Governor.

(6) The other directors of the Bank shall be appointed by the Minister.

(7) The other directors of the Bank shall hold office for three years and shall be eligible for re-appointment.

CENTRAL BANK OF NIGERIA

8. (1) There shall be a Board of Directors of the Bank which shall be responsible for the policy and general administration of the affairs and business of the Bank.

(2) The Board shall consist of a Governor, a Deputy Governor and five other directors.

(3) The Governor or, in his absence, the Deputy Governor shall be in charge of the day-to-day management of the Bank and shall be answerable to the Board for their acts and decisions.

9. (1) The Governor and Deputy Governor shall be persons of recognised financial experience and shall be appointed by the Governor-General by instrument under the public seal on such terms and conditions as may be set out in their respective letters of appointment.

(2) The Governor and Deputy Governor shall each be appointed for a term of five years and shall be eligible for reappointment: Provided that the appointment, or first appointment, of the first Deputy Governor shall be for a term of three years.

10. (1) The five other directors of the Bank shall be appointed by the Prime Minister of the Federation.

15. (1) There shall be an advisory committee of the Bank which shall consist of—

(*a*) the Minister or his alternate;

(*b*) the Minister charged with responsibility for finance in respect of each Region or his alternate;

(*c*) the Governor or Deputy Governor.

BANK OF RHODESIA AND NYASALAND

5. (1) There shall be a Governor of the Bank and a Deputy Governor of the Bank, who shall be appointed and hold office in accordance with the provisions of section (b).

(2) Subject to the provisions of subsection (3), the Bank shall be managed by the Governor, who shall be a person of proved banking experience.

(3) In the management of the Bank the Governor shall act in accordance with the policy of the Board and shall be responsible for the day-to-day management of the Bank.

6. (1) There shall be a Board of Directors which shall be responsible for the policy of the Bank and shall consist of—

(*a*) the Governor;

(*b*) the Deputy Governor; and

(*c*) seven other directors of whom at least two shall be persons who are, or have been, actively and primarily engaged in commerce or finance, at least two shall be persons who are, or have been, so engaged in industrial pursuits, and at least one shall be a person who is, or has been, so engaged in agriculture.

(3) The directors, other than the Governor and Deputy Governor, shall be appointed by the Governor-General, subject to the provisions of this Act, and shall hold office, subject to the provisions of this section, for a period of five years.

RESERVE BANK OF RHODESIA

5. (1) There shall be a Governor of the Bank and a Deputy Governor of the Bank, who shall be appointed and hold office in accordance with the provisions of section six.

6. (1) There shall be a Board of directors which shall be responsible for the policy of the Bank and shall consist of—

(*a*) the Governor; and

(*b*) the Deputy Governor; and

(*c*) not less than five and not more than seven other directors who shall be persons who are or have been actively engaged in financial, commercial, industrial or agricultural pursuits.

(3) The Governor and Deputy Governor shall be appointed by the Governor of Southern Rhodesia after consultation with the Board, each such officer to hold office, subject to the provisions of this Act, for a term of seven years.

(4) The directors, other than the Governor and Deputy Governor, shall be appointed by the Governor of Southern Rhodesia, subject to the provisions of this Act, and shall hold office, subject to the provisions of this section, for a period of five years.

(6) No person shall be appointed as a director if he—

(*a*) is a director, shareholder, officer or employee, or a member of any board or committee, of a commercial bank or accepting or discount house; or

(*b*) is a member of the Legislative Assembly; or

(*c*) is a permanent employee of the Government.

BANK OF SUDAN

11. (1) There shall be a Board of Directors of the Bank which shall be responsible for the policy and general administration of the affairs and business of the Bank.

(2) The Board shall consist of seven directors, namely a Governor, a Deputy Governor and five other Directors.

12. (2) The Governor and the Deputy Governor shall be persons of suitable qualifications and experience and shall be appointed by the Council of Ministers on the recommendation of the Minister for a term of five years on such terms and conditions as may be specified in their respective letters of appointment.

(4) The Governor and the Deputy Governor shall devote the whole of their professional time to the service of the Bank and while holding office shall not occupy any other office or employment whether remunerated or not; provided that they may, with the approval of the Minister:

(*a*) act as members of any board or commission appointed by the Government;

(*b*) become governors, alternate governors, directors or members of the Board by whatever name called, of any international bank or international monetary authority set up under any agreement or convention to which the Government shall have adhered or given support or approval.

(*c*) become directors of any institution in which the Bank may participate under Section 64.

13. (1) The five other Directors of the Bank shall be appointed as follows:

(*a*) One Director shall be appointed by the Minister to represent the Minister on the Board. The Minister may appoint an alternate to this Director who shall attend the meetings of the Board when the Director is absent.

(*b*) Four Directors shall be appointed by the Council of Ministers, on the recommentation of the Minister, from amongst persons of recognised standing and experience in affairs.

20. The Minister, with the approval of the Council of Ministers, and after consultation with the Board, may from time to time give to the Board directions of a general character as to the exercise by the Board of its functions in matters which appear to the Council of Ministers to affect the national interest; and the Board shall carry out such directions.

CENTRAL BANK OF TUNISIA

Art. 7. The direction, administration and supervision (scrutiny) of the Central Bank are entrusted respectively to a Governor, a Council of Administration (called the Council hereafter) and an Auditor.

Art. 8. (1) The business of the Central Bank will be directed by the Governor appointed by a decree of the President of the Republic.

(2) The Govt. consults the Governor everytime when it considers questions on money and credit that have repercussions on the monetary situation.

Art. 9. (1) The Governor is appointed for 6 years.

(2) The term of the Governor can be extended once or several times.

(3) The office of the Governor is incompatible with any Legislative or Governmental duty.

Art. 10. (4) He is prohibited for the same period, to advise private enterprises and to accept remuneration from them except on an authorisation of Secretary of State of the President. The Secretary determines the conditions according to which his entire remuneration or any part thereof will be continued.

Art. 11. (1). During his tenure of office, the governor is prohibited from participating or having any interest whatsoever in any private enterprise.

Art. 14. (1). The Governor is assisted by a Director General, placed directly under him and charged with the supervision of all personnel of the Central Bank.

Art. 15. (1). The Director General is appointed by President's decree on the proposal of the Governor.

Art. 19. The Council is composed of the Governor, Chairman; the Director General; and 8 Councillors appointed by the decree of the President of the Republic; 4 of whom chosen on account of high functions exercised by men in the economic and financial administration of the State or in public or semi-public institutions specialising on matters of credit or participating in the economic development of the country;—4 chosen because of their professional experience in agriculture, commerce and industry.

Art. 20. (1) The Councillors are nominated for 3 years. Their terms can be renewed once or several times.

Art. 25. (1) Within the limits of the existing statutes the Council wields extensive administrative powers over the Central Bank.

(11) It draws the annual budget of the Central Bank and makes necessary adjustments in the exercise of this function.

(12) It determines the conditions and form in which the Central Bank prepares its accounts.

(13). It approves the draft annual report on the working of the Central Bank which the Governor in his name sends to the President of the Republic.

BANK OF MOROCCO

Art. 43. The organs and administrations, directions, supervision and control of the Bank are:

(1) the Governor.

(2) the Council of the Bank named the Council.

(3) the Committee of Direction.

(4) Government Commissioner.

(5) Auditor.

The Governor is nominated by a Decree on the proposal of Ministry of Finance and cannot be relieved of his functions except in the same way.

Art. 45. The Governor administers and plans the Bank:

(1) according to conditions laid down by the present decree as well as by decrees and regulations passed before.

(2) He presides over the Council and consents to the decisions of the Council. He takes all measures of execution and all measures of conservation that he judges useful. He can delegate his powers for well determined actions.

Art. 46. The Governor is assisted either by a Vice-Governor or by a Director General. The Vice-Governor represents the governor in his absence or failure to attend. He exercises among others all other functions which are devolved on him by the Governor.

Art. 48. The Director General exercises his functions under the immediate authority of the Governor. He is nominated by a decree passed by the proposal of the governor after consulting the Ministry of Finance and the Council. The Decree nominating him fixes his remuneration.

Art. 49. The Council lays down regulations for internal discipline for the organisation of branches and agencies, also for operations of the Bank. It lays down the Statutes and the general rules for fixing the remuneration of personnel of the Bank, gives its advice on the nomination of the Governor or Vice-Governor or of the Director General. On the proposal of the Governor it nominates the officers and fixes their service conditions. It lays down characteristics of notes issued, it decides the volume of circulation and the withdrawal of the same according to the methods mentioned in Arts—17-18-20. It fixes the basic rate of rediscounting operations. It is informed periodically of the credit operations and for excessive operations carried out by the Bank. It decides on the investment of funds owned by the Bank representing its capital, reserve and depreciation accounts. It approves the Budget. It considers all questions related to the organisation or general policy of the Bank.

Art. 50. The decisions of the Council relating to matters of rediscounting can only be executed after being approved by the Ministry of Finance.

Art. 51. Composition of the Council:

(1) Governor—President.
(2) Vice-Governor or Director General.
(3) Presidents or Directors General of Semi-Govt. institutions of credit, the list of which will be fixed by the Ministry of Finance.
(4) Two representatives respectively of the Ministry of Finance and of the Minister of National Economy, nominated by the competent ministers.
(5) One representative of the Ministry of Agriculture nominated on the proposal of the Ministry of Agriculture by the Minister of Finance.
(6) Two personalities nominated by the Ministry of Finance because of the functions they exercise on state account in the economic and financial field.

Art. 53. The Committee of Direction and the Directors:
It assists the Governor in the direction of day to day affairs.
The Governor lays down the powers and methods of work of the Council Directors.

BANK OF LIBYA

Art. 4. The Bank shall have a Board of Directors consisting of a Governor, a Deputy Governor and six Members including one representative of the Ministry of Finance.

The Governor, his Deputy and the other Members of the Board shall be Libyans having experience in finance, economics or banking. No person who has any serious interest in any other banking concern shall be a Member of the Board.

Art. 5. The Board of Directors of the Bank shall conduct its affairs and exercise the powers vasted in the Bank under this Law.

The Governor and Deputy Governor shall be appointed by Royal Decree on the proposal of the Minister for a term of five years and are eligible for re-appointment.

The other Directors shall be appointed by the Council of Ministers on the suggestion of the Minister after consultation with the Governor of the Bank for a period of three years and are eligible for re-appointment.

Art. 11. Any member of the Board shall cease to be a Member of the Board if he:

(1) Becomes bankrupt, suspends payment or compounds with his creditors.
(2) Is convicted of an offence or moral turpitude.
(3) Is appointed in a salaried public office.
(4) Becomes a candidate for election to Parliament or any Legislative Council.
(5) Becomes a manager or a member of the board of management of any other banking concern or institution or if he becomes a shareholder therein.

IV. LEGAL RESERVE REQUIREMENTS

BANK OF GHANA

15· (2) The assets of the issue department of the Bank may include only the following, that is to say,

(*a*) gold, coin or bullion;

(*b*) notes whether or not sterling, coin, bank balances and convertible currency with any other bank outside Ghana;

(*c*) Treasury Bills of the Government of any convertible currency country;

(*d*) bills of exchange bearing at least two good signatures drawn on any place outside Ghana, payable in convertible currency and having a maturity not exceeding three months exclusive of days of grace;

(*e*) securities of Governments other than the Government of Ghana expressed in convertible currency, so however, that not more than forty per centum of the total assets of the issue department is so held, such restrictions not applying if the assets are held for the financing of agricultural products or the marketing of crops;

(*f*) subject to the provisions of subsection (3) of this section,

(*i*) Treasury Bills of the Government denominated in pounds and maturing within ninety-three days;

(*ii*) other securities of the Government denominated in pounds and maturing in not more than twenty years which have been publicly issued or form part of an issue which is being made to the public at the time of acquisition.

(3) The aggregate holding of Treasury Bills and of securities under paragraph (*f*) of the immediately preceding subsection shall not at any time exceed forty per centum of the currency in circulation:

Provided that the Minister may, by legislative instrument, vary the amount of the aggregate holding of such Treasury Bills and of securities to an amount not exceeding sixty per centum of the currency in circulation.

(4) The assets of the issue department shall be available to meet only,

(*a*) the liabilities of that department, that is to say, an amount equal to the total amount of bank notes or coin which from time to time have been issued and not been held or withdrawn from circulation.

22. (1) If on any particular day the total amount of media of payment exceeds by fifteen per centum or more the total amount of media of payment which have been in existence at any time during the twelve months immediately preceding that day, the Board shall forthwith make a report to this effect to the Minister specifying the causes which in their opinion have led to that situation and their proposals to the Minister as to the steps to be taken in view thereof.

(2) For the purposes of this section, "media of payment" means the currency in circulation and current account deposits with banking institutions, not being currency in the hands of banking institutions and current deposits of the Government and of banking institutions.

CENTRAL BANK OF NIGERIA

18. The Bank shall have the sole right of issuing notes and coins throughout Nigeria and neither the Federal Government nor any Regional Government nor any other person shall issue currency notes, bank notes or coins or any documents or tokens payable to bearer on demand being documents or tokens which are likely to pass as legal tender.

25. The Bank shall at all times maintain a reserve of external assets consisting of all or any of the following:

(*a*) gold coin or bullion;

(*b*) balances at any bank outside Nigeria where the currency is sterling or is freely convertible into gold or sterling, and in such currency any notes, coin, money at call and where they bear at least two good signatures and have a maturity not exceeding ninety days exclusive of days of grace, any bill of exchange;

(*c*) Treasury Bills having a maturity not exceeding one hundred and eighty-four days issued by the Government of any country outside Nigeria whose currency is sterling or is freely convertible into gold or sterling;

(*d*) securities of or guaranteed by a Government of any country outside Nigeria whose currency is sterling or is freely convertible into gold or sterling where the securities held under this paragraph do not exceed thirty per centum of the reserve of external assets and not more than two-thirds of the securities held will mature in a period exceeding five years.

26-28. The value of the reserve of external assets shall be not less than forty per centum of the total demand liabilities of the Bank.

BANK OF RHODESIA AND NYASALAND

18. (1) The Bank shall maintain a reserve consisting of gold, sterling or foreign assets convertible into gold or sterling.

(2) The value of the reserve shall be at least twenty-five per centum of the Bank's liabilities to the public.

(3) The Minister may suspend, for a period not exceeding sixty days, the reserve requirements provided in terms of subsection (2), and may extend such period for further periods not exceeding sixty days each, but no such suspension shall continue for a period longer than six months unless the Federal Assembly by resolution approves of such continuation.

RESERVE BANK OF RHODESIA

17. (1) The Bank shall maintain a reserve consisting of gold, sterling, or foreign assets convertible into gold or sterling.

(2) The value of the reserve shall be at least twenty-five per centum of the Bank's liabilities to the public.

BANK OF SUDAN

32. (1) The Bank shall maintain at all times a reserve of gold and external assets expressed in currencies determined from time to time by the Board and consisting of all or any of the following:

(*a*) Foreign exchange.

(*b*) Bills of exchange and promissory notes denominated in foreign currency and payable at any place outside the Sudan.

(*c*) Treasury bills issued by foreign Governments determined from time to time by the Board.

(*d*) Securities issued or guaranteed by foreign Governments or international institutions, determined from time to time by the Board.

(2) The reserve stipulated in the preceding subsection shall at no time be less than 25 percent of the aggregate amount of the currency in circulation and other sight liabilities of the Bank.

BANK OF MOROCCO

Art. 21. The Bank is bound to hold reserve of gold or a reserve of foreign exchange convertible into gold. The amount of this reserve cannot be less than $\frac{1}{9}$ of the total notes in circulation. This percentage may be increased to the maximum of $\frac{1}{3}$ on a proposal by the Ministry of Finance at the demand of the Bank's council.

Art. 22. Gold cover must consist of (1) gold bullion (2) gold coin (3) gold on the account of foreign credit balances.

Art. 23. Foreign Exchange convertible into gold admitted in this cover must consist exclusively of notes and demand (en compt) deposits.

BANK OF LIBYA

Art. 31. Notes and coins in circulation shall always be covered by the following assets:

(1) Gold bullion, gold coins or foreign currencies convertible under the Article of Agreement of the International Monetary Fund or other convertible currencies provided that the overall total does not exceed twenty five per cent of the total assets of the Issue Department.

(2) Securities including Treasury Bills issued or guaranteed by the Libyan Government maturing within fifteen years provided that such securities do not exceed ten per cent of the total assets of the Issue Department.

(3) Treasury Bills issued by foreign governments whose currencies may be held under para (1) of this Article.

(4) Securities issued or guaranteed by foreign governments whose currencies may be held under para (1) of this Article maturing within five years provided that the value of such securities does not exceed sixty five per cent of the total assets of the Issue Department. Within this limit the Board of Directors of the Bank may hold foreign securities maturing within fifteen years provided the value of such securities does not exceed fifteen per cent of the total assets of the Issue Department.

V. OPERATIONS, BUSINESS AND POWERS

BANK OF GHANA

23. The Bank may,

(*a*) import, export, refine, buy, hold, sell, transfer or otherwise deal in silver, platinum, gold and other precious metals;

(*b*) acquire, hold and transfer foreign exchange and foreign Government securities;

(*c*) effect foreign exchange transactions of any kind.

24. (1) The Bank may,

(*a*) with the prior approval of the Minister,

(*i*) borrow from foreign institutions and pledge assets held by it as security for the repayment of the loan;

(*ii*) lend money or grant short-term credits to foreign institutions;

(*b*) at the request of the Minister, guarantee a loan granted to the Government or to any person in Ghana by a foreign institution.

25. The Minister may in consultation with the Board take decisions relating to the exchange rate of the pound in relation to external currencies.

26. Save as otherwise directed by the Minister the Bank shall hold, manage or control foreign exchange and the transfer of funds outside Ghana.

27. (1) The Bank may purchase and sell external currencies, and purchase, sell, discount and rediscount bills of exchange and Treasury Bills drawn in or on places outside Ghana and maturing within ninety-one days, exclusive of days of grace, from the date of acquisition.

(2) The Bank may purchase and sell securities of, or guaranteed by, the Government of a country outside Ghana.

28. Within the limits of its policy, the Bank may undertake the following credit operations with individuals, public institutions or bodies corporate whether private or public, that is to say:

(*a*) buy, sell, discount and rediscount,

(*i*) inland bills of exchange and promissory notes arising out of bona-fide commercial transactions bearing at least two good signatures and maturing within ninety days, exclusive of days of grace, from the date of acquisition by the Bank;

(*ii*) inland commercial bills of exchange and promissory notes bearing at least two good signatures drawn or issued for the purpose of financing seasonal agricultural operations or the marketing of crops, and maturing within one hundred and eighty days, exclusive of days of grace, from the date of acquisition by the Bank; and

(*iii*) hold Treasury Bills which have been publicly issued and are to mature within ninety-one days;

(*b*) purchase and sell securities of the Government which have been publicly offered for sale and are to mature within a period of twenty years;

(*c*) grant advances for fixed periods not exceeding three months against publicly issued Treasury Bills of the Government maturing within ninety-one days;

(*d*) grant advances against:

(*i*) gold, coin or bullion;

(*ii*) securities of the Government which have been publicly offered for sale and are to mature within a period of twenty years;

(*iii*) bills of exchange and promissory notes as are eligible for purchase, discount or rediscount by the Bank; or

(*iv*) warehouse warrants issued by lawfully formed general and bonded warehouses or their equivalent securing possession of goods, in respect of staple commodities or other goods duly insured and with a letter of pledge from the owner.

CENTRAL BANK OF NIGERIA

28. (1) Unless otherwise prohibited by any law relating to the control of exchange the Bank shall, on demand at its head office in Lagos:

(*a*) issue and redeem Nigerian currency against sterling, and

(*b*) at its discretion issue and reedem Nigerian currency against gold or other currencies eligible for inclusion in the reserve of external assets under this Act: provided that the rates of exchange quoted by the Bank for spot transactions shall not differ by more than one percent from the parity of the Nigerian pound with the parity of the other currency.

(2) Nothing in this section shall be construed to require the Bank to sell or buy sterling for an amount less than ten thousand pounds in respect of any one transaction.

29. (1) The Bank may—

(*a*) issue demand drafts and effect other kinds of remittances payable at its own offices or at the offices of agencies or correspondents;

(*b*) purchase and sell gold coin or bullion;

(*c*) open accounts for and accept deposits from the Federal Government, the Regional Governments, the funds, institutions and corporations of all such Governments, banks, other credit institutions and, with the prior approval of the Minister, other persons in Nigeria;

(*d*) purchase, sell discount and rediscount inland bills of exchange and promissory notes arising out of bonafide commercial transactions bearing two or more good signatures and maturing within ninety days, exclusive of days of grace, from the date of acquisition;

(*e*) purchase, sell, discount and rediscount inland bills of exchange and promissory notes bearing two or more good signatures, drawn or issued for the purpose of financing seasonal agricultural operations or the marketing of crops, and maturing within one hundred and eighty days, exclusive of days of grace, from the date of acquisition;

(*f*) purchase, sell, discount and rediscount Treasury Bills of the Federal Government which have been publicly offered for sale and are to mature within ninety-three days;

(*g*) purchase and sell securities of the Federal Government maturing in not more than twenty-five years which have been publicly offered for sale or form part of an issue which is being made to the public at the time of acquisition: Provided that the total amount of such securities of a maturity exceeding two years in the ownership of the Bank (other than securities held in terms of paragraph (*h*) or held by the Bank as collateral under sub-paragraph (*ii*) of paragraph (*k*) shall not together at any time exceed thirty-three and one third percent of the total demand liabilities of the Bank.

(*h*) with the approval of the Minister, subscribe to, hold and sell shares of any corporation set up with the approval of, or under the authority, of the Federal Government for the purpose of promoting the development of a money market or securities market in Nigeria or of improving the financial machinery for the financing of economic development: Provided that the total value of any holding of such shares shall not at any time exceed fifty per centum of the aggregate of the Bank's paid-up capital and of the General Reserve Fund of the Bank;

(*i*) grant advances for fixed periods not exceeding three months against publicly issued Treasury Bills of the Federal Government within ninety three days;

(*j*) grant advances for fixed periods not exceeding three months at a minimum rate of interest at least one per cent above the Bank's minimum rediscount rate against promissory notes secured by the pledge with Bank of:

(*i*) gold coin or bullion;

(*ii*) securities of the Federal Government which have been publicly offered for sale and are to mature within a period of twenty-five years: Provided that no advance so secured shall at any time exceed seventy-five percent of the market value of the security pledged and that the total of such securities held by the Bank is within the limitations imposed by paragraph (*g*);

(*iii*) such bills of exchange and promissory notes as are eligible for purchase, discount or rediscount by the Bank up to seventy-five percent of their nominal value;

(*iv*) warehouse warrants, or their equivalent (securing possession of goods), in respect of staple commodities or other goods duly insured and with a letter of hypothecation from the owner; Provided that no such advance shall exceed sixty percent of the market value of the commodities in question;

(*k*) purchase and sell external currencies, and purchase, sell, discount and rediscount bills of exchange and Treasury Bills drawn in or on places abroad and maturing within one hundred and eighty-four days, exclusive of days of grace, from the date of acquisition;

(*l*) maintain accounts with central banks and other banks abroad;

(*m*) purchase and sell securities of or guaranteed by any Government whose currency is sterling or is freely convertible into gold or sterling or securities issued by international financial institutions, of which Nigeria is a member, which are also expressed in currencies which are sterling or are freely convertible into gold or sterling;

(*n*) undertake the issue and management of loans publicly issued in Nigeria by the Federal or Regional Governments or by Federal or Regional public bodies;

(*o*) promote the establishment of bank clearing systems and give facilities for the conduct of clearing business in premises belonging to the Bank;

(*p*) subject to as expressly provided in this Ordinance, generally conduct business as a bank, and do all such things as are incidental to or consequential upon the exercise of its powers or the discharge of its duties under this Act.

BANK OF RHODESIA AND NYASALAND

9. (1) Subject to the provisions of section (10) the Bank may:

(*a*) make or cause to be made and issue bank notes and coins in accordance with the provisions of this Act;

(*b*) accept money on current account and collect money for customers;
(*c*) grant loans and advances;
(*d*) buy, sell, discount, or rediscount:
(*i*) bills of exchange or promissory notes drawn or issued for commercial, industrial, or agricultural purposes;
(*ii*) bills of the Federal or Territorial Governments; and
(*iii*) short-term obligations of bodies corporate established by or under authority conferred by the provisions of any Federal or Territorial law;
(*e*) buy and sell securities;
(*f*) buy and sell foreign currencies, foreign bills of exchange, and bills of foreign governments;
(*g*) open credits and issue guarantees;
(*h*) open accounts in foreign countries and act as agent or correspondent for the International Monetary Fund or for any bank carrying on business in or outside the Federation;
(*i*) make arrangements or enter into agreements, subject to the consent of the Minister, with any bank or financial institution in a country outside the Federation, to borrow, in such manner, at such rates of interest, and upon such other terms and conditions as it may deem fit, any foreign currency which it may deem expedient to acquire;
(*j*) underwrite any loan proposed to be raised by the Federal Government, a Territorial Government, a local authority, or any other body corporate established by or under authority conferred by the provisions of any Federal or Territorial law;
(*k*) undertake, as agent, the issue and management of loans raised or to be raised within the Federation by any Government, local authority, or body corporate mentioned in paragraph (*n*);
(*l*) perform, as agent, such duties and carry out such functions as may be authorised by any law, or by the Minister in terms of any law, relating to foreign exchange or other financial control;
(*m*) organize and provide facilities for the collection and clearance of cheques and similar instruments;
(*n*) regulate the proceedings and conduct of its business, including the proceedings at meetings and the recording of minutes;
(*o*) do any other banking business incidental to or consequential upon the provisions of this Act and not prohibited by this Act.

(2) The Bank shall fix and announce from time to time its minimum rates for discounts and rediscounts.

RESERVE BANK OF RHODESIA

9. The Bank may:

(*a*) make or cause to be made and issue bank notes and coin in accordance with the provisions of this Act;
(*b*) accept money on current account and collect money for customers;
(*c*) grant loans and advances;
(*d*) buy, sell, discount or rediscount:

(*i*) bills of exchange or promissory notes drawn or issued for commercial, industrial, or agricultural purposes;

(*ii*) bills, notes or other obligations of the Government;

(*iii*) obligations of bodies corporate established by or under authority conferred by the provisions of any law or enactment, or constituted or reconstituted by the Federation of Rhodesia and Nyasaland (Dissolution) Order in Council, 1963;

(*iv*) bills, notes, or other obligations issued by itself;

(*e*) buy and sell securities;

(*f*) buy, sell or deal in precious metals, and hold in safe custody for other persons gold, securities, or other articles of value;

(*g*) buy and sell foreign currencies, foreign bills of exchange, and bills or other obligations of foreign governments;

(*h*) open credits and issue guarantees;

(*i*) open accounts in foreign countries and act as agent or correspondent for the International Monetary Fund or for any bank carrying on business in or outside Southern Rhodesia;

(*j*) make arrangements or enter into agreements, subject to the consent of the Minister, with any bank or other financial institution in a country outside Southern Rhodesia, to borrow, in such manner, at such rates of interest, and upon such other terms and conditions as it may deem fit, any foreign currency which it may deem expedient to acquire;

(*k*) underwrite any loan proposed to be raised by the Government or any body corporate established by or under authority conferred by the provisions of any law or enactment, or constituted or re-constituted by the Federation of Rhodesia and Nyasaland (Dissolution) Order in Council, 1963;

(*l*) undertake, as agent, the issue and management of loans raised or to be raised within Southern Rhodesia by the Government or a body corporate such as is mentioned in paragraph (*n*);

(*m*) perform, as agent, such duties and carry out such functions as may be authorised by any law or enactment or by the Minister in terms of any law or enactment, relating to foreign exchange or other financial control;

(*n*) organize and provide facilities for the collection and clearance of cheques and similar instruments;

(*o*) regulate the proceedings and conduct of its business, including the proceedings at meetings and the recording of minutes;

(*p*) do any other business incidental to or consequential upon the provisions of this Act and not prohibited by this Act.

BANK OF SUDAN

33. The Bank shall be the depository of Sudan's official external reserves.

34. The Bank may—

(*a*) buy, sell or deal in gold coins or bullion or other precious metals at home and abroad and hold gold coins or bullion or other precious metals in safe custody for others;

(*b*) buy, sell or deal in foreign exchange using for these purposes any of the instruments commonly used by bankers;
(*c*) purchase and sell Treasury Bills and other securities issued or guaranteed by foreign governments or international financial institutions;
(*d*) open and maintain accounts and appoint agents and correspondents abroad;
(*e*) open and maintain accounts and act as agent or correspondent for foreign banks, governments and government agencies and international institutions.

35. The Bank shall (save in special circumstances) deal in connection with the operations enumerated in Section 34 only with banks operating in the Sudan, the Government and its boards and agencies, Local Government bodies, foreign central and commercial banks, foreign governments and government institutions and international institutions.

36. The Bank may grant loans to, or receive loans from, any of the institutions specified in paragraph (*e*) of Section 34. Provided that such loans shall be of a short term character and consistent with the functions of the Bank as a central bank.

37. The Bank shall from time to time determine the rates at which it will buy and sell specified foreign currencies. Provided that buying and selling rates for spot foreign currency shall be fixed in accordance with obligations which the Government has under the Articles of Agreement of the International Monetary Fund.

38. The Bank shall carry out as agent such functions and duties relating to control of foreign exchange transactions as may be authorised by any law, or by the Minister pursuant to any law.

39. In case of a change in the par value of foreign currency in which any of the external assets of the Bank are denominated or a change in the par value of the Sudanese Pound, any revaluation profit or loss shall be for account of the Government.

62. The Bank may:
(*a*) with the prior agreement of the Minister open accounts for and accept deposits from persons other than those enumerated in paragraph (*e*) of Section 34 and in Sections 40, 53 and 56;
(*b*) hold as long as it thinks fit such accounts as it may take over from the offices of the National Bank of Egypt pursuant to Section 77.

63. (1). The Bank may with the prior agreement of the Minister enter into credit operations with persons other than banks and the Government.

64. The Bank may, with the approval of the Minister, subscribe to, buy, hold and sell shares of any enterprise, the participation in or the initiation of which promotes the Bank's aims or is generally in the interest of the national economy.

CENTRAL BANK OF TUNISIA

Art. 35. (1) The Central Bank exercises on behalf of the state the extensive privilege of issuing over the territory of the Republic notes and pieces of metallic money.

Art. 39. (1) The operations of the Central Bank generating the issue of money comprise:

(*a*) operations in gold and in foreign exchange;
(*b*) credit operations;
(*c*) purchase and sale of bills in the money market;
(*d*) accommodation granted to the Treasury.

Art. 40. (1) The Central Bank can buy or sell gold.

(2) It can buy and sell instruments of payment drawn in foreign currency and assets in foreign currency. It ensures the conduct of these assets and their investment in short-term bills.

(3) It can borrow short-term credit from banks in other countries and can extend short-term credit to these banks.

Art. 41. (1) The Central Bank can rediscount or hold on behalf of the banks bills representing commercial transactions and binding three solvent persons (physical or legal).

(2) The maturing of these bills cannot exceed 3 months. This maturity can always be carried to six months at most within the rules fixed by the Council.

Art. 42. (1) The Central Bank can according to previous agreement rediscount bills of exchange from banks accompanied by at least two signatures of solvent positions and created in the representation of companies agreed to by the banks.

(2) These bills ought to be drawn for a maximum period of 3 months. They are renewable, but the total duration with the consent of the Central Bank cannot exceed 9 months.

Art. 43. (1) The Central Bank can offer rediscounting facilities to all banks or all institutions specially accepted by the Secretary of State for Finance on the proposal of the Central Bank, dealing with medium term credit operations, or bills representing medium-term credit with 3 months maturity and renewable for a maximum period of 5 years.

(2) The bills must fulfil the following conditions:

(*a*) They must carry in addition to the signature of the party concerned, signatures of two other solvent persons of whom one can be replaced by the guarantee of the state.

(*b*) They must have one of the following objectives:
development of the means of production;
financing of exports;
construction of residential buildings;

(*c*) These bills, after having received the previous consent of the Central Bank, may be subjected by the Central Bank to the concessions of unconditional guarantee of the State.

Art. 44. The Council fixes from time to time the total amount of accommodation that can be given for rediscounting bills representative of medium-term credit operations.

Art. 45. (1) The Central Bank may consent to grant advances to banks on securities other than Govt. securities on condition that these securities are quoted in an official market. It can also grant advances on gold and on foreign exchange.

(2) The Council draws the list of securities, papers involving gold or foreign exchange admitted as guarantee and fixes the percentages of advances.

(3) These advances may be made for a maximum period of 3 months and

subject to the limitation of a total period of 9 months, these advances may be renewed.

(4) The borrower gives an undertaking to the Central Bank to repay the Central Bank the entire amount of credit granted on the maturity of these loans; this undertaking includes the obligation of the borrower to pay the Central Bank any fraction of the credit granted corresponding to the depreciation affecting the value of the collaterals everytime this depreciation is of the extent of 10% or over. Failure on the part of the borrower to satisfy this condition makes the amount of credit legally binding, (unquestionable) and immediately due.

Art. 46. The Central Bank can consent to the following operations on good securities issued or guaranteed by the State.

(*a*) Discounting or rediscounting securities with less than three months maturity except those at the Treasury and public institutions;

(*b*) Holding of the same securities at the banks;

c) Accommodating, according to the ratios and time limits fixed by the council, advances on Govt. securities the list of which is drawn by the council. The borrower gives an undertaking to the Central Bank which has been previously mentioned in Art. 45, Sub-Section 4.

BANK OF MOROCCO

Art. 10. The Bank of Morocco participates in the establishment of provisions for receipts and expenditure of foreign exchange and for elaboration of programmes of importing.

Art. 11. The Bank may be charged by the Ministry of Finance for the creation of certain financial institutions of general interest under the control of the state or the guarantee of the state.

Art. 12. The Bank is the financial agent of all institutions and establishments endowed with a public character for their banking and credit operations all over Morocco as well as abroad.

Art. 13. This Bank is held responsible for watching the application of the legal and regulatory powers in relation to the exercise of the banking provision as well as in relation to the organization of the money and capital market.

Operations constituting the counterpart of the Issue:

Art. 26. (1) operations on gold and foreign exchange. The Bank can proceed with all operations on gold. The Bank can equally proceed with (1) operations in foreign exchange notes using generally all instruments of payments drawn in foreign money and utilised in international transfers. (2) Demand deposits in foreign exchange, (3) commercial bills to (sight) order drawn in foreign exchange in Morocco on the foreigners and responding to the conditions of eligibility of bills which may be discounted by the Bank (4) Bills issued by or guaranteed by foreign states of a maximum of maturity 3 months.

Loss resulting from devaluation will be reimbursed by the State. Gain is to be appropriated by the State.

Credit Operations:

Art. 28. (1) Discount, buy, sell or deal in commercial bills of exchange of a maximum maturity of 120 days from the date of discounting. Bills issued or guaranteed by the State on the conditions that these bills are not acquired directly from the Treasury or any department issuing such bills.

(2) The Bank may grant loans and advances for a fixed period if guaranteed by (*a*) gold coin or gold bullion, (*b*) foreign exchange or credits in foreign exchange, (*c*) Securities or bills issued or guaranteed by the State and (*d*) commercial bills of exchange (*e*) all other real assets accepted by the Bank and guaranteed by the state.

Art. 29. Commercial bills which are discounted must have 3 signatures, one signature may be replaced by one of the guarantees enumerated in Art. 28.

Art. 30. Bills created by industrial and agricultural companies will require 2 signatures.

Art. 31. Commercial bills representing medium term credit which are discounted must have at least 3 signatures of which one is a credit agency specialised in medium term credit approved by the Ministry of Finance. These bills may have a maximum duration of 5 years, from the date of presentation to the Bank, having exclusively for their object the development of the means of production transport, equipment, construction of residential buildings and the financing of certain exports and imports.

Art. 32. The loans and advances of Art. 28 may have a maximum duration of 9 months excepting those guaranteed by the State or public institutions which will have a maximum duration of 1 year.

Art. 33. Subject to the provisions of Arts 7-12, the credit operations mentioned in Arts. 28-32 with the exception of operation affecting State funds or public bills can only be effected in favour of banks and other credit agencies.

Art. 35. Financial accommodation accorded to the state by the Bank of Morocco provides advances to the State or to some other public organisations.

The Bank can discount and deal in obligations underwritten at the order of the Treasury within the conditions fixed by the Ministry of Finance having a maximum period of maturity of 90 days.

The Bank may advance to the State in the form of cash facility limited to $\frac{1}{10}$ of the ordinary budget revenue of the last budgetary year on condition that the total duration of these advances does not exceed 240 days, consecutive or not, during one calendar year.

All financial accommodation to the State other than those mentioned in paragraphs 1-3 of the present Art. and also those mentioned in Arts 9 and 28 of the present decree can only be provided according to an agreement with the State and the Bank approved by a Royal Decree.

Other Operations

Art. 36- The Bank can open and hold current accounts and deposit accounts; receive in deposit securities, precious metals, and money and let safe deposit vaults, procured on all operations for the collections of securities, to effect all operations of exchange ready as well as term.

Obtain short-term credit from foreigners with or without security guarantees.

In a general manner make all banking operations on the order and in the account of third parties in as much the covers of the above operations are furnished or assured to the satisfaction of the Bank.

Art. 39. The Bank can with the authorisation of Ministry of Finance subscribe to the capital of financial institutions registered by particular legal regulations or placed under the control of the State.

The Bank can under the same conditions subscribe to the loans issued by the same institutions.

BANK OF LIBYA

Art. 14. In carrying out its activities the Bank may:

(1) Purchase, sell, import and export gold coin and bullion and deal therein in any manner whatsoever.

(2) Purchase and sell foreign exchange.

(3) Rediscount inland bills of exchange and promissory notes arising out of bona fide commercial transactions, bearing two or more good signatures and maturing within six months.

(4) Purchase and sell securities and bills issued or guaranteed by the Government and maturing within fifteen years.

(5) Purchase and sell securities issued or guaranteed by foreign Governments and maturing within ten years.

Art. 15. The Bank may undertake credit operations with banks which are subject to the provisions of this Law, in accordance with the conditions and terms laid down by the Board.

Art. 16. In case of financial disorders or any other emergency affecting the stability of credit or requiring the Bank to provide for the essential needs of the financial market the Bank may, after the approval of the Council of Ministers, grant exceptional loans to the banks secured by such assets and under such conditions as may be specified by the Board.

Art. 17. The Bank shall undertake monetary control and supervise Libyan internal and external transfers of currency.

VI. PROHIBITED BUSINESS

CENTRAL BANK OF NIGERIA

30. The Bank may not:

(*a*) engage in trade or otherwise, have a direct interest in any commercial, agricultural, industrial, or, save as provided in paragraph (*i*) of section 29, any other undertaking, except such interests as the Bank may in any way acquire in the course of the satisfaction of debts, due to it, and provided that all such interests so acquired shall be disposed of at the earliest suitable moment:

(*b*) save as provided in paragraph (*ii*) of section 29, purchase the shares of any corporation or company including the shares of any banking company;

(*c*) grant loans upon the security of any shares;

(*d*) subject to the provisions of section 34, grant unsecured advances or advances secured otherwise than as laid down in paragraphs (*j*) and (*k*) of section 29; Provided that in the event of any debts due to the

Bank becoming in the opinion of the Bank endangered, the Bank may secure such debts on any real or other property of the debtor and may acquire such property, which shall be resold at the earliest suitable moment;

(*e*) purchase, acquire or lease real property except in accordance with the provision to paragraph (*d*) and except so far as the bank shall consider necessary or expedient for the provision, or future provision of business premises for the Bank and its agencies and any clearing houses set up in terms of section 42, and of residences for the Governor, Deputy Governor, officials and other employees;

(*f*) draw or accept bills payable otherwise than on demand;

(*g*) allow the renewal or substitution of maturing bills of exchange purchased, discounted or rediscounted by or pledged with the Bank save in exceptional circumstances when the Board may by resolution authorise one renewal or one substitution only in either case of not more than fifty percent of the original amount of any such bills for a period not exceeding ninety days;

(*h*) pay interest on deposits;

(*i*) accept for discount, or as security for an advance made by the Bank, bills or notes signed by members of the Board or by the Bank's officials or other employees;

(*j*) open accounts for and accept deposits from persons other than as provided in paragraphs (*c*) and (*o*) of section 29.

BANK OF RHODESIA AND NYASALAND

10. The Bank may not—

(*a*) save with the consent of the Minister, purchase the shares of any banking institution or grant loans or advances upon the security thereof;

(*b*) lend or advance money on immovable property secured by mortgage, pledge, notarial, or other bond.

(*c*) make unsecured loans and advances, except to the Federal and Territorial Governments;

(*d*) lend or advance moneys to, or directly purchase Treasury bills or notes from, the Federal Government so that the amount outstanding at any one time exceeds twenty per centum of the estimated revenues of the Federal Government for its financial year in which such advances are made, nor shall such advances be made unless they are repayable within three months of the termination of the financial year in which they are made;

(*e*) buy or discount bills of exchange or promissory notes issued or drawn for commercial and industrial purposes which have a maturity exceeding one hundred and twenty days;

(*f*) buy or discount bills of exchange or promissory notes issued or drawn for agricultural purposes which have a maturity exceeding six months;

(*g*) invest in securities of the Federal Government with a longer maturity than six months a sum exceeding the capital and general reserve fund of the Bank, plus twenty per centum of its liabilities to the public in the Federation.

RESERVE BANK OF RHODESIA

9(2). The Bank may not—

(*a*) lend or advance moneys to, or directly purchase Treasury Bills or notes from, the Government so that the amount outstanding at any one time exceeds twenty per centum of the estimated revenues of the Government for its financial year in which such advances are made, nor shall such advances be made unless they are repayable within three months of the termination of the financial year in which they are made;

(*b*) invest in securities of the Government with a longer maturity than six months a sum exceeding the capital and general reserve fund of the Bank plus twenty per centum of its liabilities to the public in Southern Rhodesia.

VII. RELATIONS WITH THE GOVERNMENT

BANK OF GHANA

35. (1). The Bank may purchase and sell, on the market, securities of the Government and other securities which are obligations to make payment in Ghana currency and which bear interest at a fixed rate.

(2). The Bank shall exercise its power under this section whenever in the opinion of the Governor this is necessary in order to increase or reduce the amount of media of payment within the meaning of section 22 of this Act, or carry out any of the objects specified in section 3 of this Act.

(3). The Bank may, after consultation with the Minister, issue securities of its own, prescribe conditions therefore and sell or purchase them.

36. (1). The Bank shall be the sole banker and fiscal agent in Ghana of the Government, and may act as banker to any Government institution or agency.

(2). The Bank shall not receive from the Government a remuneration for its services under this section, save in cases determined by agreement with the Minister.

(3). The Bank shall pay, receive, collect and remit money, bullion and securities on behalf of the Government and undertake and transact any other business which the Government may from time to time entrust to the Bank.

(4). No interest shall be paid by the Bank on amounts deposited in any Government account.

(5). In any place where the Bank shall have no branch the Bank may appoint a banking institution to act as its agent for the collection and payment of Government moneys.

37. (1) The Bank may make temporary advances to the Government in respect of temporary deficiencies of budget revenue and the total amount of such advances shall not at any time exceed ten per centum of the estimated budget revenue, as laid before the National Assembly, for the financial year in which the advances are made;

(2) Subject as aforesaid the Bank may in certain cases make advances not exceeding fifteen per centum of the estimated budget revenue if the President so requests.

(3). Any advances made under this section shall be repaid within three months of the end of the financial year to which it relates; and if any such advances remain unpaid after that date the power of the Bank to make further advances in any subsequent financial year shall not be exercisable unless the amounts due in respect of outstanding advances have been repaid.

(4). The Bank shall charge interest on such advances at a rate to be determined by the Board in consultation with the Minister.

38. The Bank shall be entrusted with the issue and management of Government loans publicly issued upon such terms and conditions as may be agreed between the Government and the Bank.

CENTRAL BANK OF NIGERIA

32. (1). The Bank shall be entrusted with the Federal Government's banking and foreign exchange transactions in Nigeria and abroad.

(2) The Bank shall receive and disburse Federal Government moneys and keep account thereof without remuneration for such services.

34. (1). Notwithstanding the provisions of paragraph (*d*) of section 30, the Bank may grant temporary advances to the Federal Government in respect of temporary deficiencies of budget revenue at such rate or rates of interest as the Bank may determine.

(2). The total amount of such advances outstanding shall not at any time exceed twelve and one half per cent of the estimated recurrent budget revenue as laid before the Federal legislature for the Federal Government financial year in which the advances are granted.

(3). All such advances shall be repaid as soon as possible and shall in any event be repayable by the end of the Federal Government financial year in which they are granted. If after that date any such advances remain unrepaid the power of the Bank to grant further such advances in any subsequent financial year shall not be exercised unless and until the outstanding advances have been repaid.

35. The Bank shall be entrusted with the issue and management of Federal Government loans publicly issued in Nigeria upon such terms and conditions as may be agreed between the Federal Government and the Bank.

BANK OF RHODESIA AND NYASALAND

11. (1). The Bank shall act as banker to the Federal Government and to any of the Territorial Governments which may request it so to act.

(2). Nothing in this section contained shall prevent the Federal Government or the Territorial Governments from carrying on transactions in such manner as they may require at places where the Bank has no branches or agencies. In its capacity as banker to the Governments the Bank shall make the necessary arrangements to this end.

(3). The Bank, when authorized by the Minister to do so, shall act as agent for the Federal Government in the payment of interest and principal and generally in respect of the issue and management of the public debt of the Federation and, at the request of the Government of a Territory, may act likewise in respect of the public debt of that Territory.

RESERVE BANK OF RHODESIA

10. (1). The Bank shall act as banker to the Government.

(2). The Bank, when authorized by the Minister to do so, shall act as agent for the Government in the payment of interest and principal and generally in respect of the issue and management of the public debt of Southern Rhodesia, and may act likewise in respect of the debts of any body corporate established by or under authority conferred by the provisions of any law or enactment, or constituted or reconstituted by the Federation of Rhodesia and Nyasaland.

BANK OF SUDAN

52. The Bank shall be the banker and fiscal agent of the Government.

53. (1) The Bank shall be the depository of Government's funds.

(2) The Bank shall receive and disburse Government monies and keep account thereof without remuneration for such services. No interest shall be paid by the Bank on amounts outstanding on Government accounts.

54. The Bank shall be entrusted with the issue and management of Government loans publicly issued in the Sudan upon such terms and conditions as may be agreed between the Government and the Bank.

55. The Bank may act generally as agent for the Government on such terms and conditions as may be agreed between the Government and the Bank, when it can do so consistently with the provisions of this Act and with its duties as a central bank.

56. The Bank may act as Banker and fiscal agent to Government Boards and Agencies and to Local Government bodies on such terms and conditions as may be agreed.

57. The Bank may grant temporary advances to the Government at such rate or rates of interest as the Bank may determine. Provided that the total of such advances outstanding at any time shall not exceed 15 per cent of the estimated ordinary revenue of the Government for the financial year in which such advances are granted. Provided further that all such advances shall be repaid at the latest within six months following the end of the financial year in which they are granted.

57A. The Bank may, with the approval of the Minister, advance monies and grant credit facilities to Government boards, agencies and Local Government bodies for periods not exceeding one year and at such rate or rates of interest as the Bank may determine. The amounts of such advances and credits shall be deductible from the maximum amount of temporary advances to the Government permissible under Section 57.

58. The Bank may purchase and sell securities issued by the Government which were publicly offered for sale or form part of an issue which is being made to the public at the time of the acquisition, provided that the total amount of such securities owned by the Bank and held by the Bank as collateral pursuant to item (*iv*) of paragraph (*c*) of Section 41 does not exceed at any time one-half of the total of the paid in capital of the Bank and the General Reserve Fund.

CENTRAL BANK OF TUNISIA

Art. 49. The Central Bank can discount or hold guaranteed bills or obligations issued under orders accountable to the Treasury within the conditions fixed by the Secretary of State for finance. These bills may have maturity for a maximum period of 3 months.

Art. 50. (1) In view of permitting the regular functioning of the Treasury of the State and of the normal execution of public expenses, the Central Bank can, within the limit of a maximum amount of 5% of the ordinary receipts of the state in the last budgetary year, grant the Treasury overdrafts on current account. The duration of such overdrafts cannot exceed 240 days in a calendar year, whether consecutive or not.

(2) The Central Bank gets by virtue of overdrafts mentioned above, a commission for operations of which the rate and the modes are fixed mutually by consultation with the Secretary of State for Finance.

Art. 55. (1) The Central Bank is the financial agent of the Govt. for all its cash, banking and credit operations.

Art. 57. The Central Bank assists the government in its relation with the international financial institutions. The Governor and the agents of the Central Bank deputed for this purposes may represent the govt. in these institutions as well as in international conferences.

Art. 58. (1) The Central Bank participates in negotiations which have the objective of concluding agreements on payments and compensation. It is entrusted with the execution of these agreements. It can conclude all conventions regarding methods of application necessary for this purpose.

(2) The agreements mentioned above are executed on behalf of the State which receives all the profits, bears all the risks, expenses, commissions, interest and whatever other charges and guarantees to the Central Bank, the repayment of all loss of exchange or other loss that it might incur on these accounts.

BANK OF MOROCCO

Art. 6. The Bank is the financial Adviser to the Government. The Government consults the Bank on all matters on money which affect the prerogatives and functions of the Bank defined by the present decree. The Bank submits to the government advice and all suggestions relative to the same matters.

Art. 7. The Bank is the agent of the Treasury for all banking and credit operations all over Morocco as well as abroad; for this purpose the Bank is charged, within conditions fixed by the order of the Ministry of Finance, with the operations of issue, conversion and repayment of public debt and in a general manner to provide financial service for the loans issued by the state. It may be equally charged for assuring financial service for loans guaranteed by the state. It participates in the negotiation of foreign lending and borrowing concluded on state account or with the guarantee of the state.

It may represent the state in the above negotiations according to the directives of the Minister of Finance.

Art. 8. The Bank of Morocco assists the Govt. in its relations with the financial institutions of an international character created with a view to promote international co-operation in the monetary and financial fields where the Bank represents the Govt.

Art. 9. The Bank participates in the negotiation of international financial agreements and is held responsible for their execution. It concludes all conventions useful for agreement. The state will compensate the Bank for any possible exchange loss on any transactions on behalf of the state.

BANK OF LIBYA

Art. 18. The Bank shall be the banker for the Government, Provinces and public concerns with body corporate, it shall undertake their banking transactions and they shall deposit their balances therewith.

No interest shall be paid by the Bank on funds and balances deposited in Government and Provincial accounts, neither shall the Bank collect charges on any banking services rendered thereto.

Art. 19. The Government shall entrust the Bank with the issue and management of all Government loans and shall service and redeem such loans. The Bank shall give its advice before any loans are concluded.

Art. 20. The Bank may extend temporary advances to the Government to cover any temporary deficit in budget revenue. Such advances shall not exceed ten percent of the total revenue estimated in the Budget and shall be repayable by the end of the Government's fiscal year in which they were made.

No advance may be made to the Government in any fiscal year unless all advances made in the previous financial year have been repaid.

The conditions under which such advances may be made shall be agreed upon between the Government and the Bank according to the monetary and credit situation prevailing at the time.

Art. 21. The Government may entrust the Bank with the functions and duties arising out of Government membership in international financial institutions and may delegate the Bank to represent the Government in contacts, negotiations and transactions with foreign governments and international organisations in respect of monetary, financial, economic or commercial matter.

Art. 22. The Minister shall specify by agreement with the Board of the Bank the ordinary commercial operations which may be undertaken by the Bank together with the conditions under which such operations shall be undertaken provided that the accounts of such operations shall be kept separate and distinct from all other accounts.

In making commercial loans the Bank may not use the deposits of commercial banks or their reserves.

Art. 24. The Bank shall have the sole right to issue currency throughout the United Kingdom of Libya. In implementing this article currency means bank-notes and coins.

VIII. BELATIONS WITH OTHER BANKS: CONTROL OF BANKING BUSINESS

BANK OF GHANA

29. (1). The Bank may, after consultation with the Minister, prescribe that banking institutions shall hold liquid assets of a specific amount and composition and may fix such amounts either as a certain percentage of all its deposit liabilities

or in any other manner; and may also fix different percentages for different classes of deposits or assets, as may be defined in the prescription in any particular case.

(2) Any doubt arising as to whether a particular liability of a banking institution is to be regarded as a deposit shall be resolved by the Board and its decision thereon shall be subject to appeal to the Minister.

(3) Every banking institution shall, at any such time and in respect of any such period as the Bank may require, render to the Bank a report on its liquid assets.

(4). Any prescription made by the Bank under this section shall be made by notice addressed to the banking institution concerned and may be published in the Gazette.

30. (1). Any banking institution which fails to hold liquid assets in accordance with section 29 of this Act, commits an offence and shall be liable in addition to any other penalty to pay an interest to the Bank, at a rate to be prescribed by the Board in consultation with the Minister, on the difference between the total amount of liquid assets which it is required to hold and the total amount of assets held by it, in respect of any period during which such a difference exists; and the Bank may direct that during a period specified in the direction such banking institution shall discontinue or limit, in a manner specified in the direction, the grant of credit or the making of investments and shall not distribute dividends to its shareholders.

(2). Any banking institution which, without the approval of the Bank, makes, during the existence of any deficiency in the amount of its specified liquid assets, any fresh advance to any person commits an offence.

(4). The Bank may from time to time require any banking institution operating in Ghana to furnish, by a specified date, such information in such form as it may deem necessary to ensure compliance with the requirements of this section; and any banking institution which fails to furnish the information required under this subsection within the period specified commits an offence and shall be liable to a fine not exceeding fifty pounds for every day during which the default continues.

31. (1). The Bank may from time to time request any banking or financial institution to furnish statements of its own accounts and other information relating thereto which the Bank may require.

(2). Whenever it deems it necessary, the Bank shall, through its agents appointed for the purpose, examine the books and accounts of banking and financial institutions.

(3). In the exercise of the functions conferred by the preceding subsection the agents shall have the right to demand from such institutions inspected all information and the making available to them of all books, registers and documents which they shall consider useful for their inspection and for a correct assessment of the position of any such institution.

(4). A report of the findings of each inspection containing the proposition of any measures considered necessary to avoid the repetition of irregularities or shortcomings found shall be addressed to the Governor.

32. The Bank shall be consulted on

(*a*) the establishment of a banking institution;
(*b*) the closing of banking institutions;
(*c*) the change of capital or name of a banking institution;

(*d*) the merger of two or more banking institutions; and shall be informed on the opening or closing of branches or agencies of banking institutions and the change of place of a branch or agency of a banking institution.

33. The Bank may, with the prior approval of the Minister, in relation with-or generally or in respect of a particular class of credits or investments, direct banking institutions to refrain, generally or for a specific period, from increasing the total amount of credit granted or invested by them in other assets or to refrain from increasing it beyond a limit specified in the direction.

34. The Bank may, by notice, in the Gazette, fix the minimum amount of the paid-up capital and of the balance of undistributed net profits which a banking institution shall hold as a certain percentage of the total amount of its assets.

CENTRAL BANK OF NIGERIA

38. The Bank may act as banker to other banks in Nigeria and abroad.

39. The Bank shall wherever necessary seek the co-operation of, and co-operate with, other banks in Nigeria:

(*a*) to promote and maintain adequate and reasonable banking services for the public.

(*b*) to ensure high standard of conduct and management throughout the banking system;

(*c*) to further such policies not inconsistent with this Act as shall be in the national interest.

40. (1) The Bank may prescribe from time to time by publication in the Gazette the minimum amount of specified liquid assets which each bank operating in Nigeria under the Banking Act is required to hold.

(2). The minimum amount so prescribed shall be expressed as a percentage of the demand liabilities of each such bank, together with a percentage of the time liabilities of each such bank arising out of its time and savings deposits. No bank shall be required to maintain a higher percentage than any other bank.

42. It shall be the duty of the Bank to facilitate the clearing of cheques and other credit instruments for banks carrying on business in Nigeria. For this purpose the Bank shall at any appropriate time and in conjunction with other banks, organise a clearing house.

BANK OF RHODESIA AND NYASALAND

23. (1). Every commercial bank carrying on business within the Federation shall, on or or before the twenty-first day of every calendar month, make up and send to the Bank at its head office a return, certified correct by the chief executive officer and the chief accounting officer employed by!such commercial bank within the Federation, showing:

(*a*) the amount of its demand liabilities to the public in the Federation;

(*b*) the amount of its time liabilities to the public in the Federation; and

(*c*) the amount of its reserve balance maintained with the Bank in terms of subsection (2);

(2). As from a day to be appointed by the Governor General, every commercial bank operating in the Federation shall maintain against its liabilities to the public within the Federation, as shown in the last preceding monthly return furnished to the Bank in terms of subsection (1), a minimum reserve balance with the Bank calculated in terms of subsection (3).

(3). The minimum reserve balance which a commercial bank shall maintain with the Bank shall be equal to percentages, which the Bank shall determine and may from time to time amend, of the various classes of liabilities to the public of the commercial bank concerned, so, however, that the percentages so determined or amended shall not be less than six per centum nor more than twenty-five per centum of demand liabilities of that bank in the Federation, and shall not be less than three per centum nor more than ten per centum of its time liabilities in the Federation.

(4). The Bank shall give the commercial banks reasonable notice of the date on which any amendment of a percentage determined in terms of subsection (3) is to become effective.

RESERVE BANK OF RHODESIA

21. Every commercial bank and accepting house shall, on or before the twenty-first day of every calendar month, make up and send to the Bank at its head office a return, certified correct by the chief executive officer and the chief accounting officer employed by such commercial bank or accepting house within Southern Rhodesia, showing:

(*a*) the amount of its demand liabilities to the public in Southern Rhodesia;
(*b*) the amount of its time liabilities to the public in Southern Rhodesia; and
(*c*) the amount of its reserve balance maintained with the Bank in terms of subsection (1) of section twenty-two

22. (1) Every commercial bank and accepting house shall maintain against its liabilities to the public in Southern Rhodesia as shown in the last preceding monthly return furnished to the Bank in terms of section twenty-one a minimum reserve balance with the Bank calculated in terms of subsection (2).

(2) The minimum reserve balance which every commercial bank and accepting house shall maintain with the Bank shall be equal to percentages, which the Bank shall determine and may from time to time amend, of the various classes of liabilities to the public in Southern Rhodesia, of the commercial bank or, as the case may be, of the accepting house concerned, as shown in the last preceding monthly return furnished to the Bank in terms of section twenty-one.

(3) The Bank shall give the commercial banks and accepting house concerned reasonable notice of the date on which any amendment of a percentage determined in terms of this section is to become effective.

(4) In addition, the Bank may call upon every commercial bank and accepting house to increase the reserve balances maintained in terms of subsection (1) by an amount representing a percentage, which the Bank may determine and may amend from time to time, of the advances and bills discounted of each commercial bank and accepting house. The Bank may fix one percentage for commercial banks and a different percentage for accepting houses.

(5) The Bank may further prescribe that in respect of any increase in advances and bills discounted of the commercial banks and accepting houses after notice has been given by the Bank, every commercial bank and accepting house shall increase its reserve balance by an amount representing a percentage of such

first-mentioned increase, so, however, that the percentage shall not be more than three times the percentage fixed in terms of sub-section (4).

(6) The Bank may, with the permission of the Minister, vary the percentage prescribed for the minimum holding of liquid assets in terms of paragraph (*a*) and, either additionally or alternatively paragraph (*b*) of subsection (1) of section 24 of the Banking Act, so, however, that no variation in terms of this subsection shall reduce the percentages to less than twenty-five per centum in the case of a commercial bank and twenty per centum in the case of an accepting house. Any variation made in terms of this subsection shall be notified by the Minister by notice in the Gazette.

(7) If the Bank certified that it would be in the public interest to reduce the percentage prescribed for the minimum holding of liquid assets in terms of paragraph (*a*) and, either additionally or alternatively, paragraph (*b*) of subsection (1) of section 24 of the Banking Act, the Minister may, by notice in the Gaeette, fix a lower percentage to be effective for such period as he may specify in that notice.

23. (1) The Bank may, if it thinks it necessary in the public interest, request information from and make recommendations to banker and may, if so authorized by the Minister, issue directions to any banker for the purpose of securing that effect is given to any such request or recommendation:

Provided that:

(*a*) no such request or recommendation shall be made in respect of the affairs of any particular customer of a banker;

(*b*) before authorizing the issue of any such direction the Minister shall give the banker concerned or such person as appears to him to represent such banker, an opportunity of making representations with respect thereto.

BANK OF SUDAN

40. The Bank may open accounts for, and accept non-interest bearing deposits from, banks and other credit institutions operating in the Sudan.

41. The Bank may:

(*a*) purchase, discount or rediscount from banks Bills of Exchange or Promissory Notes drawn or issued for commercial, industrial or agricultural purposes, bearing two or more good signatures and maturing within three months from the day of acquisition. Provided that Bills of Exchange or Promissory Notes drawn or issued for the purpose of financing seasonal agricultural operations or marketing of crops may mature within nine months of the day of acquisition. And provided further that the Bank may when it considers necessary extend the limits of the maturity as specified above from three to six months and from nine to twelve months respectively;

(*b*) purchase, discount or rediscount from banks Treasury Bills of the Government which have been publicly offered for sale and are maturing within three months;

(*c*) grant to banks loans, advances and overdrafts for a period not exceeding six months against the collateral of:

(*i*) credit instruments specified in paragraphs (*a*) and (*b*) of this Section;

(*ii*) warehouse warrants or any other documents securing sole possession of goods issued in respect of staple commodities or other goods duly insured: provided that the Bank shall determine from time time the maximum percentage of advances in relation to the current value of such commodities or goods.

(*iii*) Treasury Bills or other securities issued or guaranteed by foreign governments;

(*iv*) securities issued or guaranteed by the Government or any of its agencies, subject as provided in Section 58.

(*d*) issue guarantees for liabilities of banks provided that the amount of guarantee outstanding at any time in respect of any bank shall not exceed the value of the cash deposit made by that bank together with any commodities or goods accepted as collateral security as described in sub-paragraph (*c*) (*ii*) of this section.

42. The Bank shall fix as announced from time to time its rates for discounts, rediscounts, loans or advances. It may establish differential rates for various classes of transactions or maturities

43. The Bank may sell, discount or rediscount to banks in the Sudan or abroad any of the credit instruments acquired as a result of operations enumerated in paragraphs (*a*) and (*b*) of Section 41.

44. (1) The Bank may require banks to maintain reserves in the form of deposits at the Bank or in such other form as the Bank may stipulate in a specified ratio to their sight and time liabilities.

(2) Due notice shall be given to banks before the first requisition under the preceding sub-section is made.

(3) The maximum reserve ratio required of banks shall not exceed 20 per cent.

(4) Provided the maximum specified in the preceding sub-section is not exceeded, the Bank may from time to time alter the required reserve ratio and may establish differential ratios for sight and time liabilities.

(5) Any bank which fails to maintain the required reserve shall pay to the Bank interest on the amount of the deficiency calculated at a rate exceeding by 5 per cent per annum the highest rate fixed at the time by the Bank pursuant to Section 42 for any of its operations.

54. (1) The Bank may:

(*a*) require that all applications to banks for loans above a specified amount be submitted by banks to the Bank for approval;

(*b*) fix ceilings on the volume of loans, advances and discounts outstanding at each bank for different categories of such loans, advances and discounts;

(*c*) fix a ceiling on the aggregate amount of loans, advances and discounts granted by any bank and outstanding at any time;

(2) Any bank which exceeds any of the ceilings fixed by the Bank under the preceding sub-section may be required to pay to the Bank interest on the excess calculated at a rate exceeding by 5 per cent per annum the highest rate fixed at the time by the Bank pursuant to Section 42 for any of its operations.

46. (1) The Bank may require banks to submit:

(*a*) within three months from the end of the financial year a certified copy of the balance sheet audited by an independent firm of public accounts together with a certified copy of the auditors' report;

(*b*) within 30 days from the end of each month a certified statement of the assets and liabilities of the bank as at the end of the preceding month in the form specified by the Bank;

(*c*) such other information as the Bank may require.

(2) The Bank may require any bank to open its books for inspection and to supply such other evidence as may be deemed by the Bank under Sections 44, 45 46. and 49. The Bank shall wherever necessary seek the co-operation of, and co-operate with, other banks in the Sudan to promote and maintain adequate services for the public, to ensure high standards of conduct and management throughout the banking system and to further such policies not inconsistent with this Act as shall be in the national interest.

50. The Bank shall at an appropriate time and in conjunction with other banks organise a clearing house in Khartoum and in such other place or places as may be desirable in premises provided by the Bank.

CENTRAL BANK OF TUNISIA

Art. 33. (4) It can compel all banking establishments to furnish all figures and information which it thinks necessary for knowing the development of credit and the economic situation. It is charged particularly to ensure in its headquarters all banking risks.

Art. 47. (1) For working on the volume of credit and for regulating the money market, the Central Bank can buy from the banks short term Govt. securities of less than 6 months to maturity and private securities admissible for rediscounting. It can resell these previously acquired securities.

Art. 48. The total amount of operations fixed on Govt. securities conforming to articles 46 and 47, cannot exceed 10% of the ordinary receipts of the state during the last budgetary year.

Art. 60. In view of ensuring the application of the regulation of foreign exchange, the Central Bank can demand from the banks all information and can give them all instruction.

BANK OF LIBYA

Art. 36. Commercial banks shall maintain reserves with the Bank of Libya without interest against their deposit liabilities. The Board of Directors of the Bank shall specify the kind of these deposit liabilities and the percentage of reserves to each component of these deposits provided such percentage shall be within:

(*a*) five per cent to twenty per cent on time and savings deposits, and

(*b*) ten per cent to forty per cent on demand deposits, unused balances and uncovered credit facilities.

Any upward change in the percentage within the above limits shall be made as gradual as possible and except in emergencies, banks shall be notified at least fifteen days prior to effecting this change. Such reserves shall be made in Libyan pounds unless the Board of Directors of the Bank allows some of these reserves to be in the form of other assets.

Art. 50. Every institution shall be deemed to be a commercial bank if it regularly conducts the business of accepting deposits in current accounts payable on demand or deposits payable on time, opening of credits, paying and collecting of cheques drawn or deposited by customers, making advances and other banking transactions.

A bank which conducts mainly the business of real estate, agricultural or industrial financing and which does not make the business of receiving demand deposits a principal part of its activities shall not be considered a commercial bank under this Article.

Art. 51. No bank may conduct banking business unless it is in possession of a licence provided for in Article 479 and 645 of the Commercial Code with the exception that the licence in this case shall be granted by the Minister in consultation with the Governor of the Bank of Libya.

Any institution which is not in possession of a licence issued under this Law to conduct banking business shall not use the word "bank" or its synonyms or any similar expression in any language whether for its private name, commercial title or advertisements.

Art. 53. The Bank of Libya shall be informed of any changes intended to be made in the statute of a bank, its organization or in any of the other statements submitted at the time of applying for the licence.

Art. 65. Every bank shall submit to the Bank of Libya tho following:

(1) Monthly statements of its financial position according to the forms prescribed by the Board of Directors of the Bank of Libya within a period not exceeding fifteen days form the end of each month; such statements shall include the particulars of all unsecured advances and credit facilities made by the bank to the company or companies in which the bank or any of its directors is interested as a member of the board of directors or as manager, agent or guarantor.

(2) A copy of its last audited balance sheet within a period of four months from the end of its financial year.

(3) A copy of each report presented to the shareholders, on the operation of the bank within five days from such presentation and a copy of the minutes of every meeting of the general assembly within thirty days from the date of holding such meetings for banks whose head office is situated in Libya.

(4) A statement on every change in the composition of the board of directors of the bank within fifteen days from the date of such change.

(5) Any statement or explanation required by the Bank of Libya on the operations undertaken by the Bank in such form and within such time as shall be specified by the Bank.

Art. 67. No bank may merge with another bank without the approval of the Minister after consultation with the Bank of Libya. In this case, the Minister shall prescribe after consultation with the Board of Directors of the Bank of Libya the necessary procedures to be followed.

Art. 68. No bank may suspend its operations unless it has obtained a prior permission from the Board of Directors of the Bank of Libya.

Art. 69. The cancellation of the licence shall be decided by the Minister after consultation with the Bank of Libya except in the case stated in Para (2) of this Article where cancellation will be by decision of the Council of Ministers.

Art. 70. The decision for the cancellation of the licence shall result in the suspension of the bank's operations. In this event, the Board of Directors of the Bank of Libya may decide to liquidate the bank immediately or may permit it to carry out the operations outstanding at the time of such cancellation according to the conditions specified by the Board.

Annexure 1

SCHEDULE OF NATIONAL CURRENCY UNITS*

AND

STERLING/FRANC/DOLLAR EQUIVALENTS

Country	Unit		Equivalent
1. Ghana	Ghanaian Pound £ G 1	=	1 Pound sterling originally
	(1 U.S. Dollar on 31.12.55	=	.3571 G pounds)
	Since 1965 1 Cedi (C)	=	8s.4d = 100 d.
	Parity of the Cedi	=	1.03678 grams fine gold
2. Libya	Libyan Pound £ L1	=	1 Pound sterling
		=	2.7910 (U.S. dollars)
	Parity of the Libyan Pound	=	2·48828 grams fine gold
3. Nigeria	Nigerian Pound £ N1	=	1 Pound sterling
	Parity of the Nigerian Pound	=	2.48828 grams fine gold
4. Sudan	Sudanese Pound £ S1	=	1.025 pounds sterling
	Parity of the Sudanese Pound	=	2.872 U.S. dollars
		=	2.55187 grams of fine gold
5. Rhodesia	Rhodesian Pound £ R1	=	1 Pound sterling
6. Morocco	Dirham 1 Dirham	=	0.9756 New French Franc
		=	20 U.S. Cents.
7. Tunisia	Dinar 1 Dinar (after devaluation in September, 1964)	=	£ 0.68

*Sources: Charters and Annual Reports of the Central Banks. Also *Statistical Year Book*, United Nations, 1965. Tables 180 pp. 542-545 and 186 pp. 575-579.

Annexure 2

THE SUDAN CURRENCY BOARD

The Sudan Currency Board, created under the Currency Act of June 17, 1956, laid the foundations of the issue of the new Sudanese currency. The Board was modelled on the lines of the Currency Boards operating in many British colonies but must be sharply distinguished from them in its composition, seat of operations and objectives. According to the provisions of the Currency Act the standard unit of currency in Sudan should be the Sudanese pound, which was to be divided into 10 equal units each of which was to be called a millieme. The par value of the Sudanese pound was laid down at 2.55187 grams of fine gold. The Board, empowered to issue currency in the Sudan, was to be composed of (1) the Deputy Permanent Under Secretary of the Ministry of Finance and Economics who should be the Chairman (2) the Director of the Ministry of Commerce, Industry and Supply, ex-officio and (3) the following non-official members appointed by the government (*a*) a Sudanese national possessing suitable qualifications and (*b*) three other suitably qualified persons acceptable to government. The term of office of the non-official members should be three years. Members of Parliament and directors/officers/shareholders/employees of any banking institution were not qualified for appointment as chairman or member of the Board. The seat of the Board was to be at Khartoum. The constitution of the Board was obviously different from that of the WACB in that the members were appointed by the national government and the seat of the Board was local.

The principal duties of the Board were (1) to meet any preliminary expenses and to discharge any liabilities incurred in connection with the issuing of notes and coins (2) to make all necessary arrangements for the printing of notes and minting of coins, for the issue, reissue and redemption of notes and coins, for the destruction of cancelled notes and coins unfit for further use etc (3) to establish a Currency Reserve Fund and to maintain the Funds so as to provide for the redemption of currency (4) to credit to the Currency Reserve Fund the proceeds of the issue of notes and coins and to debit to it any expenditure incurred other than for the redemption of notes and coins as well as any provision for depreciation of the Board's assets (5) to ensure that the currency reserve fund should not be less than the value of currency in circulation and (6) to invest the currency reserve fund in gold, prescribed foreign currencies, bank balances in prescribed foreign currencies, securities issued or guaranteed by any prescribed government or by the Sudan Government. The amount invested in the securities issued or guaranteed by the Sudan Government should not, however, exceed half of the total amount of currency issued. The pound sterling was prescribed as the appropriate currency for the purpose of investment of the Currency Reserve Fund which could be invested in securities denominated in sterling provided they were issued or guaranteed by the U. K. Government. The Board should make such arrangements as might be necessary for the issue of currency sufficient for the redemption of foreign notes and coins in circulation in Sudan over such period as might be prescribed. The Board should issue on demand notes and coins against prepayment in any foreign currency prescribed from time to time as a currency appropriate for this purpose.

The Board might charge a commission for such transactions, the rates of commission charged being published in the official gazette. Without prejudice to any law pertaining to exchange control, the Board should receive currency notes and coins in Sudan and on demand issue in exchange mail or telegraphic transfers of equivalent value in any foreign currency prescribed from time to time as a currency appropriate for such purpose. The Board could charge a commission for such purposes but would have to publish the rates thereof from time to time. When any person surrendered Sudanese currency to the Board it should deliver to that person in exchange on demand and without charge notes and coins of equivalent value.

Advances might be made by the government to the Board to meet the preliminary expenses incurred in issuing notes and coins. These advances together with interest at agreed rates must be repaid. If at any time the liquid assets of the Board were inadequate to meet its liabilities, it might borrow on the security of its investments such sums as might be necessary to meet the liabilities falling due.

The surplus income of the Board at the close of every financial year should be credited to the government. In case of a deficiency in the Currency Fund Income Account, the government should make good the deficiency.

The Board should submit to the government a half yearly statement showing the amount of notes and coins in circulation and the position of the Currency Reserve Fund Income Account, and an annual report of the transactions for each financial year for the purpose of presentation to both the Houses of Parliament.

The Board should with the approval of the Minister of Finance appoint a Currency Controller and a Deputy Currency Controller and other officers as necessary. One or more banks could be appointed to conduct its banking business.

The Minister of Finance and Economics might, after consultation, give directions of a general character as to the performance by the Board of its functions affecting public interest and the Board must carry out such directions.[1] This is reminiscent of the relevant provision of the charter of the Bank of England which transformed it into a State-owned institution in 1946.

The position of the Sudan Currency Board was affected by an amendment of the Currency Act, 1956. The Chairman of the Board was allowed to continue in office even after his appointment as Governor of the Bank of Sudan. The Bank was set up as the Central Bank of the country by an Act of December 1, 1959. The Sudan Currency Board was to transfer all its assets and liabilities to the Bank on the appointed day 22nd February 1960 and was thereafter to go into liquidation. The Board was also permitted by the amendment Act to accept deposits of money from banks operating in the Sudan[2]. The object was to enable the Board to absorb foreign exchange without having to issue notes in excess of the normal requirements of circulation.

The actual exchange of notes was undertaken by the provincial, district and local treasuries and by the various banks which agreed to serve the general public as well as their own customers. The period of exchange was fixed as from April 8,

[1] Sec. 38, The Currency Act. 1956.

[2] The Currency Act, 1956 (Amendment) Act 1959, Sec. 17A.

1957 to July 7, 1957 after which date Egyptian notes would be no longer legal tender.

On 7th October 1957, the total amount of Egyptian notes exchanged was £E 23,757,454 and an equivalent amount of Sudanese notes was issued. The first Sudanese coins were issued on January 19, 1957. The legal period for the exchange of foreign coins was fixed as beginning from October 1,1957 and ending on 31st December, 1957[1].

The stocks of exchanged Egyptian notes as well as British and Egyptian coins were the property of the Sudan government who made agreements with the governments of these countries for their redemption. The government was responsible for the necessary cover, including the foreign assets, for the currency issued by the Board for the purpose of the exchange operation. According to the provisions of the Law the currency cover was to consist of gold, sterling balances, securities issued or guaranteed by the U.K. Government within the prescribed limits and securities issued or guaranteed by the Sudanese government. On the basis of these provisions the Board agreed to accept from the government one half of the cover for the currency issued in the form of 90 days government treasury bills carrying interest at 2% p.a. By mutual agreement the amount of Sudan Government treasury bills in the cover was not to exceed at any time one half of the currency in circulation. The balance of the cover was provided by the government in the form of sterling assets. The Board's policy was to maintain a relatively high proportion of the foreign assets in very liquid form. As much as 45% of the sterling assets was thus partly invested in British treasury bills and partly held in the form of balances with the Bank of England[2]. The policy of maintaining the foreign assets in a highly liquid form was adopted with a view to prevent fluctuations in the market values of the securities held by the Board from affecting its position. Subsequent increases in the Board's sterling assets were invested in British treasury bills in conformity with this policy.

At the close of business on February 21, 1960, the amount of currency issued by the Board stood at LS 22,549,137. This was a fall of nearly LS 20 million since August 31, 1959 when it had reached a total of LS 43,781,743. Continuing balance of payments surpluses had been responsible for a heavy inflow of foreign exchange. In order to provide the government with sufficient Sudanese currency to absorb this foreign exchange, the Board had to issue to the government notes against payment insterling. The subsequent decline in the note issue was to be attributed to the redemption of currency notes for which the Board paid to the government the equivalent in sterling. It has been observed that the Board was empowered to accept deposits from banks operating in the Sudan. In exercise of this power the Board withdrew from the National Bank of Egypt, Khartoum all notes not required for the current business by the Institution[3].

In accordance with the provisions of the Law establishing the central bank, the assets and liabilities of the Sudan Currency Board were transferred to the Bank of Sudan on 22nd February, 1960.

---

[1] First Report of the Sudan Currency Board December, 1957.

[2] First Report of the Sudan Currency Board—31 December 1957. pp. 5-6.

[3] Fourth Report of the Sudan Currency Board—1st July 1959—21 February, 1960. p. 6.

A copy of the balance sheet of the Sudan Currency Board, dated 21st February, 1960, is reproduced below[1]:

SUDAN CURRENCY BOARD

Liabilities	LS	Assets	LS
Currency in circulation	22,549,137	Sudan Government treasury bills (at cost)	12,977,812
Deposit Account—National Bank of Egypt-Khartoum	20,272,750	Investments at Market Value*	8,523,782
		British Government Treasury Bills	22,338,814
Currency Fund Income Account	1,191,069	Balances with the Bank of England	106,087
			43,946,495
		Balance with National Bank of Egypt, Khartoum	19,532
		Interest accrued on Sudan Government Treasury Bills	46,929
LS	44,012,956	LS	44,012,956

* Investments—British Govt. Stocks	Market Value LS
$2\frac{1}{2}$% Funding Stock 1956/1961	1,937,980
$4\frac{1}{2}$% Conversion Stock 1962	4,206,082
$4\frac{3}{4}$% Conversion Stock 1963	2,379,720
	LS 8,523,782

[1] Fourth Report of the Sudan Currency Board, 1st July, 1959-21st February, 1960, pp. 12-13. p. 15.

Select Bibliography

BOOKS

1. H. W. Arndt—The Australian Trading Banks, 1958.
2. J. Aschheim—Techniques of Monetary Control, 1961.
3. Hans Aufricht—Central Banking Legislation (IMF), 1961.
4. S. K. Basu—Industrial Finance in India, (Calcutta University), 4th Edition, 1961.

   S. K. Basu—A Survey of Contemporary Banking Trends (Book Exchange Calcutta) Third Edn. 1965.

   S. K. Basu—Theory and Practice of Development Banking (Asia Publishing House, Bombay) 1965.
5. C. V. Brown—Government and Banking in Western Nigeria (OUP), 1965.
6. L. V. Chandler—Central Banking and Economic Development, (Bombay University), 1962.
7. H. C. Coombs—Development of Monetary Policy in Australia, 1956.
8. W. F. Crick (Ed)—Commonwealth Banking Systems (Clarenden Press, Oxford), 1965.
9. A. G. Davies (Ed)—Central Banking in South and East Asia. (Hong Kong University Press), 1960.
10. E.E. Jucker-Fleetwood—Money and Finance in Africa (George Allen and Unwin), 1964.
11. P. G. Fousek—Foreign Central Banking: The Instruments of Monetary Policy, 1957.
12. N. A. Cox George—Finance and Development in West Africa: The Sierra Leone Experience (Dennis Dobson) London, 1961.
13. Ida Greaves—Colonial Monetary Conditions (HMS Office) 1953.
14. D. L. Grove—New Guatemalan Bank Law.
15. Benjamin Higgins—Economic Development, Principles, Problems and Policies (Constable) London, 1959.
16. Bert Hoselitz—Sociological Aspects of Economic Growth (Free Press, London), 1964.
17. H. V. R. Ienger—Monetary Policy and Economic Growth, (Vora and Company), 1962.
18. G. G. Johnson—The Treasury and Monetary Policy, 1933-38.
19. J. M. Keynes—A Treatise on Money, Vols I-II.
20. Majid Khadduri—Modern Libya. (John Hopkins Press), 1963.
21. C. H. Kisch and W. A. Elkin—Central Banks (Macmillan), 1928.
22. De Kock—Central Banking, 1954.
23. E. Nevin—Central Funds in Underdeveloped Countries, (Macmillan) 1961.
24. W. T. Newlyn and D. C. Rowan—Money and Banking in Colonial Africa, (Oxford), 1954.
25. A. F. W. Plumptre—Central Banking in the British Dominions 1940.
26. R. S. Sayers—Central Banking After Bagehot, 1957.

    R. S. Sayers—Modern Banking (6th Edition) 1964.
27. R. S. Sayers (Ed)—Banking in the British Commonwealth.

28. S. N. SEN—Central Banking in Underdeveloped Countries (Book Land-Cal) 1952.
29. R. TRIFFIN—Monetary and Banking Reform in Paraguay.
30. H. W. WALLICH and R. TRIFFIN—Monetary and Banking Legislation of the Dominican Republic 1947 (F.R.B. of N.Y. 1953).
31. PARKER WILLIS—Theory and Practice of Central Banking with particular reference to the Federal Reserve System.

2. ARTICLES AND LECTURES

JOACHIM AHRENSDROFF, "Central Bank Policies and Inflation," IMF Staff Papers, Vol. III, October, 1959.

B. A. ALLEN, "The Commonwealth Banking Corporation and the Trading Banks," The Bankers' Magazine, October, 1966.

J. ASCHHEIM, "Reconsideration on Theoretical and Practical grounds of the choice between the V.R.R. and O.M.O.", The Economic Journal, December, 1959.

H. W. ARNDT, "Central Banking in Developing Countries," Indian Economic Review, January-March, 1965.

G. A. BLOWERS and A. N. MCLEOD, "Currency Unification in Libya," IMF Staff Papers, November, 1952.

A. F. BRIMMER, "Banking and Finance in the Sudan," S. A. Journal of Economics, Vol. 28, No. 1, March, 1960.

E. A. BRINBAUM and M. QUERISHI, "Advance Deposit Requirements For Imports," IMF Staff Papers, Vol. VIII, 1960.

C. V. BROWN, "Evolution of Banking Power in West Africa," The Bankers' Magazine, March, 1966.

A. G. CHANDAVARKAR, "Central Banking in Libya," The Bankers' Magazine, June, 1960.

LORD COBBOLD, "Some Thoughts on Central Banking" Stamp Memorial Lectures, 1965.

G. L. M. CLAUSON, "The British Colonial System," The Economic Journal, April, 1944.

R. L. CROUCH, "The Inadequacy of New Orthodox Methods of Monetary Control," The Economic Journal, December, 1964.

C. S. DORRANCE, "Instruments of Monetary Policy in Countries without highly developed money markets," IMF Staff Papers, July, 1965.

C. D. DESHMUKH, "Balance between Monetary Policy and other Instruments of Economic Policy in a Developing Economy," Per Jacobsson Foundation Lecture, October, 1965.

ARTHUR HAZLEWOOD, "Central Banking in Nigeria," The Bankers' Magazine, 1960.

RODRIGO JARAMILLO, "Central Bank Discount Rates," IMF Staff Papers, Vol. XIII, March, 1966.

H. G. JOHNSON, "Monetary Theory and Policy," American Economic Review, June, 1962.

J. W. KRATZ, "The East African Currency Board," IMF Staff Papers, Vol. XIII., July, 1966.

M. A. KRIZ, "Central Banks and the State To-day," American Economic Review, September, 1948.

A. R. LOW, "The Varied Role of Central Banks," Economic Record, December, 1958.

JORGE MARSHALL, "Advance Deposits on Imports," IMF Staff Papers, Vol. VI. No. 2, April, 1958.

J. O. W. OLAKANPO, "Monetary Management in Dependent Economies," Economica, November, 1961.
"Commercial Banking in Nigeria," The Bankers' Magazine, Jan, 1965.
"Money and Banking Problems in Nigeria," *Ibid*, March, 1966.

A. C. PORTER, "Narrow Markets and Monetary Policy," Economic Development and Cultural Change, October, 1965.

F. O. N. PERKINS, "Central Banking in Australia," The Bankers' Magazine, Oct, 1966.

V. G. PENDHARKAR & NARASIMHAN, "Recent Evolution of Monetary Policy in India," Reserve Bank of India Bulletin, April, 1966.

L. Rasminsky "Role of the Central Banker Today" (Per Jacobsson Foundation Lecture, November 1966).

V. P. ROMILLY, "The Money Market in Rhodesia and Nyasaland," The Bankers' Magazine, December, 1962.

P. F. ROSE, "Recent Developments in the Australian Money Market," The Bankers' Magazine, October, 1966.

R. V. ROOSA, Place of Monetary Policy in the Economic Policy of the United States. (Per Jacobsson Foundation Lecture, October 1965).

S. P. SCHATZ, "Capital Shortage Illusion," Oxford Economic Papers, July, 1965.

Reserve Bank of India Bulletin, March 29, 1965. Speech of the Governor, Reserve Bank of India, at the Dinner Meeting of the Calcutta Bankers' Association,

FEDERAL Reserve Bank of New York, Monthly Review, Oct. 1960 and July, 1964, "New Central Banks."

British Banking 1965, The Economist, June 19, 1965.

African Research Bulletin, August, 1966.

The Statesman Year Book,

The Statesman, December 3, 1966. Art. by R. W. Howe, "Ghana sheds no tears for the gods that failed."

Barclays Bank Monthly Review, May, 1953, "New Bank for the Gold Cost,"

Barclays Bank Monthly Review, May, 1958, "Central Banking in Africa."

3. OFFICIAL REPORTS AND PUBLICATIONS AND LETTERS

(*a*) Banks

African Countries

GHANA

The Bank of Ghana Ordinance, 1957.

The Bank of Ghana Act, 1959.

The Bank of Ghana Amendment Act, 1963.

Annual Reports of the Board of Directors, Bank of Ghana for the financial years ending June 1958-1964.
The National Investment Bank Act, Ghana, 1963, and Bye Laws, 1963.
Reports of the Board of Directors, National Investment Bank, 31 December, 1963.
Letter to the writer from Mr. G. N. Parry, Actg. Secretary, Bank of Ghana dated 14 October, 1965.
Letter to the writer from the Secretary, National Investment Bank of Ghana, 24 November, 1966.

LIBYA

Law No. 30 of 1955, Establishing the National Bank of Libya.
Banking Law No. 4 February 1963, Libya.
Annual Reports of the National Bank of Libya, First to Eighth, 1957-1964.
Ninth and Tenth Annual Reports of the Bank of Libya, 1964/65 and 1965/66.
Inflation in Libya, Economic Research Department, National Bank of Libya, 1961.
Monthly Economic Bulletin, Bank of Libya, Published by the Research Department, Bank of Libya, Vols. I-V.
Letter to the writer from the Acting Director, Research Dept. Bank of Libya, dated February 9, 1966.

MOROCCO

Statutes of the Bank of Morocco 30 June, 1959. Amendment 30 Dec. 1962.
Structure Et Distribution Du Credit Au Maroc.
Statuts, Banque Nationale Pour le Developpment Economique.
Annual Reports, Bank of Morocco, 1963/1964 and 1965 Rabat. (*Rapport Banque du Maroc Exercise 1965*).
Banque Du Maroc—Etudes Et Statistiques 1956-65.

NIGERIA

The Central Bank of Nigeria Ordinance, 1958.
The Central Bank of Nigeria Act. 1958 As Amended, 1962.
Annual Reports and Statements of Accounts, Central Bank of Nigeria, 1960-1965.
Economic and Financial Review, Central Bank of Nigeria, Vol. 3, 1965, Vol. 4, 1966.
Memorandum and New Articles of Association, Nigerian Industrial Development Bank (Adopted by special Resolution January 6, 1964 and confirmed 22 January, 1964).
Explanatory Memorandum and Guide to Applicants issued by the NIDB.
Annual Reports and Accounts, Nigerian Industrial Development Bank, 1964 and 1965.

RHODESIA AND NYASALAND

The Bank of Rhodesia and Nyasaland Act. 1956.
Annual Reports of the Bank of Rhodesia and Nyasaland 1960-64.
Memorandum of the Governor of the Bank of Rhodesia and Nyasaland, Radcliffe

Committee, Vol. I. Also Oral Evidences. Radcliffe Committee.

The Reserve Bank of Rhodesia Act, 1964.

SUDAN

Bank of Sudan Act. 1959. as amended by Bank of Sudan Act, 1962.

Economic and Financial Bulletin, Bank of Sudan. Vols. VI-VII, 1965-66.

Prospectus of the Industrial Bank of Sudan.

The Industrial Bank of Sudan Act, 1961 and Bye Laws, 1962.

Annual Reports of the Industrial Bank of Sudan for the years ending 1960, 1961, 1962, 1963, 1964 and 1965.

TUNISIA

Textes Organiques Banque Centrale de Tunisie.

Annual Reports of the Central Bank of Tunisia 1958-59 to 1963-1964.

Bulletin Banque Centrale de Tunisie, 1964-1965.

Statistical Tables relating to the Central Bank of Tunisia.

Statuts, La Societe Tunisienne de Banque.

Annual Reports of the Board of Directors *Societe Tunisienne de Banque* 1959-1965.

Quarterly Review, Central Bank of Tunisia.

OTHERS

Annual Reports of the Industrial Finance Corporation and Industrial Development Bank of India.

Annual Reports of the Bank of England.

Report on Currency and Finance, Reserve Bank of India.

Reserve Bank of India Bulletin.

Federal Reserve Bulletin.

Federal Reserve Bank of New York, Monthly Review.

Barclays Bank, Monthly Review.

Annual Reports of the State Bank of Pakistan and Speeches of the Governor upto 1965-66, Karachi.

Bank of Korea Act, April 21, 1960.

Organic Law of the Central Bank of Costa Rica, 1953 as amended up to June, 1960.

Organic Laws of the Bank of Paraguay (1944), Bank of Guatemala, 1946 and the Central Bank of the Dominican Republic 1947.

Memorandum of the Governor of the Reserve Bank of South Africa, Radcliffe Committee.

Report by Sir Cecil Trevor on "Banking conditions in the Gold Coast on the question of a Central Bank," Accra, 1951.

Report by J. B. Loynes on the Establishment of a Nigerian Central Bank, Lagos, 1957.

Report by J. L. Fisher on the desirability and practicability of establishing a Central Bank in Nigeria as an Instrument for promoting the economic development of the country. (Photostat copy) Lagos, 15 December, 1952.

Report of the Radcliffe Committee, Written Memoranda and Oral Evidences.

Report by Dr. Erwin Blumenthal on the working of the East African Currency Board and the possibility of establishing an East African Central Bank, Tanganyka.
Annual Reports of the East African Currency Board.
Annual Reports of the Sudan Currency Board.

INTERNATIONAL ORGANISATIONS

Eight Central Banks. BIS Publication.
IMF Staff Papers.
IBRD Mission, Economic Development of Libya.
IBRD Mission, Economic Development of Nigeria.
Measures for the Economic Development of Underdeveloped Countries. United Nations.
International Currency Experience (L of N) Geneva.
Annual Reports of the IBRD and IDA, Washington up to 1965-66.
Annual Reports of the International Finance Corporation, Washington up to 1964-65.
Annual Reports of the Bank of International Settlements, Basle.

Index